Oregon

Trips & Trails

NORDSTROM

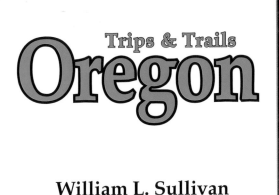

Trips & Trails
Oregon

William L. Sullivan

Navillus Press
Eugene

A Navillus Press book

www.oregonhiking.com

©2006, 2004, 2003 William L. Sullivan

Maps and photographs by the author.
All rights reserved. No part of this book may
be reproduced in any form without written
permission from the publisher.

Published by the Navillus Press
1958 Onyx Street
Eugene, Oregon 97403
Printed in Korea. ISBN 978-09677830-38

Front cover: Eagle Cap, mountain goats,
balsamroot, Baker City. Spine: Clark's nutcracker, aster, Mount Hood from Lost Lake.
Back cover: Heceta Head. Page 1: Portland.
Page 2: Lemolo Falls. This page: Crater Lake
in April.

CONTENTS

The regions of Oregon are color-coded throughout the book for easy orientation.

Wheelbarrows at Oswald West State Park help campers carry their gear to Short Sands Beach *(see p93).*

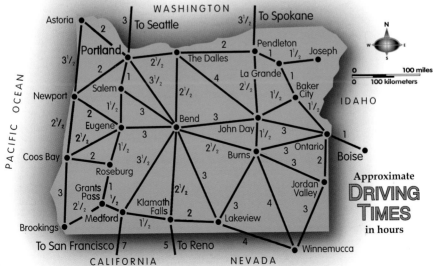

Approximate DRIVING TIMES in hours

Huckleberry leaves turn crimson in fall in the alpine meadows surrounding Mount Jefferson in the Central Oregon Cascades *(see p162).*

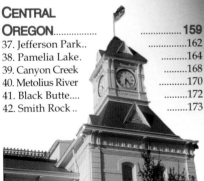

Corvallis, in the Willamette Valley, has one of the West's oldest county courthouses still in use *(see p153).*

The Warner Lakes of Southeast Oregon's high desert country fill with water and teem with birdlife in wet years, but dry to alkali puddles by fall *(see p265)*.

NORTHEAST OREGON
(page 231)

SOUTHEAST OREGON
(page 259)

◁ **The Imnaha River emerges from the Eagle Cap Wilderness of Northeast Oregon at Blue Hole.**

INTRODUCTION

Since pioneer days, the word "Oregon" has been a call to beauty and exploration.

They called it "Polyanna," an "earthly Paradise," and "the land at Eden's gate." In the 1840s, the fabulous tales that filtered out of the nearly mythical land of Oregon inspired thousands of Americans each year to abandon their old lives and set off in covered wagons on the Oregon Trail—risking everything they had on a two-thousand-mile trek across the wilderness.

For every believer who followed the Oregon dream, a thousand skeptics stayed behind. The doubters scoffed that no land could be as beautiful as the reports of Oregon claimed.

Those who live in Oregon know that the skeptics were wrong. To this day, a tour across Oregon is a journey through unparalleled scenery. The diversity of this beauty makes it all the more inspiring.

To the west, rainforest canyons descend to a wild coast of wave-smashed headlands and hidden beaches. In the Willamette Valley, daffodils and shade oaks surround white clapboard farmhouses amid rolling croplands. In the Cascade Range, glaciers writhe down 10,000-foot volcanoes toward turquoise lakes. And in the cliff-lined canyons of Southeast Oregon's high desert, forgotten rivers curve past hot springs and ancient petroglyphs.

Let this book be your guide as you chart your own Oregon Trail, exploring the fabled beauty that still inspires Oregonians to love, cherish, and protect their paradise.

◁ **The Devils Cauldron in Oswald West State Park** *(see p93).*   △ **The Hoffer Lakes in Northeast Oregon** *(see p243).*

How to
USE THIS BOOK

Start your tour of Oregon by choosing one of the state's ten geographic regions. Throughout this book, the chapters about these regions are identified by color-coded page corners. Each chapter begins with an overview map, followed by articles about the region's star attractions, scenic trails, and top features. Chapters end with a list of places to stay.

The Coquille River Lighthouse overlooks Bandon's old town *(see p124)*.

 ## Star Attractions

 ## Scenic Trails

Whether you're planning a week-long tour of Oregon's far corners or a quick afternoon outing, keep an eye out for the **red stars** in this book. These star attractions are the state's top travel destinations—places worth a journey, where you could easily spend half a day or more.

Turn to the **regional overview maps** at the start of each chapter to locate the star destinations for that area. The numbers on the stars are keyed to more detailed articles later in the chapter.

Many of the recommended destinations are free. When prices and open hours are listed, they are subject to change.

All of the state's most interesting **hot springs** are featured. For a complete listing, turn to the "hot springs" entry in the index.

Hiking is popular in Oregon because many of the state's most beautiful places are accessible only by trail.

The 65 featured paths have been chosen for their outstanding scenery. The paths are numbered consecutively throughout the book. Trails rated **Easy** are generally less than 3 miles round-trip and gain less than 500 feet of cumulative elevation. **Moderate** trails range from about 3 to 5 miles and may gain 1000 feet of elevation. **Difficult** hikes vary from 4 to 8 miles with up to 2000 feet of elevation gain. Trails rated **Very Difficult** demand top physical condition, with a strong heart and strong knees.

Distances are given in round-trip mileage. **Elevation gains** are measured cumulatively, adding all the uphill segments. The **open dates** estimate when the trail will not be blocked by snow.

Key to
MAP SYMBOLS

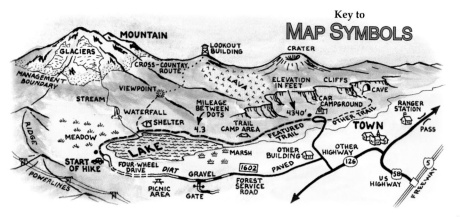

The **use** listing tells whether a trail is open to horses and bicycles as well as hikers. **Dogs** are allowed on nearly all trails; where there are rules they are mentioned in the text.

The text also notes which hikes require **trailhead parking permits.** The most common type of permit, a Northwest Forest Pass, costs $5 per car per day or $30 per season. Buy it at Forest Service offices or outdoor stores.

For the **maps** listed in the hike notes, or for more information about Oregon's outdoors, check with the **Nature of Oregon Information Center** (*www.naturenw.org*, 503-872-2750), at 800 NE Oregon Street, Portland, 97232, near the Lloyd Center MAX light rail stop.

Many hikes pass through **Wilderness Areas,** where bicycles and vehicles (except wheelchairs) are banned. Group size is usually limited to twelve, and campfires are banned within 100 feet of water or trails.

The 1904 Mosier House is one of many historic Oregon homes open as a bed & breakfast inn.

WHERE TO STAY

This guide suggests a variety of the most interesting alternatives to motels, from posh bed & breakfast inns to free, rustic campgrounds. Look for the symbols below on the book's ten regional overview maps, and then flip to the "Where to Stay" section at the end of each chapter for more details.

 Campgrounds are sometimes free. Those marked "$" cost $10 or less. Campgrounds are open all year unless otherwise noted.

 Bed & Breakfast inns and quaint hotels offer elegant alternatives. Room prices are for two people. Unless noted, pets are not allowed.

The dangers of Wilderness are often over-rated. No one has been killed by a black bear or cougar in Oregon's history, and grizzlies are extinct in the state. Rattlesnakes are so rare that hikers go thousands of miles without finding one.

The biggest danger in the woods is getting lost and cold. Always bring a knapsack with a warm, waterproof coat, a flashlight, a map and compass, a fire starting device, and enough water for the trip. Drink from lakes or streams only if you have filtered the water to protect against *Giardia*, a paramecium that causes malaria-like symptoms.

In the woods, follow the **no-trace ethic.** Leave no litter and pick no flowers.

Borax Hot Springs boils up in pools near Steens Mountain. For a complete list of hot springs, see "hot springs" in the index.

Groups to Explore With

If you enjoy the camaraderie of a group, or if you're new to hiking, consider joining one of Oregon's three largest outdoor clubs. These groups offer several hikes each week, but also organize snowshoe tours, climbs, canoe trips, cabin retreats, and sometimes even guided bus tours.

Chemeketans (Salem). Meetings at 360½ State Street, Salem. *www.chemeketans.org.*

Mazamas (Portland). Meetings at 909 NW 19th Avenue, Portland. *www.mazamas.org.*

Obsidians (Eugene). News at YMCA, 2055 Patterson Street, Eugene. *www.obsidians.org.*

Oregon's Climate and GEOGRAPHY

Portland's skyline rises from the west bank of the Willamette River.

Oregon's geography seems like something assembled by committee, with a rainforest here, a desert there, and everything else in between. In fact, because North America has been sliding westward for millions of years, Oregon has been collecting mountain ranges, one after the other. These barriers chop the state into distinct climate zones, from wet (in the west) to dry (in the east).

Portland Area

Despite its rainy reputation, the Portland area enjoys sun all summer. Lots of winter drizzle, with wind and an occasional ice storm, add up to 41 inches of annual precipitation.

Oregon Coast

Heavy rains from November to March supply most of the coast's 75 inches of annual precipitaion. Storms with 40-foot waves narrow beaches in winter, but the sand returns with gentler waves and some surprisingly pleasant weather in spring. When summer heats inland areas into the 90°s F, fog forms over the beach at night, and often doesn't burn off until afternoon.

Baker Beach, near Florence, is the northern edge of a 40-mile-long stretch of dunes.

Willamette Valley

Pioneer farmers claimed that crops never failed in the mild climate of this broad inland valley. Summers are rainless, with only a couple of truly hot days near 100° F. The winters are wet, pushing annual precipitation to 40 inches, but on average they bring only a day or two of snow.

Lower Table Rock's mesa overlooks the Medford area.

Southern Oregon

Although the Medford area is sunny and dry, with just 19 inches of annual precipation and a dozen summer days above 100° F, Crater Lake in the Cascade Range to the east sees 44 feet of snowfall a year.

Although 70% of Oregon's population lives in the Willamette Valley and Portland areas, restrictions protect farmland from urbanization (here, Willamette Mission State Park).

Cascade Range

This string of glacier-clad 10,000-foot volcanoes acts as a cloud barrier, keeping Eastern Oregon five times drier than Western Oregon. Summers in the Cascades are cool and mostly dry, but 40 feet of snow falls from November to April, enticing skiers and leaving a snowpack until July. Most of the volcanoes are extinct, but the range averages one eruption every 100 years.

Snow covers trails near the Cascade Range's major peaks (here, North Sister), from about November to July.

The 9000-foot granite peaks of Northeast Oregon's Wallowa Mountains resemble the Rocky Mountains.

Northeast Oregon

Hot, dry summers and cold winters mark this land of sagebrush canyons and irrigated wheatfields. Annual precipitation rarely tops 15 inches, except in the snowy Blue Mountains and Wallowa Mountains.

High Desert

In the starkly beautiful sagebrush lands of Oregon's high desert, rivers drain to alkali playas to die. Afternoon thunderstorms in the hot summers and snow flurries in the freezing winters add up to a mere 12 inches of precipitation. Treeless, wedge-shaped mountains dominate the vast landscape.

Paulina Lake fills a volcano's caldera in Central Oregon.

Central Oregon

In the rain shadow of the Cascade Range's magnificent snow-capped peaks, the sunny center of Oregon sees just 10 inches of annual precipitation. Easy access to skiing, whitewater rafting, and hiking have led to the spread of recreation homesites in the area's pine and juniper forests.

Steens Mountain towers above the Alvord Desert.

The Green Lakes nestle at the foot of South Sister. ▷

Oregon's
HISTORY

Oregon was one of the last blank spots to be charted on the map of North America. Palisaded by a harborless seashore on the west and the chasm of Hells Canyon on the east, the state remained a retreat for Native American tribes until Oregon Trail pioneers ventured here in the mid 1800s. Oregonians today are still pathfinders, defending their natural heritage with zeal.

A Klamath tribal legend says Crater Lake formed in a battle of the gods.

An Age of Ice

The first people in Oregon arrived here by 13,200 BC. They had crossed a land bridge between Siberia and Alaska laid dry by the Ice Age. That cooler, damper era increased the polar ice packs, lowering the oceans hundreds of feet. In Oregon, Ice Age glaciers carved countless alpine valleys. A glacier in Montana launched up to a hundred massive Missoula Floods that poured through the Columbia Gorge, inundating the Willamette Valley with meltwater from the Rocky Mountains.

The 70 sagebrush sandals from Fort Rock Cave date to 7050 BC.

The wetter climate allowed giant lakes to form in what is now the desert country of Southeast Oregon. In Fort Rock Cave, beside one of these vanished lakes, archeologists in 1938 unearthed some of the earliest human artifacts in Oregon—a surprising cache of 70 sandals woven from sagebrush bark.

Tales and Legends

Klamath tribal legends describe how a vengeful god destroyed a mountain, creating a lake. In fact, a cataclysmic eruption in 5700 BC reduced 12,000-foot Mount Mazama to a 6-mile-wide caldera, which filled to become Crater Lake. The blast's ash blanketed much of North America.

A later "Bridge of the Gods" legend suggested that people could once walk across the Columbia River with dry feet. The unlikely tale also has a basis in fact. A massive landslide in 1300 AD dammed the Columbia River for as much as two months. The dam washed out to create the Cascades, a rapids that lent its name to the adjacent Cascade Range.

The Explorers

Early European visitors to Oregon's harborless shore were not impressed. The first, Spanish pilot Bartolome Ferrelo in 1542, turned back at the Rogue River mouth in a torrential rainstorm. The English pirate Sir Francis Drake complained of Oregon's "most

Captain Cook named Cape Perpetua on a 1778 voyage.

TIMELINE

12,000 BC	10,000 BC	8000 BC	6000 BC	4000 BC	2000 BC	0

10,000 BC Last Ice Age flood inundates Willamette Valley.

7500 BC House of poles and mats built at Paulina Lake.

4000 BC Basalt flow from Mount Newberry creates Lava Cast Forest.

1300 AD Bridge of Gods landslide dams Columbia River.

1577 AD Francis Drake sails by Oregon.

11,200 BC Humans build campfires in Fort Rock Cave.

7050 BC Weavers leave 70 sagebrush sandals in Fort Rock Cave.

5700 BC Mount Mazama erupts, collapses to form Crater Lake's caldera.

0 Mount Hood eruption creates Crater Rock.

1543 AD Ferrelo of Spain sails by Oregon.

1700 AD Tsunami devastates Coast.

vile, thicke, and stinking fogges" in a brief 1577 visit.

Later British explorers hoped to find a Northwest Passage through Oregon—perhaps the fabled River of the West—enabling direct trade between England and China. British explorer George Vancouver was narrowly beaten to the discovery of the great river in 1792 by an American merchant, Captain Robert Gray, who named it the Columbia after his ship.

Meriwether Lewis and William Clark (shown here in a Seaside statue) led the Corps of Discovery to Oregon.

Lewis and Clark

President Thomas Jefferson envisioned an American empire extending to the Pacific Coast. After negotiating the Louisiana Purchase of French lands to the Rocky Mountains, he secretly ordered Lewis and Clark to explore a thousand miles farther, to the Oregon shore. Their 1804-06 expedition backed up the United States' claim to the Oregon Country by planting a flag at the mouth of the Columbia River. The Corps of Discovery spent a rainy winter in Fort Clatsop, a log stockade they built 7 miles south of present-day Astoria.

Early Settlements

Just five years after Lewis and Clark's return, business tycoon John Jacob Astor sent two troops to Oregon to found a fur-trading empire. After many mishaps, they built Fort Astoria in 1811, the first permanent American settlement west of St. Louis. After the US and Britain fought the War of 1812, Astor sold his fort to a British company rather than risk

losing it by force.

Both the US and Britain claimed the Oregon Country, but the two sides agreed in 1818 to "joint occupancy" of the region.

In 1825 British fur traders built a large settlement at Fort Vancouver. In 1834 American Jason Lee founded a Methodist missionary outpost on the Willamette River near Salem.

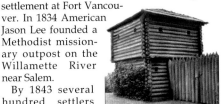

Replica of 1811 Fort Astoria.

By 1843 several hundred settlers lived in Oregon. Many of them met that May at the Willamette River settlement of Champoeg, where they narrowly voted to form a provisional government on an American model, effectively declaring that Oregon should be American and not British. Britain dropped its claim to the area in 1846. Oregon became a US Territory in 1848 and won statehood in 1859.

The Oregon Trail

After Lewis and Clark's harrowing description of the Rocky Mountain crossing, the idea of a wagon route to Oregon was widely ridiculed as impossible. But a determined missionary couple, Marcus and Narcissa Whitman, managed to pull a battered wagon with horses as far west as Idaho in 1838. Two years later, mountain man Joe Meek hitched a wagon to oxen and dragged

The Oregon Trail Interpretive Center near Baker City (see p244) includes a replica covered wagon on the actual Oregon Trail route.

1778 Captain James Cook sails by Oregon, launches sea otter fur trade.	1792 Captain Robert Gray of Boston discovers Columbia River.	1811 American fur traders found Fort Astoria; sell to British in 1813.	1825 British fur company builds Fort Vancouver on north side of Columbia River.	1840 First wagon crosses Oregon Trail; emigration peaks at 8000 a year by 1853.	1848 California Gold Rush; Oregon becomes US Territory.
1780	**1800**		**1820**	**1840**	
1779 The word "Oregon" first appears in print; origin unclear.	1792 British explorer Captain Vancouver overlooks Columbia River.	1805-06 Lewis and Clark explore Columbia, winter at Fort Clatsop.	1818 Britain and US agree to joint occupancy of Oregon Country.	1834 Jason Lee founds Methodist mission on Willamette River.	1843 Vote at Champoeg creates Oregon government on American model.

it all the way to the Columbia River. Word spread like wildfire among the restless souls of America: The impossible Oregon Trail was open after all.

By 1853, at the peak of the trail's popularity, 8000 people a year trekked overland 2000 miles from Missouri to Oregon, bringing cattle and wagons full of gear. In 1845 a Lost Wagon Train with 1000 people attempted a shortcut across Central Oregon, eventually straggling north to The Dalles with many fatalities. In 1853 a second Lost Wagon Train of 1500 people attempted a similar shortcut. They abandoned their wagons in the Cascade Range's forests but safely reached Eugene, doubling the population of Lane County.

Indian Wars

Smallpox, measles, and other diseases spread by contact with explorers in the late 1700s and early 1800s killed perhaps 90 percent of the native population in the Willamette Valley. As a result, Oregon Trail pioneers encountered little resistance to settlement there.

In Southern Oregon, gold miners and settlers formed vigilante troops that massacred natives indiscriminately with the goal of extermination. In the Rogue River War of 1853-56, the Takelma and Tututni tribes retaliated by killing settlers and ambushing soldiers. The US Army killed hundreds in a final battle May 27-28, 1856, and then deported 1400 tribespeople — virtually the entire native population of Southern Oregon — to reservations on the Northern Oregon Coast, where most

A plaque at Wallowa Lake honors the father of Chief Joseph, leader in the 1877 Nez Perce War.

died of disease.

In Northeast Oregon, the Wallowa band of the Nez Perce tribe was ordered by the US Army in 1877 to move to a small Idaho reservation, following the terms of a treaty signed by a different band. Chief Joseph led the 400-member Wallowa band out of Oregon, but after an altercation, battled the Army on a 1000-mile retreat toward what Joseph hoped would be political sanctuary in Canada. The Nez Perce were defeated in Montana 20 miles short of their goal and, despite international sympathy for their cause, were exiled to distant reservations.

The Gold Rush

The discovery of gold in California in 1848 inspired half the male population of Oregon to head south. Most returned by 1850 with gold dust and mining experience.

Gold strikes in Southern Oregon in 1850-51 drew thousands to Jacksonville. Later gold

The City Hall of Granite remains from the boom years of Eastern Oregon's gold rush.

discoveries in Eastern Oregon in 1860-61 created boomtowns of 10,000 people at Canyon City and Auburn, near present-day Baker City. In each case, after miners had panned or sluiced the easy gold out of the creekbeds, companies brought in heavy hydraulic hoses to wash away entire hillsides in the search for gold.

Transportation Develops

The Oregon Country's first railroad used a wooden track and mules to haul carts on a portage route around the Columbia River's dangerous Cascades rapids in 1851. Steel rails and a tiny locomotive improved the short line

TIMELINE

1853-56 Rogue River Indian War.	**1862** First locomotive; gold discovered in Eastern Oregon.	**1883** First transcontinental railroad arrives in Portland.	**1893** Cascade Range Forest Reserve created; becomes Nat'l Forests in 1908.	**1905** Lewis and Clark Exposition draws 3 million to Portland.

1860	1880	1900	1920

1859 Oregon becomes a state.		**1877** Nez Perce Indian War; Chief Joseph leaves Oregon.	**1894** Flood changes river courses, inundates Portland.	**1902** Crater Lake National Park created.	**1912** Women win right to vote in Oregon.
1850-51 Gold discovered in Southern Oregon.					**1915** Columbia River Highway opens.

The "Stump Dodger" railroad near Baker City once hauled timber and gold ore, but now is open to tourists.

ism, and Bonneville Dam, the first of many Columbia River dams that would provide cheap hydroelectric power.

The anti-Japanese hysteria that came with World War II led to the unconstitutional internment of thousands of Oregonians of Japanese descent in camps east of the Cascade Range. Despite blackouts and coastal patrols by blimps, a Japanese submarine succeeded in shelling Fort Stevens and bombing a Southern Oregon forest in 1942.

in 1862. In 1883, however, full-sized locomotives arrived in Portland on a new transcontinental track. By the early 1900s, railroads criss-crossed the state, with many temporary lines built to log remote forests.

Early highways, such as the scenic 1915 Columbia River Highway east of Portland, were built primarily for pleasure drives, but later replaced railroads in importance.

Depression and War

The Great Depression left a third of Oregon's work force unemployed and caused half of the banks to fail by 1933. In that year, President Franklin Roosevelt created the Civilian Conservation Corps (CCC), a program that employed young men from welfare families to work in the woods, building campgrounds, trails, and roads.

The federal programs in Oregon culminated in 1937 when President Roosevelt toured the state to open the spectacular new Timberline Lodge, built on Mount Hood by 7250 Northwest artisans to promote tour-

Pathbreaking Preservation

Haphazard postwar development and intense clearcutting of the National Forests in the 1960s and 1970s inspired a movement to preserve the beauty that had attracted Oregonians from the first. The Wilderness Act of 1964 protected key mountain areas; major additions since then have preserved many old-growth forests as well. Oregon led the nation with the Beach Bill of 1967, guaranteeing public access to beaches, and

The Capitol in Salem was built in 1939. Oregon has become known for pioneering legislation, including laws protecting the state's quality of life.

the Bottle Bill of 1971, requiring deposits on bottles and cans to reduce litter.

In 1971 Governor Tom McCall dared to stand up against pro-development business interests and denounce constant growth. On a nationwide broadcast the maverick governor urged people to visit Oregon if they liked, "but, for heaven's sake, don't come here to live."

Oregonians reelected McCall by a landslide. The Oregon Trail was no more, and quality of life, rather than quantity, had become the new goal.

A Japanese submarine attacked Oregon in WWII.

1933 Tillamook Burn torches 240,000 acres.	1948 Flood washes away Vanport, pop. 18,500, near Portland.	1961 Freeway completed from Portland to Salem.	1967 Oregon beach bill preserves public beach access.	2000 Steens Mountain Wilderness, Cascade-Siskiyou National Monument created.
1937 Bonneville Dam, Timberline Lodge built.			1995 Reinstated Grand Ronde tribe opens Spirit Mountain Casino.	
1940		**1960**	**1980**	**2000**
1935 Capitol burns; replaced with marble building 1939.	1942 Japanese submarine shells Fort Stevens, bombs Southern Oregon.	1954 Klamath, Siletz, and Grand Ronde Indian Reservations terminated.	1971 Governor McCall tells nation: Visit Oregon but don't stay.	1997 Assisted suicide law enacted, first in nation.
			1964 Wilderness Act protects Mount Hood, other areas.	

PORTLAND

Ranked among the nation's most livable cities, Portland is Oregon's urban heart.

The Portland area is home to nearly a third of Oregon's 3.5 million residents, but it remains a surprisingly laid-back metropolis. Even business executives here often wear athletic shoes and backpacks to work.

No other American city of Portland's size claims so many bookstores, bicycles, microbreweries, and hiking trails per person. Where else would the locals call themselves "Webfeet" and prize independent thinking so highly that the number one religious affiliation is "none of the above"?

Portland is anchored at the confluence of the Willamette and Columbia Rivers, a region born of water. From 18,000 to 12,000 years ago, Ice Age glaciers in the Rocky Mountains repeatedly launched floods that funneled through the Columbia River's gorge, deluging the Portland area with 400 feet of water and leaving the gravel plains on which the city now stands.

Two businessmen platted Portland in 1843, correctly guessing that the head of easy navigation on the Willamette River would become Oregon's major port. The founders flipped a penny to decide whether to name it after Boston or Portland, Maine—their home towns. The 1833 coin is now displayed in the city's Oregon Historical Center.

Today Portland has become an easy city to visit, with modern rapid transit trains connecting a lively downtown with the airport, the riverfront, the zoo, and even the Wildwood Trail, a 30-mile path through the forests of Portland's vast park system.

◁ **Pioneer Courthouse Square.**   △ **MAX rapid transit offers free rides in downtown** *(here, Ankeny Square).*

Exploring
PORTLAND

Wedged between the Willamette River and a wall of steep, forested parks, Portland's downtown packs most of its attractions within walking distance: museums, shops, galleries, bookstores, a riverfront promenade, and even a Chinatown. It's easy to get here on MAX, the rapid transit train that runs from the airport. If you're driving, avoid workday rush hours and look for one of downtown's many parking garages.

Chinatown
The Portland Classical Chinese Garden *(see p30)* offers a quiet one-block retreat in Chinatown. Chinese restaurants are nearby.

Washington Park
Famed for its success in breeding elephants, the Oregon Zoo in Washington Park *(see p34)* is just a ten-minute trip from downtown by light rail. Nearby are the World Forestry Center, the Childrens Museum, an extensive Rose Garden, the Japanese Garden *(see p35)*, and the start of the 30-mile Wildwood Trail *(see p32)*.

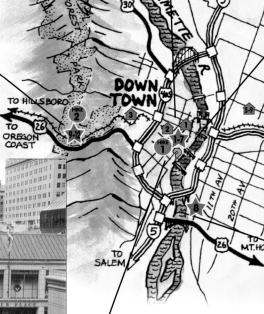

Downtown
In the heart of Portland's downtown district, the MAX rapid transit train passes the 1869 Pioneer Courthouse *(see p24)* and countless shops, including Pioneer Place (with sky bridge, in foreground). Other top downtown attractions include the Portland Art Museum *(see p31)*, the Oregon History Center *(see p30)*, Saturday Market *(see p28)*, and Old Town *(see p25)*, with its historic buildings and lively pubs.

Willamette Riverfront

A promenade through downtown's McCall Waterfront Park *(see p28)* passes a steam-powered sternwheeler and small sightseeing cruise ships.

Getting Around

Tri-Met's buses (above), the MAX light rail, and the Portland Streetcar make access to downtown easy. Rides are free within downtown's large Fareless Square zone. Tri-Met information is behind the waterfall in Pioneer Courthouse Square.

KEY

⭐ 5	Star attraction
HIKE 12	Featured hike
2	Campground
6	B&B or quaint hotel
?	Information:

Portland Oregon Visitors Association
26 SW Salmon St.
Portland, OR 97204
800-345-3214 *www.pova.com*

OMSI

On the Willamette River's east bank, the Oregon Museum of Science and Industry *(see p31)* includes an Omnimax theater and a visitable submarine.

Pioneer Courthouse Square

In the middle of downtown, this brick plaza bustling with commuters, students, tourists, and shoppers is affectionately known as "Portland's living room." Make yourself at home by sitting on the curving brick steps.

The square is the hub of the city's rapid transit and bus lines. Across Sixth Avenue stands the **Pioneer Courthouse**, an 1869 stone building with an octagonal wood cupola. The building first opened as a post office. Restored as a courthouse, it is the Northwest's oldest public building still in use.

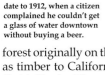

Portland's Benson fountains date to 1912, when a citizen complained he couldn't get a glass of water downtown without buying a beer.

Pioneer Courthouse Square itself has seen many changes since the city founding in 1843. The dense forest originally on this site was shipped as timber to California during the 1848 Gold Rush. The resulting stumps, painted white to prevent pedestrians from tripping over them in the dark, won Portland the disparaging nickname "Stumptown on the Willamette."

A bronze commuter with an umbrella is one of many whimsical statues at Pioneer Courthouse Square. Look for otters, bears, beavers, and a deer nearby.

Portland's first real schoolhouse was built here in 1858. But the school came down in 1883 to make way for the Portland Hotel, a seven-story Queen Anne chateau that fell in 1950 to make way for a parking lot. In the 1970s, 64,000 citizens donated money to create the present public plaza. Their names remain engraved on the square's paving bricks.

GETTING THERE: Catch any MAX train or Tri-Met bus to downtown and get off by the Pioneer Courthouse at 6th Avenue and Yamhill Street. If you're driving, look for one of several parking structures a few blocks away; expect to pay $1 an hour.

TRAVELING WITH MAX

Why fight freeway traffic when you can take MAX? The sleek electric trains of Portland's Metropolitan Area Express (MAX) glide through the city at about ten-minute intervals all day — and at about half-hour intervals most of the night.

From downtown the blue line runs west to Hillsboro (tunneling through the hills) and east to Gresham. The red line runs east from downtown to the airport. Art decorates many of the stations.

No fees are charged for rides in the downtown area. Fares are $1.65 to the zoo and $1.95 to the airport. The same tickets are valid on Tri-Met buses and on the Portland Streetcar. An all-day pass costs $4.

Be sure to pay your fare and validate your ticket at an automat where you board, because there are no conductors to accept fares on the train itself.

MAX rapid transit trains have become so popular that they are often standing-room-only in the free downtown area.

Old Town

Portland began as a riverside clearing where Multnomah Indians gathered campfire wood. When entrepreneur Asa Lovejoy stopped for lunch in that clearing with a drifter named William Overton in 1843, he offered to front the 25-cent filing fee if Overton would claim the site as a homestead and deed him half the land. They marked the site with tomahawk blazes.

Sandstone detail on the 1892 Dekum Building.

Today Portland's Old Town encompasses roughly the first three blocks west of the Willamette River, from the Burnside Bridge area south to the Morrison Bridge. Several of the 19th-century stone, brick, and cast-iron-fronted buildings are lively pubs, but not as many as in the 1870s, when Portland had one saloon for every 40 inhabitants. In those days, riverfront docks were two-storied, with an upper level used during spring's high water. The lower levels became hangouts for shanghai men, who delivered unwary passersby for forced service on merchant ships to China.

Highlights in Old Town today include the **New Market Theater** at Second Avenue and Ankeny Street, built in 1875 as a posh twin of London's Covent Garden, the neighboring **Skidmore Fountain**, the 1879 **Bishop's House** at 219 Stark Street, and the 1892 **Dekum Building** at 519 SW Third Avenue.

GETTING THERE: Take any MAX train downtown to the Skidmore Fountain stop. If you're driving north on Interstate 5, follow City Center signs to exit 1A, follow the Naito Parkway north along Waterfront Park 1.3 miles, and turn left a block on Oak Street.

The Portland Streetcar line opened in 2001, a modern reminder of the dozen streetcar companies that crisscrossed the city with tracks a century earlier.

PORTLAND STREETCARS

Modern streetcars, built in the Czech Republic, shuttle across downtown every 13 minutes on a four-mile route from 23rd Avenue to Portland State University, RiverPlace, and the Oregon Heatlh Sciences University aerial tram.

Rides are free in Fareless Square, which includes the entire downtown area. Beyond that zone the fare is $1.65, payable inside the streetcar after you board.

Because the streetcar route crosses the MAX rapid transit route at right angles near the center of town (*see map p27*), transfers are easy.

Built in 1879 beside a Catholic cathedral, the Bishop's House on Stark Street between Second and Third Avenues became a Chinese tong's headquarters and a speakeasy before being converted to a restaurant.

HIKE 1

Downtown Portland

Easy
2.3-mile loop   100 feet elevation gain
Open all year   Use: hikers, bicycles
Map: free brochure at Powell's Bookstore

At the Portland Arts Center, a movie theater's "Paramount" sign was relettered to spell "Portland."

Portland's downtown is compact enough to explore on a two-hour walking tour, but allow extra time to stop at museums and shops. If you tire along the way, simply catch a streetcar, train, or bus—they're all free downtown.

Begin at Pioneer Courthouse Square, a brick plaza with a coffeeshop above ground and a travel bookstore below ground. The bookstore offers free maps of downtown.

For the recommended walking loop, head across the square to Yamhill Street and walk downhill alongside the 1869 Pioneer Courthouse, *(see p24)*. At the next corner, veer left into Pioneer Place, cutting diagonally through this four-story shopping atrium *(photo p29)*.

Then zigzag another two blocks toward the river to the Dekum Building, an ornate office tower built in 1892 solely from materials native to Oregon. Walk onward another block to Stark

Street and you'll pass the gothic 1879 Bishop's House *(see p25)*.

Turn left at the corner onto Old Town's Second Avenue. Notice the high-water marks of Willamette River floods on the stone building at 133 Second Avenue.

Then turn right on Ankeny Street at the New Market Theater, an 1875 building modeled after London's Covent Garden. Cross First Street to the soothing water sounds of the 1883 Skidmore Fountain.

The next block fills with the arts and crafts vendors of Saturday Market on weekends from March through December. Cross the Naito Parkway to the lawns of Governor Tom McCall Waterfront Park and turn right on a promenade along the riverbank's concrete seawall. Here you'll pass the salvaged mast of the 1893 *USS Oregon*.

A few blocks beyond the Morrison

Critics of the post-modern 1983 Portland Building have relented, perhaps swayed by *Portlandia*, a two-story-tall copper statue crouched triumphantly above the door.

Getting There

It's easiest to take a MAX train to Courthouse Square at 6th Avenue and Yamhill Street. If you're driving, park in one of several parking structures a few blocks away.

Street bridge, head inland to Salmon Street Springs, a gigantic fountain with 185 computer-controlled jets. After a few blocks on Salmon Street, angle across Lownsdale Square, a park block donated in 1852 at a time when an elk was still said to graze here. The current elk statue dates to 1900.

As you continue up Main Street from the elk you'll pass the Portland Building, a postmodern office tower that raised eyebrows in 1983 for its daring angles and its teal-rust-cream color scheme.

A few more blocks up Main Street brings you to the Portland Center for the Performing Arts. Beyond this concert

A Portland druggist left a bequest of $5000 to quench the thirst of "horses, men, and dogs" with the Skidmore Fountain, unveiled in 1888.

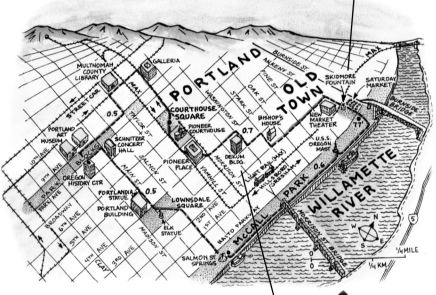

hall, detour briefly left along the Park Blocks to the Oregon History Center (*see p30*) and the Portland Art Museum (*see p31*), both worth an extended visit.

Then turn around and walk north through the park blocks. At Taylor Street, detour left to visit the stately Multnomah County Central Library, built in 1913 and renovated in 1997. A block later, turn right at the corner of the Galleria. With a 75-foot atrium, this building opened in 1910 as the first department store west of the Mississippi. Then walk back beside the MAX rail lines to conclude your loop hike at Courthouse Square.

Sandstone sculpture decorates the 1892 Dekum Building.

A popular riverfront promenade extends for a mile through Tom McCall Waterfront Park, between downtown and the Willamette River.

3   Tom McCall Waterfront Park

Portland replaced its original wooden waterfront docks with a seawall in 1929 and then buried the Willamette riverfront with a freeway in 1943. A "return to the river" movement in 1974 spurred the city to replace concrete with lawns.

Today the mile-long park between the Naito Parkway and the river is a great place to stroll and enjoy the river view. But there are other attractions as well: the changing water jets of the Salmon Street Springs fountain, historical monuments, and a maritime museum housed aboard the 1947 steam-powered sternwheeler *Portland.* Docked at the foot of Pine Street, the ship is open Friday-Sunday 11am-4pm. Admission runs $5 per adult and $3 for children ages 6-17.

GETTING THERE: Ride MAX to the Skidmore Fountain stop and walk a block east. Or drive Interstate 5 north and follow City Center signs to Naito Parkway exit 1A *(see map p27).*

4   Saturday Market

Open Sat-Sun, March-December. Free.

Rain or shine, artisans and craftspeople set up colorful booths to display their wares every weekend from March to Christmas at this freewheeling outdoor bazaar, the largest such market in continuous operation in the country.

This is the place to find local pottery, jewelry, and tie-dyed shirts—or just to buy a burrito and watch the crowds. By the market's own rules, everything must be made in Oregon and sold by the actual craftsperson.

GETTING THERE: Ride MAX to the Skidmore Fountain stop. Or drive Interstate 5 north, follow City Center signs to exit 1A, and take the Naito Parkway 1.3 miles to the Burnside Bridge *(see map p27).*

Pioneer Place, across Sixth Avenue from the Pioneer Courthouse, features an atrium with 70 shops. ▷

A CITY OF BOOKSTORES

Is it Portland's seemingly endless winter drizzle that makes reading so popular? Portland boasts more bookstores per capita than any other city its size in America.

One of the largest bookstores in the world, Powell's City of Books, fills an entire downtown block at 10th Avenue and Burnside Streets. Its shelves hold more than a million new and used books. The store provides fold-out maps to help visitors find their way through the maze of color-coded rooms.

Powell's operates six branches throughout the city, including Powell's Travel Store beneath Pioneer Courthouse Square. But Portland book lovers have many other favorite hangouts, including the Looking Glass Book Store at 318 SW Taylor, Twenty-Third Avenue Books at 1015 NW 23rd Avenue, and of course the Multnomah County Central Library. This stately 1913 building, restored to its original splendor, has more than 17 miles of bookshelves.

From the Chinese garden's teahouse, the view includes the Moon-Locking Pavilion—and a downtown skyscraper.

5 Chinese Garden

Open daily 10am-5pm Nov-Mar; 9am-6pm Apr-Oct. Adults $7, seniors $6, students $5.50, kids under 5 free.

Craftsmen from Portland's Chinese sister city, Suzhou, built this classical Ming Dynasty garden on a full city block in Portland's Chinatown district.

The tranquil, walled retreat features a bridged lake, curving walkways, a waterfall, 500 tons of Suzhou stone, and nine tile-roofed pavilions. A two-story teahouse offers 24 kinds of tea (about $4 a cup) and light Chinese snacks.

GETTING THERE: Ride MAX to the Chinatown stop and walk west (away from the river) three blocks to Everett Street and Fourth Avenue. Or drive Interstate 405 to exit 2B and follow Everett Street east 11 blocks.

6 Oregon History Center

Open daily 9am-9pm. Adults $10, seniors and students $8, children (age 6-18) $5. Kids under 5 free.

With four floors of exhibits and a research library, the Oregon History Center showcases the collection of the Oregon Historical Society.

Permanent exhibits include "Treasures of Oregon," including artifacts from the Lewis and Clark expedition, and displays about Portland's pioneer history, including the penny that was flipped to determine the city's name.

For more information call 503-222-1714 or check *www.ohs.org*.

GETTING THERE: Ride MAX to Courthouse Square and walk four blocks south to 1200 SW Park Avenue. Or drive Interstate 405 to exit 2A, take Salmon Street east five blocks, and look for parking.

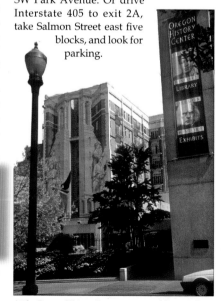

At the Oregon History Center, an eye-catching mural with a 3-D look features scenes from Oregon's past.

The Portland Art Museum's complex includes a five-floor exhibit hall.

7 Portland Art Museum

Open Tue-Wed and Sat-Sun 10am-5pm; Thu-Fri 10am-8pm. Adults $15, kids (age 5-18) $6.

Founded in 1892, this five-floor complex alongside downtown's west Park Blocks displays 35 centuries of the world's art.

The largest and oldest museum of its kind in the Northwest, the center regularly hosts major traveling exhibitions from Europe and the Far East.

Although traveling exhibits get top billing, don't miss the extensive permanent displays of Native American art (with intricate basketry), Asian Art (with elaborate lacquered Chinese cabinets), Northwest Art, and works by European masters, including Monet's 1914 *Water Lilies*.

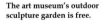

The art museum's outdoor sculpture garden is free.

No admission is charged to visit the museum gift shop, cafe, and adjacent outdoor sculpture garden—a pleasant spot for lunch or a rest stop on a walking tour.

GETTING THERE: Ride MAX to Courthouse Square and walk four blocks south and two blocks west to 1219 SW Park Avenue, or drive Interstate 405 to exit 2A, take Salmon Street east five blocks, and look for parking.

8 OMSI

Open Tue-Sun 9:30am-5:30pm. Adults $9, children age 3-13 and seniors $7.

Hands-on exhibits and live science demonstrations make the Oregon Museum of Science and Industry (OMSI) a particularly big hit with kids.

On the Eastbank Esplanade bike path, OMSI has sweeping views of downtown's skyscrapers across the Willamette River.

At OMSI you can experience a simulated earthquake measuring 5.5 on the Richter scale ($4 per ride), walk through a gigantic model of a heart, or experiment with pendulums.

Some popular attractions in the museum complex require separate admission:

A World War II-era submarine is docked beside OMSI.

▶ Climb aboard the *USS Blueback* submarine ($5.50).

▶Experience a giant-screen Omnimax movie ($8.50 adults, $6.50 kids).

▶ Watch a planetarium show ($5.50).

▶ See a laser light show ($5.50-$7).

Package rates are available. For more information call 503-797-4000 or check *www.omsi.edu.*

GETTING THERE: Drive north on Interstate 5 across the Willamette River bridge in Portland, take Water Street exit 300B, and follow signs to OMSI at 1945 SE Water Street.

OMSI's main building is a radically renovated former Portland General Electric power plant.

HIKE 2 — Wildwood Trail

Easy (to Hoyt Arboretum)
3.6-mile loop   500 feet elevation gain
Open all year   Use: hikers only
Map: Forest Park (Portland Parks & Rec)

Moderate (to Pittock Mansion)
7-mile loop   800 feet elevation gain

Very Difficult (entire trail)
30.2 miles one way   2500 feet elevation gain

A walk on the famous Wildwood Trail through Washington Park is a reminder of what's so wonderful about Portland. What other city would have a forest path leading from a world-class zoo, past a Japanese garden, to a mansion with a mountain view?

Although the Wildwood Trail stretches for 30.2 miles, mostly

Signs at every junction make it easy to follow the winding Wildwood Trail.

through the surprisingly wild woods of Forest Park, the relatively short hikes recommended here take only two or three hours.

From Washington Park's MAX light rail station, you can walk up the road 100 yards to a sign marking the start of the Wildwood Trail on the left. But along the way you'll pass the steps for the entrance to the Vietnam Veterans Memorial — and it's actually more dramatic to start your hike here, going under the memorial's bridge and following its spiral path up to the Wildwood Trail.

From there on, expect trail junctions

The Vietnam Veterans Memorial's path spirals up past polished stone walls engraved with names.

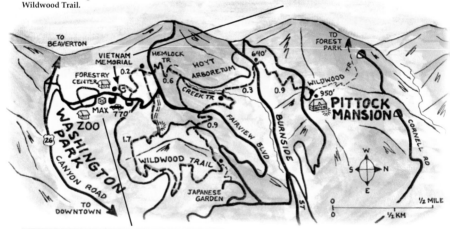

The MAX station at Washington Park is hundreds of feet underground, so you ride an elevator to the surface.

every few hundred yards. Just keep an eye out for the Wildwood Trail signs. Within 0.4 mile you'll cross a paved road and pass a huge green water tank to a viewpoint of Mt. St. Helens, Mt. Rainier, and the Pittock Mansion, a potential goal of your hike.

After 1.7 miles you'll get a glimpse down through the forest to the Oriental bridges and manicured greenery of the Japanese Garden (see p35). Detour

Almost all of the Wildwood Trail's 30.2-mile route traverses wild parks with native ferns and trees.

On a forested ridge beside the Wildwood Trail, the Pittock Mansion has a sweeping view of Portland and Mount Hood.

PITTOCK MANSION

Built in 1909-14 by *Oregonian* editor Henry L. Pittock, this elegant 16,000-square-foot mansion is surprisingly modern, with an elevator, intercom, and central vacuum cleaning.

Tours are available daily between noon and 4pm (adults $6, kids $3).

To drive here from downtown Portland, take Burnside Street west 1.6 miles and follow signs to the right half a mile.

The mansion exhibits Old World craftsmanship and surprisingly modern innovations.

down to the right to visit the garden if you have time.

Otherwise continue on the Wildwood Trail, which now climbs, crossing several paved roads and a ridgecrest before descending into the Hoyt Arboretum.

Arboretum means "tree museum," and in fact this entire valley is filled with native and exotic trees. You'll switchback down through ponderosa pines and then traverse an impressive grove of redwoods and sequoias. Finally you'll reach a footbridge over a creek.

If you're tired or if you're hiking with children, turn left onto the Creek Trail here to complete the shorter, 3.6-mile loop. In this case, follow the Creek Trail across a paved road, turn left onto the Hemlock Trail, and take that path over the ridge (crossing Fairview Boulevard) back to the Vietnam Memorial.

Getting There

Take the MAX light-rail train to the underground Washington Park station and ride the elevator up. If you're driving, head west from Portland on Highway 26 (Canyon Road) toward Beaverton, take the zoo exit, and park at the far end of the zoo's huge parking lot beside the MAX station, opposite the World Forestry Center.

If, however, you've got enough energy for a 7-mile hike, continue on the Wildwood Trail through the Hoyt Arboretum. Soon the path crosses Burnside Street — a busy, frightening highway you'll have to cross at a run. Then the trail climbs 0.9 mile through forest, crosses a paved road, and reaches the Pittock Mansion parking lot. Walk through the portico on the manion's left side to the spacious front lawn where there's a magnificent view of downtown Portland.

To complete your hike, return on the Wildwood Trail to the Hoyt Arboretum footbridge, turn right onto the Creek Trail until it hits the Hemlock Trail, and then follow this path left, over the ridge to the Vietnam Veterans Memorial.

Elephants have been a specialty at Portland's zoo since 1962, when Packy became the first Asian elephant born in North America in 44 years.

9 Oregon Zoo

Gates open daily 9am-6pm April 15 to September 15, otherwise 9am-4pm.
Adults $9.50, seniors $8, kids age 3-11 $6.50.

Penguins, elephants, and bears! Surrounded by the forests of Washington Park, the Oregon Zoo exhibits animals from around the world in natural-looking settings.

When you walk through the zoo entrance you'll pass a hillside with mountain goats and cross a bridge across the zoo train's tracks. Beyond the tracks, pavilions and exhibits are in all directions.

Keep to the right if you'd like to ride the zoo's miniature train. The 35-

Polar bears and penguins draw crowds, but the zoo also features native Oregon species such as elk and otters.

minute trip (open in summer) doesn't offer many views of animals, but instead wends through the forest to a station beside the Rose Garden and Japanese Garden. Fares are $3.50 for adults and $2.75 for seniors or children ages 3-11.

GETTING THERE: Take MAX or drive Highway 26 west of town to Washington Park.

10 World Forestry Center

Open daily 10am-5pm. Adults $7, seniors $6, children (age 5-18) $5.

Exhibits in this educational center explore the natural history of Oregon's forests and the uses of wood.

The center opened in a huge log building built for the 1905 Lewis and Clark Exposition. When that structure burned, the center moved here. Interactive exhibits now allow visitors to simulate a parachute smoke jump, a whitewater raft trip, a mechanical tree harvest operation, and a Siberian forest train ride.

GETTING THERE: Take MAX or drive Highway 26 west of town to Washington Park.

The World Forestry Center is both a museum about Oregon's forests and a center for programs.

Whimsical cows stand outside the Children's Museum building as part of a temporary art display.

 Japanese Garden

Open Mon noon-7pm and Tue-Sun 10am-7pm April-Sept; Monday noon-4pm and Tue-Sun 10am-4pm Oct-March. Adults $8, seniors $6.25, students $5.25, kids under 6 free.

Nestled amid the forests of Washington Park, this authentic Japanese garden includes a teahouse, waterfall, rock garden, zigzag bridge over a pond, and a dramatic view across Portland to Mount Hood.

Opened in 1967, the garden includes a stone pagoda from Portland's sister city Sapporo and carefully follows historic Japanese design, yet blends with the mossy native woods.

While in the area, don't miss the free formal **Rose Test Garden,** across the street from the Japanese Garden's bus stop and parking lot.

Lanterns and azaleas line winding paths in the Japanese Garden.

GETTING THERE: Take Tri-Met bus #63. Or drive Highway 26 west of downtown, take the Washington Park/Zoo exit, and follow signs past the zoo a mile.

 Children's Museum

Open Mon-Sat 9am-5pm, Sun 11am-5pm. Admission $7 (ages 1-54), seniors $6.

Known as CM2, the Children's Museum 2nd Generation offers hands-on fun for children age 12 and under. The museum's building is the former home of OMSI, another popular destination for inquisitive kids *(see p31).*

GETTING THERE: Take MAX or drive Highway 26 west of town to Washington Park.

A zigzag path leads through iris beds to a waterfall in the Japanese Garden's strolling pond garden.

<table>
</table>

HIKE 3

Sauvie Island

Moderate
7 miles round trip   No elevation gain
Open except in May floods
Use: hikers only
Map: St. Helens (USGS)

At the tip of Oregon's largest island, this woodsy hike along the Columbia River leads to a miniature lighthouse and a secluded, sandy beach.

Because the route is within the Sauvie Island Wildlife Area, you can expect to spot great blue herons, geese, or even a bald eagle—particularly in winter. It's also fun to watch ocean-going freighters steam past. Overnight camping and unleashed dogs are prohibited. High water sometimes closes the trail here in May—and can hatch mosquitoes in June.

Start the hike by walking through a fence opening at the far right end of the parking area to the beach. Then head to the left. Sharp eyes will already be able to spot the Warrior Rock Lighthouse

3 miles ahead. When the sand narrows near the third beacon tower, climb up to the left and continue on an old road that parallels the beach.

It's a good idea to wear boots because

Ocean freighters steam past the trail on Sauvie Island.

this road can be muddy after winter floods and for about a month after the Columbia River's usual high water from mountain snowmelt in May.

After 2.8 miles the road fades in a meadow and forks. Keep right to find the road leading 0.2 mile through the woods to the lighthouse's small rocky headland. A white-sand beach nearby makes an ideal lunch spot. For a viewpoint of the town of St. Helens, hike to the end of the beach and follow a trail 200 yards across the island's tip.

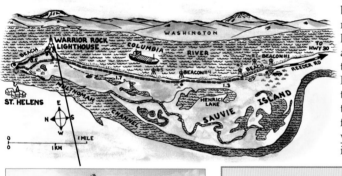

Though small, the Warrior Rock Lighthouse still serves as a navigational beacon on the Columbia River channel.

Getting There

Drive north of downtown Portland on Highway 30 toward St. Helens 10 miles, turn right across the Sauvie Island Bridge, turn left on Sauvie Island Road, and stop at the Cracker Barrel Grocery to buy Sauvie Island Wildlife Area's required $3.50 parking permit. Then drive 1.8 miles past the store on Sauvie Island Road, turn right onto Reeder Road, and follow this road for 10.6 paved miles and 2.2 miles of gravel to road's end.

WHERE TO STAY

Campgrounds (map pp22-23)

	Campsites	Water	Showers	Flush Toilet	Fee
1 MILO McIVER STATE PARK. Visit a fish hatchery on the Clackamas River. Drive 25 miles southeast of Portland to Estacada, turn south on Hwy 211 a mile. Info: 800-551-6949. Reservations: 800-452-5687.	54	●	●	●	$$
2 OXBOW REGIONAL PARK. The whitewater Sandy River loops around old-growth forest, trails, and a boat ramp. From exit 19 of I-205, follow Division Street east through Gresham 13 miles and follow signs. No pets. Gates locked sunset to 6am. Info: 503-797-1850.	67	●	●	●	$$

◁ The Sandy River at Oxbow Park.

B&Bs and Quaint Hotels (map pp22-23)

	Rooms	Private bath	Cont. breakfast	Full breakfast	Rate range
11 72ND AVENUE STUDIOS. Toward the airport, this affordable 1914 bed and breakfast inn has an elegant garden. 3415 NE 72nd Avenue, Portland, OR 97213. Info: 503-288-8501 or www.72ndavenuestudios.com.	2	2	●		$55-65
2 HEATHMAN HOTEL. A personal concierge serves you at this 1927 art deco hotel with an arts/literature theme. Pets OK. 1001 SW Broadway, Portland, OR 97205. Info: 800-551-0011 or www.heathmanhotel.com.	150	●			$159-259
1 HOTEL LUCIA. This 1920s downtown hotel has wireless Internet access and a 24-hour gym. Special floor for pets, smoking. 400 SW Broadway, Portland, OR 97205. Info: 877-225-1717 or www.hotellucia.com.	127	●			$155-305
5 KNOTT STREET INN. This bed & breakfast in a 1910 Craftsman home is a mile from the Lloyd Center at 2331 NE Knott St., Portland, OR 97212. Info: 503-249-1855 or www.knottstreetinn.com.	3	●		●	$125
6 THE LION & THE ROSE. In a 1906 Queen Anne mansion, this bed & breakfast inn at 1810 NE 15th Ave., Portland, OR 97212 is within walking distance of the Lloyd Center and small upscale shops. Afternoon tea included. Info: 800-955-1647 or www.lionrose.com.	6	●		●	$94-179
3 MacMASTER HOUSE. This grand 1895 Victorian bed & breakfast with a huge porch is near downtown and Washington Park at 1041 SW Vista Ave., Portland, OR 97205. Info: 800-774-9523 or www.macmaster.com.	8	2		●	$55-169
12 McMENAMINS EDGEFIELD. The buildings of a 1911 poor farm have been renovated as a hotel with a brewery, movie theater, golf course, and two hostels. Near I-84, east of Portland 12 miles at 2126 SW Halsey St., Troutdale, OR 97060. Info: 800-669-8610 or www.mcmenamins.com.	114	90			$30-115
10 McMENAMINS KENNEDY SCHOOL. This 1915 school now houses 5 bars, a brewery, and a movie theater. 5736 NE 33rd Ave., Portland, OR 97211. Info: 888-249-3983 or www.mcmenamins.com.	35	●			$84-109
7 PORTLAND'S WHITE HOUSE. This large bed & breakfast inn occupies a 1911 replica of the White House at 1914 NE 22nd Ave., Portland, OR 97212. Info: 800-272-7131 or www.portlandswhitehouse.com.	8	●		●	$125-225
4 RIVER'S EDGE. On Sauvie Island 20 minutes from town, this modern bed & breakfast has a private beach. 22502 NW Gillihan Rd., Portland, OR 97231. Info: 503-621-9856 or www.riversedge-bb.com.	2			●	$95-155
8 SULLIVAN'S GULCH. Wild West art decorates this 1908 bed & breakfast inn near the Lloyd Center at 1744 NE Clackamas St., Portland, OR 97232. Pets OK. Info: 503-331-1104 or www.sullivansgulch.com.	4	2		●	$95-125
9 TUDOR HOUSE. Antiques, a grand piano, and eclectic art fill this 1930 bed & breakfast inn a mile from the Lloyd Center at 2321 NE 28th Ave., Portland, OR 97212. Info: 503-287-9476.	2	●		●	$90-135

The Lion & The Rose. ▷

COLUMBIA GORGE

The Columbia River breaks through the Cascade Range in a spectacular chasm.

Several worlds collide in the Columbia Gorge, where the mile-wide Columbia River cuts through the lofty Cascade Range.

In the west, moss-covered rain forests cling to misty green cliffs. A few miles east, only scrub oaks dot a semiarid scabland. And in between, a colonnade of more than twenty major waterfalls separates the alpine meadows of the Cascade Range from the mudflats of the Columbia River, nearly at sea level.

The columnar basalt that forms the Gorge's cliffs was originally part of massive lava outpourings that inundated eastern Washington, eastern Oregon, and Idaho from 10 to 17 million years ago. These rock floods surged down the ancient Columbia to the sea, pushing the river north to its present location. As the Cascade Range grew taller the river kept pace by cutting its canyon deeper and deeper.

Much of the Gorge's present scenery dates to colossal Ice Age floods unleashed 18,000 to 12,000 years ago when a retreating Montana glacier undammed a gigantic lake. As the water poured through the Gorge 800 feet deep, it undercut the cliffs, leaving the graceful waterfalls visible today.

Many visitors first experience the Columbia Gorge by stopping along Interstate 84 to admire 542-foot Multnomah Falls, Oregon's tallest cascade. But many other marvels await between Portland and The Dalles — wildflower fields, slot-like canyons, tunnels, rock monoliths, historic towns, and of course, plenty of waterfalls.

◁ Oneonta Gorge (see p46).   △ The Columbia River cuts past Dog Mountain (see p54) and Indian Point.

Exploring the
COLUMBIA GORGE

The Columbia River's winding chasm through the Cascade Range has long been a channel for travelers—first for the canoes of powerful Indian trading nations and later for the covered wagons of Oregon Trail pioneers. Today Interstate 84 whisks traffic east of Portland through this dramatic gorge in an hour, but it pays to set a lazier pace, enjoying the scenic backroads, discovering the hidden waterfalls, and visiting the historic old river towns along the way.

Waterfalls

Dozens of cascades plunge from the cliffs on either side of the Columbia Gorge, including Multnomah Falls and Elowah Falls (*above*).

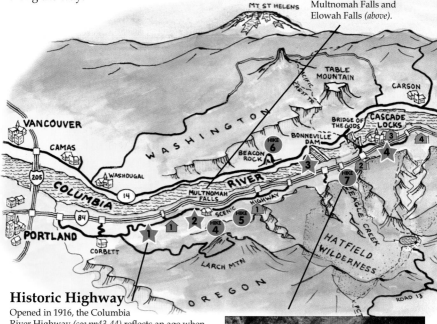

Historic Highway

Opened in 1916, the Columbia River Highway (*see pp43-44*) reflects an age when automobiles were used primarily for pleasure drives. Several sections of the route between Portland's outskirts and The Dalles are still drivable. Others are open as trails, including the Tooth Rock section (*below*) near Bonneville Dam.

Eagle Creek

Blasted out of the cliffs in the 1910s, the breathtaking trail up Eagle Creek's canyon passes Punchbowl Falls (*above*) and tunnels through the rock behind a waterfall at Tunnel Falls (*see p52*).

Hood River

This sunny riverside village still serves as the center of a major fruit-growing region, but it has also become an upscale hangout for windsurfers, who use the area's reliable winds to zip their sailboards back and forth across the Columbia River. The town itself has a charming historic district *(at right)* with quaint hotels, artsy shops, an excursion railroad, and popular brewpubs *(see p55)*.

KEY

5	Star attraction
HIKE 12	Featured hike
2	Campground
6	B&B or quaint hotel
?	Information:

Columbia River Gorge NSA
902 Wasco Ave., Suite 200
Hood River, OR 97031
541-386-2333
www.fs.fed.us/r6/columbia

UMATILLA HOUSE
1857–1930

The Dalles

Long an Indian trading center, this bend of the Columbia River became an important stop on the Old Oregon Trail. Today travelers stop in The Dalles to visit the Columbia Gorge Discovery Center or to tour the town's many historic buildings and museums *(see p58)*. At left, a mural on a downtown building depicts the pioneer Umatilla House hotel.

The historic Columbia River Highway loops around Vista House, a 1918 viewpoint and rest stop atop Crown Point.

Scenic Drive

Designed as one of the world's prettiest roads, the 1916 Columbia Gorge Highway still shows off the area's splendors, looping around viewpoints and arching past waterfalls on graceful bridges.

Loop at Rowena's plateau.

Two portions of the original 74-mile route remain suitable for pleasure drives. A 22-mile western section passes Crown Point's panorama and half a dozen waterfalls, including Multnomah Falls. A 15-mile eastern section loops down from a scenic plateau at Rowena.

GETTING THERE: For the western section, drive east of Portland 18 miles on Interstate 84 to Troutdale and follow "Historic Highway" signs from Lewis & Clark State Park exit 18 to Ainsworth Park exit 35. For the eastern section, follow signs from Mosier exit 69 of Interstate 84 to The Dalles exit 82.

Multnomah Falls

Oregon's tallest waterfall is such a popular stop for travelers that it has its own exit of Interstate 84.

Multnomah Falls plummets 542 feet in two tiers, with a scenic stone footbridge between the two cascades. Admire the falls from a stonework plaza, stroll a few hundred yards up to the misty footbridge between the falls, or explore farther on a network of hiking trails (*described on pp44-45*).

GETTING THERE: Drive Interstate 84 east of Portland to Multnomah Falls exit 31, park, and walk under the overpass.

The 1925 Multnomah Falls Lodge has an information center, gift shop, ice cream stand, and elegant restaurant.

Bonneville Dam

Open daily 9am-5pm except holidays. Free.

When President Roosevelt opened Bonneville Dam in 1937, it was the first federal dam on the Columbia.

Surprisingly, there's a lot to do at this Columbia River dam, and it's all free.

At the entrance, turn left to visit the park-like grounds of a fish hatchery. Automats sell fish food that you can throw into the trout tanks, but the top

At Bonneville Dam's fish hatchery you can watch 10-foot-long sturgeons from an underwater window.

draw here is watching giant sturgeons.

If you turn right at the entrance and drive a mile, you'll cross the dam's navigational lock to a visitor center with excellent historical displays. Self-guided tours take you to the dam's generators, the locks, and a basement window where you can count salmon swimming up a fish ladder.

GETTING THERE: Drive Interstate 84 east of Portland 40 miles to Bonneville Dam exit 40.

HISTORIC COLUMBIA RIVER HIGHWAY

Assigned to survey a Columbia Gorge excursion road for new-fangled automobiles in 1913, engineer Samuel Lancaster based his design on tourist roads he had studied in the Swiss Alps. No curve would be tighter than a 100-foot radius, and no grade steeper than five percent. He intentionally detoured the Oregon road to viewpoints and waterfalls.

Completed from Portland to Hood River in 1915, and from Hood River to The Dalles in 1922, Lancaster's road won international acclaim for its grace and beauty.

Today, sections at either end of the 74-mile route are still drivable (see p42).

Also, two significant portions of the historic road have been reopened as trails for hikers, bicyclists, and equestrians:

Park at the Tooth Rock Trailhead (at Bonneville Dam exit 40 of Interstate 84) and hike the old road east a mile to Tooth Rock, where bridge-like viaducts hug cliffs (see p40).

Park at the Hatfield East Trailhead (take Mosier exit 69 of Interstate 84 and follow signs) and hike the old road west 0.7 mile to a pair of scenic tunnels.

The twin tunnels at Mosier were built in 1919-21, filled with rubble in 1953, and reopened in 1999.

Views from the old road's Mosier Twin Tunnels are far more dramatic than from the freeway below.

HIKE 4 · Multnomah Falls

Moderate (to top of falls)
2.2 miles round trip   700 feet elevation gain
Open all year
Use: hikers only
Map: Trails of the Columbia Gorge

Difficult (to Wahkeena Falls)
5.4-mile loop   1600 feet elevation gain

Oregon's most popular trail climbs to viewpoints at Multnomah Falls, a 542-foot, two-tiered plume that plummets into a misty, mossy forest grotto. The classic hike here follows

Wahkeena Falls, a 242-foot triple cascade, has its own uncrowded parking pullout and trail, but you can also hike there from Multnomah Falls on a 5.4-mile loop.

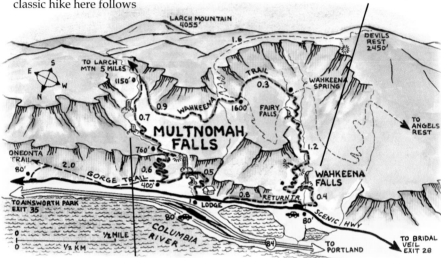

Above Multnomah Falls the trail becomes less crowded and passes a series of charming upper waterfalls.

a paved 1.1-mile path to the top of the falls. But you can beat the crowds and see half a dozen extra waterfalls if you have the energy for a longer loop.

As you start out from the parking area, you'll pass a historic 1925 stone lodge on your right (see p42), a good place to pick up a map or a quick ice cream cone. Walk straight toward the falls to find the paved trail switchbacking up to a stone bridge between the two segments of Multnomah Falls' long cascade.

The trail here has seen more than its share of natural drama. In 1991 a forest

Getting There

Drive Interstate 84 east of Portland 31 miles to Multnomah Falls exit 31, park, and walk under the overpass.

fire swept across the path, stopping just short of the lodge. In 1996 a bus-sized chunk of the waterfall's cliff broke loose, landed in the splash pool, and sprayed rock splinters past the bridge. In 1998, torrential rainstorms launched a gigantic landslide of rocks, mud, and trees that wiped out the trail and kept it closed for a year.

If your courage holds, continue on the reopened path past the stone bridge. Keep right at junctions to climb to a fenced overlook on Multnomah Falls' lip. The dizzying view aims down the cataract to the toy-sized lodge and its ant-like crowds.

If you're not yet ready to turn back, consider continuing on a 5-mile loop to

The water ouzel "flies" underwater in whitewater streams for minutes at a time in search of food.

WATER OUZELS

Naturalist John Muir called the water ouzel "the mountain streams' own darling, the hummingbird of blooming waters."

Although it doesn't look acquatic, the robin-sized water ouzel (or American dipper, *Cinclus mexicanus*) spends much of its life on the bottoms of raging whitewater streams.

If you watch very long beside nearly any Columbia Gorge creek you'll spot one of these slate-gray daredevils whirring along above the water, giving a distinctive *zeet-zeet* cry. Next, the bird is likely to land on a rock, bob a few times to eye the water's depth, and then plunge in, flapping its wings as it marches about the creek's bottom for up to two minutes at a time, looking for insect larvae among the pebbles.

Ouzels are never farther than a few feet from water, and even build their nests in cushions of moss behind waterfalls. Although this cheery species ranges throughout the American West, it lives only where creeks run wild and white.

A footbridge separates the upper 542-foot portion of Multnomah Falls from a 78-foot lower cascade.

see the area's other waterfalls. From the viewpoint at the top of Multnomah Falls, follow the Larch Mountain Trail up Multnomah Creek 0.7 mile. Then turn right on the Wahkeena Trail. This path climbs for 0.9 mile and then descends past Fairy Falls to an elegant stone bridge below Wahkeena Falls, a 242-foot triple cascade in a sculpted chute. Continue down to a parking area on the old Columbia River Highway. Rather than walk back to your car on this narrow road's shoulder for 0.8 mile, take the Return Trail that parallels the road through the woods.

HIKE 5

Oneonta Gorge

Moderate
2.7-mile loop   400 feet elevation gain
Open all year
Use: hikers only
Map: Trails of the Columbia Gorge

Next door to busy Multnomah Falls but usually overlooked by tourists, this delightful trail explores a cavern behind Ponytail Falls and then loops around Oneonta Gorge, a mossy chasm so narrow that Oneonta Creek fills it wall to wall. An optional 1.8-mile side trip leads to Triple Falls, where three plumes of water plunge 120 feet at once.

The trail starts from the historic Columbia River Highway beside 176-foot Horsetail Falls and climbs along a mossy slope of little licorice ferns. In late spring tiny white candyflowers and pink geraniums crowd the path.

After 0.2 mile turn right on the Gorge

A short side trip up Oneonta Creek leads to Triple Falls.

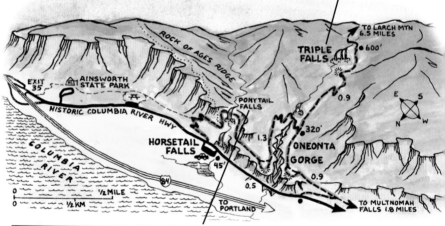

The trail around Oneonta Gorge ducks through a cavern behind Ponytail Falls.

Trail, which soon ducks behind 80-foot Ponytail Falls (alias Upper Horsetail Falls). The lava flow that created this falls' stony lip also buried a layer of soft soil. The falls have washed out the underlying soil, creating the cavern.

Beyond Ponytail Falls 0.4 mile take a right-hand fork for a quick viewpoint loop out to a cliff edge high above the highway. The view extends up the Columbia to Beacon Rock (see p49), but keep children away from the unfenced edge. Then continue on the main trail another 0.4 mile, switchback down to a dramatic metal footbridge above 60-foot Oneonta Falls, and climb to a junction with the Oneonta Trail.

Turn left here if you'd like to take the optional side trip up to Triple Falls and the perfect spot for lunch: a footbridge in a scenic creekside glen at the top of the falls. Otherwise continue the loop by turning right on the Oneonta Trail for another 0.9 mile and turning right along the road to the mouth of slot-like Oneonta Gorge. With any luck you'll be able to rest on the creek's pebble beach here while one of your party runs up the road another 0.3 mile to fetch the car.

The best way to see the inside of Oneonta Gorge is to put on sneakers

> ### Getting There
>
> Drive Interstate 84 east of Portland 35 miles to Ainsworth Park exit 35 and follow the old scenic highway 1.5 miles back to the large Horsetail Falls Trailhead parking area.

and wade knee-deep up the creek from the highway bridge. In late summer when the water's not too deep nor too icy, it's usually possible to trek half a mile through the 20-foot-wide chasm to an otherwise hidden, 100-foot falls. This adventure is not for the faint of heart, however, because the route sometimes involves clambering over a logjam or wading a chest-deep pool.

HIDDEN WATERFALLS OF THE GORGE

Most visitors to the Columbia Gorge miss the area's prettiest waterfalls—the ones tucked away in mossy side canyons not visible from the highway.

Here are three short walks that lead to five of these hidden gems.

Latourell Falls. From Portland, take Bridal Veil exit 28 of Interstate 84 and turn right on the Columbia River Highway 2.8 miles to the Latourell Falls parking area on the left. From here a 2.3-mile loop trail visits 249-foot Latourell Falls and a 100-foot upper falls.

Elowah Falls. From Ainsworth Park exit 35 of Interstate 84, turn left toward Dodson for 200 feet and turn right on

Upper McCord Creek Falls, on the Elowah Falls trail.

Frontage Road for 2.1 miles to Yeon Park. From here keep left on a path 0.4 mile to a fork. To the left 0.4 mile is 289-foot Elowah Falls. To the right 0.7 mile is 100-foot Upper McCord Creek Falls.

Wahclella Falls. Take Bonneville Dam exit 40 of Interstate 84 and turn away from the river 100 yards to a turnaround. The path loops 1.8 miles up Tanner Creek to Wahclella Falls, thundering in a canyon-end grotto.

Upper Latourell Falls splashes into a rocky pool.

Wahclella Falls spouts from a basalt slot.

The cliff-edged trail up Hamilton Mountain overlooks the Columbia River and the tip of Mount Hood.

HIKE 6 — Beacon Rock

Moderate (to Beacon Rock)
1.8 miles round trip   600 feet elevation gain
Open all year
Use: hikers only
Map: Bridal Veil (Green Trails)

Moderate (to Rodney Falls)
2.2 miles round trip   600 feet elevation gain

Washington's Beacon Rock State Park boasts two of the Columbia Gorge's most famous trails: a switchbacking path up 848-foot Beacon Rock, and the Hamilton Mountain Trail to Rodney Falls.

Lewis and Clark named Beacon Rock in 1805 while paddling past its cliffs. In 1915 a man named Henry Biddle bought the rock and arduously constructed a well-graded trail to the top. When the Army Corps of Engineers suggested the monolith be blown up for use as a jetty at the mouth of the Columbia, Biddle's family tried to make the area a state park. At first Washington refused the gift. But that decision quickly changed when Oregon offered to accept.

To climb Beacon Rock, park in one of the Highway 14 pullouts on either side of Beacon Rock and walk 50 yards along the road to the signed trailhead between the parking areas. Although nearly all of the 0.9-mile route has railings, parents should hold children's hands.

From the top the view stretches from Crown Point to Bonneville Dam. Kids love to point out Burlington Northern's toy trains chugging by, far below.

Lewis and Clark named Beacon Rock in 1805.

Tiny powerboats cut white V's in the Columbia's green shallows.

If you'd rather take the Hamilton Mountain Trail, turn off Highway 14

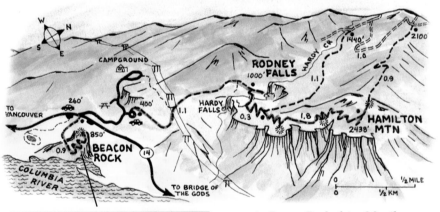

opposite Beacon Rock, drive 0.3 mile up a paved road toward the campground, and then veer to the right to the trailhead.

The trail up 848-foot Beacon Rock includes 47 switchbacks and dozens of railed catwalk bridges.

Getting There

From Portland, take Interstate 205 north across the Columbia River and turn right on Washington Highway 14 for 28.6 miles to Beacon Rock State Park. From Cascade Locks, pay $1 to cross the Bridge of the Gods, and turn left on Highway 14 for 6.9 miles. Expect to pay a $5 parking fee.

Pathfinder plant, common in the Columbia Gorge, won its name because the arrow-shaped leaves are silvery underneath, and as a result, tenderfeet roaming off-trail leave silver arrows pointing the direction they went.

The Hamilton Mountain Trail climbs through a second-growth Douglas fir forest with red thimbleberries, blue Oregon grape, and bracken fern. Soon you pass under a powerline, where a trail from the campground joins on the left.

At the 1-mile mark a side trail to the right descends to a poor viewpoint of Hardy Falls. Continue on the main trail a few hundred yards and go left on a side trail that ends at a railed cliff beside Rodney Falls, a fascinating, 50-foot cascade trapped in a rock-walled bowl. Then switchback down to a footbridge below the falls — a good turnaround point.

Athletic hikers can continue uphill at all junctions for 1.8 miles to Hamilton Mountain's summit, following a cliff-edged ridge with dizzying views.

 Cascade Locks

This Columbia Gorge town has been a legendary crossroads since Indians told of a "Bridge of the Gods" *(see below)*. The landslide that launched the legend left a rapids that pioneers circumvented with a portage railroad locomotive in 1862 and a navigational lock in 1896. Both can be seen at the city's Marine Park, which also has a museum, picnic area, camping lawn, and riverboat landing.

The Northwest's first locomotive is on display in Marine Park.

GETTING THERE: Drive Interstate 84 east of Portland 44 miles to Cascade Locks exit 44.

The sternwheeler *Columbia Gorge* leaves Marine Park for two-hour cruises daily at 11am and 2pm in summer. Tickets are $25 for adults and $10 for children.

THE BRIDGE OF THE GODS

One of Oregon's best known native legends tells of a "Bridge of the Gods" that allowed people to cross the Columbia River dry-footed at Cascade Locks.

In the legend, the two tribes on either side of the river met on the bridge for peaceful commerce — until one day an evil spirit named Loowit changed herself into a beautiful maiden, camped on the bridge, and drove the chiefs of the two tribes to a jealous war.

This so angered the great spirit Tyee Sahalie that he changed all the principal characters into mountains. The two rival chiefs became Mount Hood and Mount Adams, while Loowit became Mount St. Helens. But they kept fighting, hurling lava bombs at each other. Finally their earthquakes destroyed the bridge.

Geologists say the legend may date to a gigantic landslide that dammed the Columbia River here 550 years ago, allowing people to cross the river dry-footed for several months. The slide washed out to create the Cascades, a rapids that gave the Cascade Range its name.

Travelers on Cascade Locks' modern Bridge of the Gods, a 1926 steel span, pay a $1 toll.

WILDFLOWERS OF THE GORGE

A bridge between Western Oregon's rainforests and Eastern Oregon's sagebrush steppe, the Columbia Gorge blooms with all kinds of wildflowers. Here are favorites from the wet western canyons (on the left of this page) to the arid eastern hills (on the right).

COLUMBINE *(Aquilegia formosa).* In wet woodlands, this bloom has nectar lobes for hummingbirds.

BALSAMROOT *(Balsamorhiza sp.).* In April and May, this bloom turns entire hillsides yellow.

TRILLIUM *(Trillium ovatum).* This spectacular woodland lily blooms in April, a herald of spring.

TIGER LILY *(Lillium columbianum).* This showy June-July flower can pack a dozen blooms on one plant.

WILD ONION *(Allium acuminatum).* This onion fills Dog Mountain's meadows with tangy aroma in June.

FRINGECUP *(Tellima grandiflora).* Often overlooked, this trailside woodland stalk is cute up close.

WILD IRIS *(Iris tenax).* Also called an Oregon flag, this June bloom varies from blue to yellowish white.

DEATH CAMAS *(Zigadenus sp.).* Dangerously similar to edible camas, this bloom's root is poison.

ANEMONE *(Anemone oregana).* At higher elevations in the west, this bloom carpets forests in May.

SALSIFY *(Tragopogon dubius).* This dry June roadside flower turns to a giant dandelion-like seed puffball.

BACHELOR BUTTON *(Centaurea cyanus).* One of many showy blue composite flowers with this name.

HIKE 7

Eagle Creek

Moderate (to Punchbowl Falls)
4.2 miles round trip　400 feet elevation gain
Open all year
Use: hikers only
Map: Trails of the Columbia Gorge

Difficult (to Tunnel Falls)
12 miles round trip　1200 feet elevation gain

Built in the 1910s to accompany the opening of the Columbia River Highway, the Eagle Creek Trail is one of Oregon's most spectacular paths, passing half a dozen major waterfalls. The trail is also an engineering marvel. To maintain an easy grade through this rugged canyon, the builders blasted ledges out of sheer cliffs, bridged a colossal gorge, and even chipped a tunnel through solid rock behind 120-foot Tunnel Falls.

Today the trail is so popular the parking lot fills by 10am on sunny weekends,

After 3.3 miles, the trail spans a chasm at High Bridge.

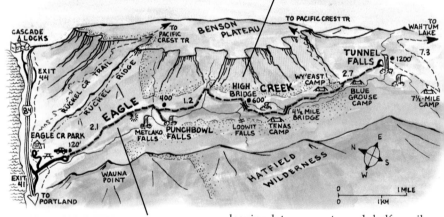

Cable railings add some security where the Eagle Creek trail has been carved into sheer cliffs.

leaving latecomers to park half a mile away. Although this is a great place to backpack, tenting along the first 7.5 miles is allowed only in four designated camp areas, where competition for weekend space is keen. Campfires are strongly discouraged. An additional caution to parents: trailside cliffs make this no place for unsupervised children.

The trail starts along the creek but soon climbs well above it along a slope of cedars and mossy maples. Look for yellow monkeyflowers and curving fronds of maidenhair fern overhanging the path. After 0.8 mile the trail traverses

Black-stalked maidenhair ferns wave above the path.

Getting There

From Portland, take Interstate 84 to Eagle Creek exit 41, turn right, and keep right along the creek for a mile to the road's end. Because the Eagle Creek exit is only accessible from the west, travelers from Hood River have to take Bonneville Dam exit 40 and double back on the freeway for a mile. Northwest Forest Pass parking permits are required at the trailhead. They cost $5 per car per day or $30 per season. Leave nothing of value in your car as break-ins are a problem here.

a cliff with cables as handrails. At the 1.5-mile mark several short side trails to the right lead down to a viewpoint of 100-foot Metlako Falls in the distance.

Continue on the main trail 0.3 mile to a ridge-end junction with the Lower Punchbowl Trail, a 0.2-mile side trail down to a broad, 15-foot falls with a bedrock bank suitable for sunbathing. Hike upstream to a gravel beach to peer ahead to picturesque, 30-foot Punchbowl Falls in a huge, mossy rock bowl.

If you're game for a longer hike, return to the Eagle Creek Trail and continue 1.2 miles to High Bridge, a metal footbridge across a dizzying, slot-like chasm. Here the creek has exposed a long crack in the earth—the fault along which this valley formed. For a nice lunch spot, continue

0.4 mile to Tenas Campground (on the right) and Skooknichuck Falls (on the left). For a still longer hike continue a couple miles further, duck behind Tunnel Falls, and 200 yards later gain a view ahead to the valley's last great, unnamed waterfall.

A classic 2- to 3-day backpacking trip continues to Wahtum Lake. Snow closes this 26.8-mile loop from mid-November until June. Start by hiking up the Eagle Creek Trail 13.3 miles to Wahtum Lake. Then veer left on the Pacific Crest Trail for 6.3 miles to the Benson Plateau, and turn left to descend the Ruckel Creek Trail back to your car.

Punchbowl Falls pours into a huge, mossy bowl.

HIKE 8   Dog Mountain

Difficult
6.9-mile loop   2820 feet elevation gain
Open all year
Use: hikers only
Map: Trails of the Columbia Gorge

Dog Mountain looms across the river from Oregon.

The most spectacular wildflower meadows of the Columbia Gorge drape the alp-like slopes of Dog Mountain, north of the Columbia River in Washington. In May and June these hills are alive with yellow balsamroot, red paintbrush, and blue lupine. Even flowerless seasons provide breathtaking views of the Columbia Gorge. Such beauty has made the steep climb popular, but with three trails to the top, you can choose your route.

For the best views, head uphill on the steep, scenic route. Then you can return on a gentler, longer loop that's easy on the knees. So start out from the far, right-hand end of the parking lot

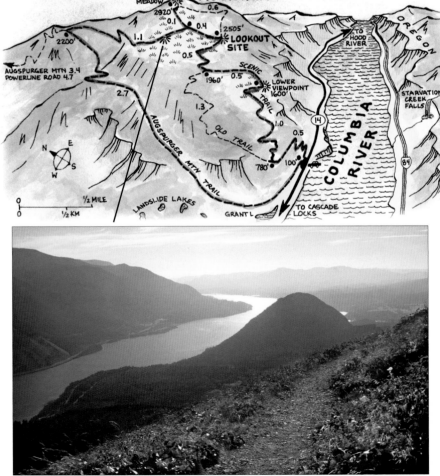

From Dog Mountain's summit meadow, the view sweeps west down the Columbia Gorge past Wind Mountain.

on the Dog Mountain Trail. After half a mile the trail forks. Ignore the left-hand path—the precipitous, viewless Old Trail. Instead turn right, through a Douglas fir forest brightened in spring by big 3-petaled trilliums and tiny 6- or 7-petaled starflowers. This path climbs almost a mile before suddenly emerging at a viewpoint on a windswept, grassy knoll.

In early summer, sunflower-like balsamroot and red paintbrush spangle this pleasant picnic spot, a satisfactory turn-around point. The view extends across the chasm of the Columbia Gorge to Starvation Creek Falls and sometimes-snowy Mt. Defiance.

The grander meadows on Dog Mountain's summit are nearly twice as high as this lower viewpoint. If your legs are up to the challenge, continue half a mile to another junction with the Old Trail. Head uphill here at a gruelingly steep grade for half a mile to an old fire lookout site in a steep wildflower meadow. Take a sharp left turn here and keep heading uphill for another half mile to your destination: the top of the meadow, afloat in panoramic vistas from Hood River to Mt. Hood and Cascade Locks.

Notice the flavorful assortment of wildflowers at this lookout: wild strawberry, chocolate lily, and wild onion.

Turn around after soaking in the view. Hike back down through the meadow 200 yards, and turn right at a sign for Augspurger Mountain. This path descends a ridge with views of its own for 1.1 mile. Then turn left at a junction. For the final 2.7 miles back to your car, the Augspurger Mountain Trail gently spirals halfway around Dog Mountain, like the flight path of an airplane slowly coming in for a landing.

Getting There

Drive Interstate 84 to Cascade Locks exit 44, take the Bridge of the Gods across the river (paying a 75-cent toll), and turn right on Washington Highway 14 for 12 miles. Between mileposts 53 and 54 park at the Dog Mountain Trailhead pullout on the left. A $5-per-car Northwest Forest Pass is required.

The Full Sail Brewery, downtown at 506 Columbia Street, has a tasting room open noon to 8pm daily.

 ## Hood River

Long a fruit-packing center for the orchards of the beautiful valley north of Mount Hood, this quaint Columbia River town has boomed with an influx of sailboarders, drawn by the sunny skies and reliable winds of the eastern Columbia Gorge (see p56).

Start your visit on

Excursion trains from Hood River traverse scenic orchards to Parkdale, at the foot of Mount Hood.

the edge of the historic downtown district at the public parking lot at Fifth Street and Cascade Avenue. Facing the lot, the employee-owned **Full Sail Brewery** has been creating specialty craft beers, ales, and lagers since 1987. Free tours are available by request on the hour.

The restored 1912 Hood River Hotel is in a historic district full of galleries, sailboard shops, and cafes.

After this heady introduction, amble through Hood River's old town to see the trendy galleries, boutiques, coffee shops, and sailboard stores. You might stop at the **Museum of Carousel Art** at 304 Oak Street, for their displays of organs, carousels, and wooden animals. It's open Monday-Saturday 11am-3pm and Sunday noon-4pm for a $5 admission ($2 for kids).

Then stroll by two hotels listed on the National Register of Historic Places, the 1912 **Hood River Hotel** at First and Oak, and the 1904 **Hotel Oregon** at Second and Cascade.

Next walk a block down First Street to the 1911 railroad station, still in use by Amtrak and by the **Mount Hood Railroad,** which offers excursion tours of the scenic Hood River Valley in historic Pullman cars. The 4-hour rides leave at 10am Wednesday through Sunday from April through October, and include a layover in the cute village of Parkdale at the foot of Mount Hood. Fares are about $23 for adults and $15 for children age 2 to 12.

GETTING THERE: Drive 63 miles east of Portland on Interstate 84 to Hood River exit 63.

Outfitted with wetsuit and flotation belt, windsurfers zip across the choppy Columbia River.

BOARDSAILING

A natural wind tunnel, the Columbia Gorge has become one of world's most popular centers for windsurfing and kiteboarding—especially in the sunny eastern end of the gorge near Hood River.

Beginners often start at Hood River's Sailpark (off exit 64 of Interstate 84), where lessons are available, and sometimes end up blown across the river to Bozo Beach in Washington. Launch sites for more experienced "boardheads" are at Mayer State Park (exit 76) and Viento State Park (exit 56).

HIKE 9 · McCall Preserve

Easy (to plateau ponds)
2.2 miles round trip   300 feet elevation gain
Open all year
Use: hikers only
Map: brochure at trailhead

Difficult (to McCall Point)
3.4 miles round trip   1100 feet elevation gain
Open May 1 to October 30

This cliff-edged plateau of oak grasslands and wildflowers belongs to the Nature Conservancy, a non-profit group that quietly purchases ecologically sensitive land. The preserve has two public trails: an easy path that passes several ponds to a cliff overlooking the Columbia River, and a steep trail that climbs to a panorama atop McCall Point.

Trail sign at Rowena Viewpoint.

The best time to visit this dry eastern end of the Columbia Gorge is spring, when flowers dot the slopes. Grass widows are at their showiest in mid March, while yellow balsamroot and blue lupine peak in early May. Avoid the heat of July and August. And remember to wear long pants if you're taking the upper trail, as it passes poison oak.

Because this is a nature preserve, dogs, horses, and bicycles are not allowed. Camping, flower picking, and off-trail hiking are also banned.

The easy path to the lower plateau starts at a stile and signboard on the opposite side of the old Columbia River Highway from the Rowena Loop

Mount Hood beckons from Tom McCall Point.

Named for the Oregon governor who helped preserve beaches and rivers in the 1960s, Tom McCall Point overlooks the lobed plateau of McCall Preserve, the Columbia River, and Mount Adams beyond.

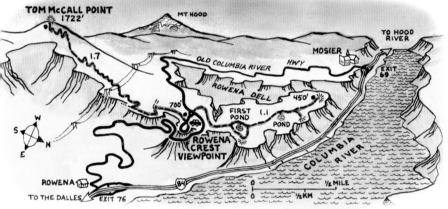

Viewpoint's entrance road. In spring, look here for balsamroot, purple vetch, bachelor buttons, and white yarrow. Ten-inch-long ground squirrels zip about the fields from February to June but hibernate the other seven months.

After 0.3 mile take a right-hand fork of the trail around a pond full of lilypads and cattails. Listen for the melodious warble of redwing blackbirds. The trail loops past a cliff-edge viewpoint and returns to the main trail. Continue out the plateau past a smaller, poison-oak-fringed pond, and reach trail's end at a cliff above the Columbia. Note the eight layers of basalt in the opposite cliffs, evidence of the lava floods that deluged Eastern Oregon and created this plateau 10 to 17 million years ago.

To try the steeper path up McCall Point (open May through October),

return to the parking area and look for a trail sign on the right at the start of the parking loop. This path joins an ancient road and turns left along the rim edge. When the trail forks at a large signboard, switchback up to the right on a steep path. The trail switchbacks steeply up the ridgecrest through scrub oak (and poison oak) to a summit meadow with glorious views of Mt. Hood, Mt. Adams, and the entire eastern Columbia Gorge.

Getting There

From Hood River, drive Interstate 84 east to Mosier exit 69 and follow "Scenic Loop" signs 6.6 miles to the Rowena Crest Viewpoint parking area. From The Dalles, take Rowena exit 76 and follow the old Columbia River Highway west to the viewpoint.

★ 6   The Dalles

The Columbia River's narrows at The Dalles has always squeezed traffic at the east end of the Columbia Gorge — first the salmon that leapt upstream past Indian spearfishers, then the wagons of Oregon Trail pioneers, and now travelers exploring east from Portland in search of wide open spaces.

The gothic Surgeon General's Quarters at Old Fort Dalles houses a fascinating collection of swords, guns, dresses, photographs, and furniture.

Museums and interpretive centers cluster about The Dalles. Start at the visitor information center at 404 W. Second Street to pick up a free map and a brochure with suggested **walking tours** to the commercial district's 47 historic buildings and the nearby Trevitt Historical Area's 54 homes.

A block behind the visitor center, take a look inside the (free) **Original 1859 Wasco County Courthouse** at 410 W. Second Place, once the seat of the largest county in the US, stretching to Montana.

A mannequin peers from a window in the historic commercial district.

Don't miss the **Old Fort Dalles Museum**, on the site of an 1860s US Army fort, a mile uphill at 15th and Garrison. Tour the museum in the Surgeon General's Quarters, check out the antique wagons in a nearby shed, and walk across the street to the

Volunteers demonstrate spinning in the Anderson House, a log cabin across the street from Old Fort Dalles.

Anderson House complex, a collection of late 1800s log cabins built by a Swedish immigrant near Dufur and moved here for restoration. Hours are 10am to 5pm daily from mid-May to early September. Adults are $3, but students get in free.

GETTING THERE: Drive Interstate 84 east to The Dalles exit 84 and head into town 0.6 mile to the visitor information center on the right.

★ 7   Columbia Gorge Discovery Center

Open daily 9am-5pm except holidays.
$6.50 for adults, $3 for kids age 6-16.

Ride a windsurfing simulator, pump a railroad handcar, or walk replica Gold Rush boomtown streets in this first-rate interpretive center. Admission includes a visit to the Wasco County Historical Museum, also housed in the center's dramatic stone building. Even without paying the entrance fee you can stroll paths outside the building past a pond, covered wagons, a replica Indian settlement, and several historic log cabins.

GETTING THERE: Drive Interstate 84 to exit 82 (just west of The Dalles) and follow signs.

A pioneer wagon stands at the entrance to the Columbia Gorge Discovery Center in The Dalles.

WHERE TO STAY

Campgrounds *(map pp40-41)*

	Campsites	Water	Showers	Flush Toilet	Fee
1 **AINSWORTH STATE PARK.** Near Multnomah Falls, this dark, wooded park has lots of trails nearby. Open mid-March through October. Take exit 35 of Interstate 84. Info: 503-695-2301.	49	●	●	●	$$
3 **CASCADE LOCKS MARINE PARK.** The camping lawn of this riverfront city park *(see p50)* is a popular stop for long-distance Pacific Crest Trail hikers. Info: 541-374-8619.	16	●	●	●	$$
2 **EAGLE CREEK.** Walk to a fish hatchery and the Eagle Creek Trail *(see p52)* from this Forest Service campground. Take exit 41 of Interstate 84 just west of Cascade Locks. Open April through September.	17	●		●	$$
4 **HERMAN CREEK HORSE CAMP.** This quiet Forest Service camp is the best access to the Pacific Crest Trail for horses in the Gorge. Take Cascade Locks exit 44 of Interstate 84 and drive through town 4 miles.	7	●			$$
8 **MEMALOOSE STATE PARK.** On the Columbia River, this somewhat noisy camp (named for a nearby island once used for Indian burials) has a playground and windsurfing beach. Reservations: 541-452-5687.	110	●	●	●	$$
7 **TUCKER.** On the bank of the Hood River, this county park is open April through October. Take Hood River exit 62 of Interstate 84, drive into town 1.1 mile, turn right on 13th Street, and follow Odell signs 5 miles.	81	●	●	●	$$
6 **VIENTO STATE PARK.** Beside noisy Interstate 84, this convenient park accesses a Columbia River windsurfing beach. Info: 800-551-6949.	75	●	●	●	$$
5 **WYETH.** Near a freeway, this Forest Service camp is open May 20 to September 15. Take Interstate 84 exit 51, just east of Cascade Locks.	14	●		●	$$

9 **DESCHUTES RIVER.** From the shady lawns of this riverbank state park campground, hiking trails and a 17-mile bike path follow the Deschutes upstream. Expect birdlife, fly fishermen, and river rafters at the end of their runs. Take exit 97 of Interstate 84 just east of The Dalles. Reservations: 541-739-2322.

Campsites	Water	Flush Toilet	Fee
58	●	●	$$

◁ **Deschutes River a mile above camp.**

B&Bs and Quaint Hotels *(map pp40-41)*

	Rooms	Private bath	Cont. breakfast	Full breakfast	Rate range
1 **BRIDAL VEIL LODGE.** On 30 acres in the Gorge's waterfall country, this bed & breakfast is off Bridal Veil exit 28 of Interstate 84. Info: 503-695-2333 or *www.bridalveillodge.com.*	2	●		●	$90
2 **COLUMBIA GORGE HOTEL.** Amid gardens atop a 210-foot waterfall, this restored grand hotel from 1921 is on the national historic register. Take exit 62 of Interstate 84 to 4000 Westcliff Drive, Hood River, OR 97031. Pets OK. Info: 800-345-1921 or *www.columbiagorgehotel.com.*	40	●		●	$159
3 **HOOD RIVER HOTEL.** In a historic downtown district *(see p55)*, this restored 1913 hotel at 102 Oak Avenue, Hood River, OR 97031 is furnished with antiques but has a Jacuzzi, nine kitchen suites, and an Italian restaurant. Info: 800-386-1859 or *www.hoodriverhotel.com.*	41			●	$69-169
4 **MOSIER HOUSE.** This turreted 1904 mansion, now a quiet bed & breakfast inn with an impressive view, dominates the Columbia Gorge hamlet of Mosier, population 290. Between Hood River and The Dalles, take Mosier exit 69 of Interstate 84. Info: 877-328-0351 or *www.mosierhouse.com.*	5	1		●	$69-125

Mosier House Bed & Breakfast. ▷

MOUNT HOOD

Oregon's tallest peak gleams like a great white beacon above the Cascade forests.

From Portland, the graceful cone of Mount Hood beckons on the horizon, just an hour's drive away. The 11,240-foot snowpeak has long been the city's great escape—a mountaineering challenge, a winter sports playground, and a dramatic backdrop for hikes through wildflower meadows and forests.

Mount Hood also remains an active volcano, with four minor eruptions in the 1800s and one in 1907. The mountain's most famous hotel, Timberline Lodge, stands atop avalanche debris from a massive explosion and lava-dome-building eruption that rocked the peak 2000 years ago. Today climbers still encounter sulfurous steam fumaroles and hot rocks in a basin just south of the summit.

Lieutenant Broughton, an English explorer under George Vancouver's command, named the peak in 1792 for a British admiral who had outgunned the Americans in the Revolutionary War.

When pioneers traveled the Oregon Trail in covered wagons in the 1840s, the mountain marked a final barrier along the difficult road to the promised land—even after Sam Barlow opened a new, harrowing shortcut around the peak's south flank in 1845.

Although the upper portion of the mountain is always clad in ice and snow (with skiing even in August), the meadows at timberline are generally snow-free from mid-July through October, and trails in the deep, forested river canyons surrounding the mountain's base are often open for hiking all year.

◁ Mount Hood from Timberline Lodge room 245.   △ Wildflowers along the Timberline Trail.

Exploring
MOUNT HOOD

Historic Timberline Lodge serves as a popular starting point for visitors to Mount Hood. Here you can tour the lodge, stroll through alpine wildflower meadows, or even climb to the 11,240-foot summit itself. For different views of the scenic mountain, head for the campgrounds and picnic areas at Lost Lake, Trillium Lake, or Cooper Spur. Round out your visit with a hike to a waterfall or a walk among the giant old-growth trees along the Salmon River.

Ramona Falls

A stairstepped fan across a cliff of columnar basalt, this waterfall (see p74) is both a popular day hike destination and a welcome stop on the 37.6-mile Timberline Trail (see p72) around Mount Hood.

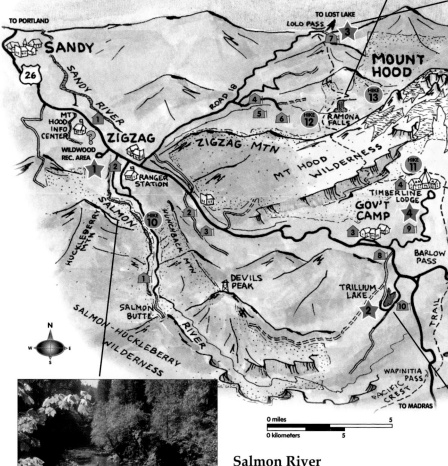

Salmon River

Some of the closest old-growth forests to Portland line the Salmon River. The Wildwood Recreation Area (see p64) offers short interpretive streamside paths, while the Salmon River Trail (see p64) explores wilder country upstream.

Lost Lake

Pretty as a postcard, Lost Lake offers a campground, cabins, and paddleboat rentals *(see p 68)*.

Cooper Spur

Historic Cloud Cap Inn is not open to the public, but the scenic Cooper Spur area includes two campgrounds and several top trails *(see p78)*.

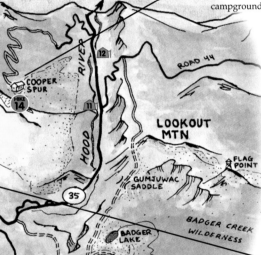

TO HOOD RIVER

COOPER SPUR

HIKE 14

12

RIVER

HOOD

11

ROAD 44

LOOKOUT MTN

FLAG POINT

GUMJUWAC SADDLE

35

BADGER CREEK WILDERNESS

BADGER LAKE

KEY

5 — Star attraction

HIKE 12 — Featured hike

2 — Campground

6 — B&B or quaint hotel

? — Information:

Mount Hood Info Center
65000 E. Highway 26
Welches, OR 97067
888-622-4822
www.fs.fed.us/r6/mthood

Timberline Lodge

Built as a make-work project in the Depression, this 1937 hotel became a grand expression of Northwest art. Tour the lodge's displays, hike the alpine wildflower meadows nearby, or go skiing in any month of the year *(see p70)*.

Trillium Lake

The closest large lake to Mount Hood, Trillium Lake has a campground, fishing dock, and shoreline loop trail, but it's also just a pleasant place to sit by the shore and watch the light change on the mountain *(see p66)*.

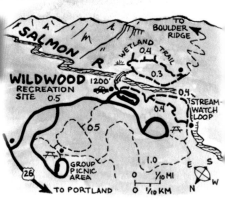

⭐ Wildwood Area

Open daily 8am to sunset, May to October.
$3 parking fee (or Northwest Forest Pass).

Picnic, fish, or hike along the wild Salmon River in this park-like area just 39 miles from Portland. Two easy interpretive loop paths, each 0.8 mile long, begin at the main trailhead parking area.

Trail benches are shaped like salmon.

The Cascade Streamwatch Trail ambles along the Salmon River and explores a small side creek, passing interpretive signs, a window with an underwater creek view, and a gravel beach suitable for sunbathing.

The Wetland Trail crosses a 300-foot bridge over the Salmon River. On the far shore, turn left onto a boardwalk that skirts a cattail slough in an alder forest.

GETTING THERE:
From Portland, drive Highway 26 toward Mount Hood 39 miles. Beyond Sandy 15 miles, turn right at a large sign for the Wildwood Recreation Site. The gate

An underwater window lets visitors watch a stream.

here is locked in winter, but hikers can always park here and walk half a mile to the trails.

The Wetlands Trail begins with a 300-foot river bridge.

HIKE 10   Salmon River

Easy   *(refer to map on opposite page)*
5.2 miles round trip   100 feet elevation gain
Open all year
Use: hikers, bicycles
Map: Salmon-Huckleberry (USFS)

A few miles upstream from the Wildwood Recreation Area, this quiet riverside path traverses an old-growth forest with ten-foot-thick red cedars and leads to small sandy beaches with deep green pools suitable for a chilly summer swim. Because a paved road parallels the route, it's easy to arrange a car shuttle so you can hike the 2.6-mile trail one way.

From the Old Salmon River Trail parking pullout, the path promptly descends to the river—a clear, 40-foot-wide mountain stream. In this ancient forest, huge Douglas firs filter sunlight for an understory of vine maple, sword fern, shamrock-shaped sourgrass, and deep green moss. Look for "nursery logs," fallen giants that provide a fertile platform above the brush for rows of seedling trees to catch light and take root.

Many side paths lead to the water's edge from the heavily used main trail. After 0.5 mile a particularly noticeable cross-path leads to a beach beside a ten-foot-deep pool in the river. Just upstream from this pleasant picnic site the river tumbles over two four-foot falls.

Continue on the main trail to the 1.3-mile mark. Then watch for another worthwhile side trail to the right. This one crosses a bouldery, mostly dry

A small beach at the half-mile mark of the Old Salmon River Trail makes a nice rest stop.

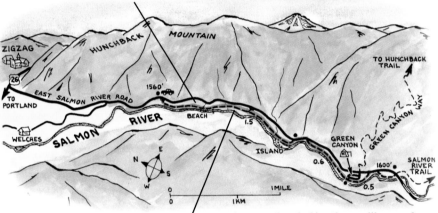

Ancient red cedars tower alongside the trail.

oxbow slough to a forested island with pebbly river beaches.

Just 250 yards after the side trail to the island, the main trail joins the paved road. Walk along the road's shoulder 200 yards until the riverside trail continues.

After another half mile you'll pass the campsites of Green Canyon Campground. Stay on the graveled path past the campground and an adjacent picnic area. Another 0.2 mile beyond, the trail joins the paved road for 200 yards and then ducks back into the woods for 0.2 mile to an upper trailhead parking area at the Salmon River Bridge.

Getting There

From Portland, take Highway 26 toward Mount Hood for 42 miles. At Zigzag turn right at a sign for the Salmon River Road and follow this paved route 2.7 miles. Two hundred yards beyond a National Forest boundary sign, park at a pullout on the right for the Old Salmon River Trail. A $5-per-car Northwest Forest Pass is required.

2   Trillium Lake

All 57 campsites at the Trillium Lake campground are often full on summer weekends, but stop here anyway for a picnic or a lakeside stroll with a stunning mirror-reflection view of Mount Hood.

The gravel 1.9-mile loop path around the lake includes several boardwalks across interesting marsh areas. The path is accessible even for wheelchairs, as are some picnic tables and campsites.

Canoeing around the lake is another popular option, made even more attractive by the fact that motors are banned.

Expect to pay a $5 parking fee if you don't already have a Northwest Forest Pass.

Trillium Lake is famous for its Mount Hood reflection.

The campground is closed from November to mid-May, but the mountain view is just as impressive in winter, when snowshoers and nordic skiers trek 1.6 miles to the frozen lake from the Trillium

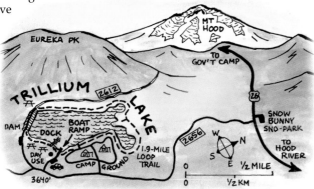

An all-accessible fishing dock at the day-use area is a popular place to plunk a fishing line or just enjoy the view.

Lake Sno-park on Highway 26.

A pioneer woman's grave in a meadow one mile north of the lake marks the Barlow Trail, an Oregon Trail route from the 1840s.

GETTING THERE: From Portland, drive Highway 26 toward Mount Hood 56 miles. Beyond Government Camp 3 miles, turn right at a Trillium Lake sign for 1.6 miles.

Picnic shelter at Trillium Lake. ▷

THE BARLOW TRAIL

Pioneers desperate for an Oregon Trail shortcut around Mount Hood to the Willamette Valley blazed the Barlow Road past Trillium Lake in 1845. Because the historic route parallels Highway 26 for many miles, modern travelers can stop to see informative displays, visit trailside graves, and hike portions of the actual trail.

Highway signs identify portions of the Barlow Road, an Oregon Trail branch.

Samuel Barlow and his wife Susannah set off from Illinois with their extended family on March 30, 1845, joining 3000 others who took covered wagons on the trail to Oregon that year. When they reached the Columbia River, however, they found an unexpected bottleneck. Hundreds of wagons were crowded on the riverbank six miles west of The Dalles, where the trail ended at the Columbia Gorge. The rapids ahead had already wrecked countless jerrybuilt rafts, drowning many travelers.

Could there be another way through the Cascade Range? Sam noticed a low point on the horizon south of Mount Hood and announced, "God never made a mountain without a way over it or under it, and I'm going to try." He led eleven wagons up toward the mountain, and another 17 followed a few days later. When they reached the Cascades' forests the group arduously chopped, sawed, and burned trees, trying to clear a path. Discouraged, they finally built a log cabin four miles east of Trillium Lake to store their goods, left their wagons, and hiked on to Oregon City on foot.

The next year Barlow built a crude road to rescue the stranded wagons and began charging other travelers a toll—even though his route was so rough in places that wagons had to be

Before the wagon route around Mount Hood, the overland Oregon Trail ended at The Dalles.

lowered down rocky chutes on ropes.

For a quick look at Laurel Hill, the most harrowing part of the Barlow Trail, drive Highway 26 east from Portland 51 miles toward Mt. Hood. Just before milepost 51, park at an Oregon History signboard on the right and walk 0.5 mile to the top of a rocky chute where Barlow Trail wagon ruts are still visible.

Barlow's trail down Laurel Hill was a rocky chute.

3 Lost Lake

Closed by snow mid-November through April.

Boardwalks of the all-accessible Old Growth Trail traverse the campground area for more than a mile.

Lost Lake was known to the Hood River Indians as "Heart of the Mountains." When white explorers had trouble finding the lake in 1880 they declared they were not lost; the lake was.

Today, famed for its picture-postcard view of Mount Hood, the lake has a large campground, a picnic area, a resort, rentable cabins, and a network of trails. Stop at the resort's store to pay campground fees or buy a $5 day-use

Lost Lake's resort rents canoes, rowboats, and paddleboats. Powerboats are banned.

parking pass, if you don't already have a Northwest Forest Pass. For the best view of Mount Hood, keep right past the store to a picnic area at road's end. This is also the start of a spectacular 3.4-mile lakeshore loop trail.

GETTING THERE: From Interstate 84 in Hood River, take West Hood River exit 62, drive into town 1.1 mile, turn right on 13th Street, and follow signs for Odell 5 miles. After crossing a bridge fork to the right past Tucker Park for 6.3 miles, then fork to the right to Dee, and follow signs 14 miles to Lost Lake's entry booth.

For a rougher but shorter route from Portland, take Highway 26 toward Mount Hood 42 miles and turn left at the Zigzag store onto East Lolo Pass Road 18 for 10.5 miles. At Lolo Pass turn right onto gravel McGee Creek Road 1810 for 7.7 miles until it rejoins Road 18. Continue on pavement 7 miles and turn left onto Road 13 for 6 miles.

△ Sunrise at Lost Lake brings pink reflections.   The lakeshore trail begins at a picnic area with a first-rate view. ▷

★1 Timberline Lodge
Open daily. Free admission; rooms $75–$230

Timberline Lodge began as a make-work program in the Depression, but by the time President Roosevelt dedicated this elegantly rustic hotel in 1937 it had become a grand expression of Northwest art. Today the lodge is still a must-see stop, both in winter when it's the hub of a bustling ski resort, and in summer when it's the base for alpine hikes and climbs of Mount Hood.

Carvings of animals and native designs decorate the lodge.

Tour the lobby to see the massive stone fireplace that supports the hexagonal

A lovable Saint Bernard serves as the lodge's mascot.

hall's roof. Go upstairs to find the Ram's Head tavern and the best views of the mountains. Don't miss the historic displays and video in the lodge's basement that describe the building's construction. Across the street is the newer concrete Wy'East day lodge, with a cafeteria, gift

---

CLIMBING MOUNT HOOD

First scaled in 1857, Mount Hood has become one of the most climbed snowpeaks in the world. In 1916 climbers carried up the materials for a fire lookout that finally blew off the summit in 1941. The peak has been scaled by a man with no legs, a woman in high heels, and even a gibbon named Kandy.

Still, the climb remains technical and dangerous. Rockfalls and sudden blizzard whiteouts cause fatalaties almost every year. An ice ax and crampons are essential. Climbers must fill out a wilderness permit and are strongly encouraged to register at Timberline Lodge before setting out from there, the most popular route. To reduce the sanitation problems of crowds, climbers are urged to carry

The Mazamas, Portland's mountaineering club, organized atop Mount Hood in 1893, when 155 men and 38 women convened on the summit.

their human waste out in plastic bags.

The trek up from Timberline Lodge usually takes seven hours to the top and four to return. Plan to start before dawn to avoid the afternoon's soft snow.

The most popular climbing route ascends from Timberline Lodge to Crater Rock's spire (at far left), traverses to the right on an icy knife-edge ridge called the Hogback, and leads around a dangerous glacial crevasse to the top.

Upstairs, the Ram's Head Pub offers stunning views, inexpensive light dinners, and local microbrews.

shop, equipment rental shop, and Forest Service information center.

The 37.6-mile Timberline Trail around Mt. Hood starts behind the lodge. Most hikers sample the route with short day hikes, although backpackers can tackle the entire trail (see pp72-73).

GETTING THERE: From Portland, drive Highway 26 toward Mount Hood 54 miles. On the far side of Government Camp, turn left for 6 miles up to the lodge.

Hand-wrought iron decorates the lodge's front door.

WINTER AT MOUNT HOOD

With four downhill ski areas and 16 sno-parks, Mount Hood is the most heavily used winter sports area in the state.

Timberline Lodge's high-speed quad chairlifts cover 3500 vertical feet of elevation, topping out at 8500 feet with the Palmer Lift, open through summer. In winter, skiers and snowboarders generally prefer the lower runs through the woods between Timberline Lodge and Government Camp.

Mount Hood Meadows, a few miles east, has 11 lifts, 2770 feet of vertical drop, and more powder snow. Lift tickets run about $10 more than at

A snowboarder carves a half-pipe at Timberline in August. Olympic athletes often train here in summer when other ski resorts are closed.

Timberline, but the area's more varied terrain still draws crowds.

Mount Hood Meadows has the mountain's only full-service nordic skiing center, but most people skip the resort's groomed trails in favor of the less expensive Forest Service ski routes that radiate from 16 plowed sno-parks along Highways 26 and 35.

To take the kids sledding down a hill, head for the Snow Bunny Sno-Park on Highway 26 east of Government Camp 3 miles. For an easy snowshoe tour, start across the highway at the Trillium Lake Sno-Park and follow a snowed-under road 2 miles to the frozen lake. Sno-park permits, required for your car, cost about $3 and are available at outdoor stores.

HIKE 11 Timberline Trail

Easy (to Zigzag Canyon)
4.4 miles round-trip   500 feet elevation gain
Open mid-July through October
Use: hikers, horses
Map: Mount Hood Wilderness

Difficult (to Paradise Park)
12.2-mile loop   2300 feet elevation gain

Very Difficult (around Mount Hood)
37.6-mile loop   8500 feet elevation gain

The Timberline Trail circles Mount Hood in 37.6 spectacular miles. A short day hike samples the route, although backpackers routinely tackle the entire trail in three- to five-day treks, and marathoners have been known to jog the entire loop in a day.

Start by walking up a wide paved path on the right-hand side of Timberline Lodge. Wildflowers here include

Wildflowers spangle the slopes of Paradise Park's alpine meadow from late July through August with red paintbrush (*above*), lupine, and avalanche lilies.

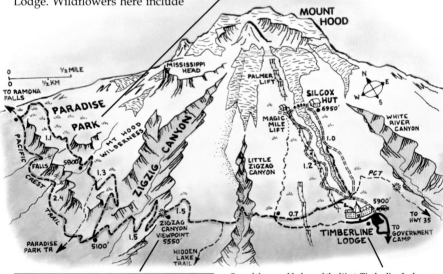

One of the grand lodges of the West, Timberline Lodge has artistic touches added by the skilled craftspeople who built it in 1937.

Zigzag Canyon stymied Oregon Trail shortcut-seeker Sam Barlow in 1845. He left his wagons behind and later built a road avoiding the 700-foot-deep chasm. The Zigzag River here still has no bridge, but hikers can often cross on rocks dry-footed.

At the 7000-foot-level on Mount Hood, the Silcox Hut is a scenic destination for a 1-mile hike from Timberline.

SILCOX HUT

The Silcox Hut served as the upper terminus for Timberline's original Magic Mile ski lift from 1939 to 1962. Restored as a chalet in 1992, it now offers a limited cafe in the European alpine tradition. Ride the modern chairlift up ($8 for adults, $6 for kids age 7-12), or hike the mile up from Timberline Lodge for free.

Groups of at least 12 can book the hut overnight, too. For about $100 a person you get dinner, bunkbeds, and breakfast. Timberline Lodge handles the reservations at 800-547-1406.

Derelict for decades, the Silcox hut was restored in authentic 1930s style by a nonprofit group in 1992.

An October sunrise along the Timberline Trail.

lupine and cushion-shaped clumps of white phlox. After 200 yards turn left at a sign for the Pacific Crest Trail—which also serves as the Timberline Trail at this point.

After a mile you'll cross Little Zigzag Canyon, and at the 2.2-mile mark you'll reach an overlook of a much larger gorge, Zigzag Canyon. Turn back here for an easy hike. For a longer day hike, continue 2.8 miles to the wildflower meadows of Paradise Park. If you're backpacking, be sure to camp under the trees and not in the fragile meadows.

Beyond this the Timberline Trail passes Ramona Falls *(see p74)*, McNeil Point *(pp76-77)*, and Cooper Spur *(p78)* on the loop back to Timberline Lodge. Note, however, that this portion of the route includes bridgeless creek crossings that can be dangerous on afternoons when snowmelt causes high water.

Getting There

From Portland, follow "Mt. Hood" signs 55 miles east on Highway 26. At the far end of Government Camp, turn left for 6 curvy, paved miles to Timberline Lodge's vast parking lot.

HIKE 12

Ramona Falls

Difficult

7.1-mile loop   1000 feet elevation gain

Open late April through October

Use: hikers, horses

Map: Mount Hood Wilderness

Like white lace, 120-foot Ramona Falls drapes across a stair-stepped cliff of columnar basalt.

The very popular trail to the shady grotto of this Mount Hood cascade starts out in a mossy alder forest beside the Sandy River's bouldery outwash plain. The pioneers who named the river thought its milky color was caused by sand. In fact the stream carries glacial silt—rock powdered by the weight of Mount Hood's glaciers.

After 1.2 miles the path crosses the Sandy River on a temporary bridge that's removed each winter to avoid floods. A few hundred yards beyond the bridge you'll reach a trail junction. The shortest route to the falls is the horse trail to the right, but it's less scenic, so leave it as a return route.

Instead veer left on a path that traverses a lodgepole pine forest to the wild Muddy Fork of the Sandy River.

Ramona Falls.

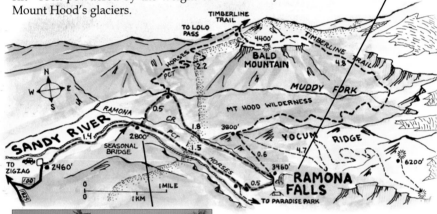

Here, turn right on a trail that soon follows the mossy bank of Ramona Creek—a delightful woodsy stream that leads up to the base of the falls.

Although camping is banned within 500 feet of Ramona Falls, a side path leads to designated campsites to the south.

Mount Hood rises above the rushing Sandy River.

Getting There

From Portland, take Highway 26 toward Mt. Hood for 42 miles. At the village of Zigzag, turn left onto East Lolo Pass Road. After 4.2 miles turn right onto paved Road 1825, and in 0.7 mile turn right across the Sandy River bridge. Continue 1.8 miles on what is still Road 1825, and then fork left onto Road 100 for half a mile to a large parking area at road's end. A $5-per-car Northwest Forest Pass is required.

WILDFLOWERS OF MOUNT HOOD

A wreath of alpine meadows around Mount Hood bursts into bloom in July and August. Some of the favorites here have showy seeds in fall too.

WESTERN PASQUE FLOWER *(Anemone occidentalis)*. This high alpine flower *(left)* is named for Easter (French: *pasque*) because it blooms so early, sometimes melting holes through the snow. By August it develops dishmop-shaped seedheads *(right)* that win it the name Old Man of the Mountain.

BUNCHBERRY *(Cornus canadensis)*. A miniature version of the dogwood tree, this 6-leaved plant carpets mid-elevation forests each June with 4-petaled blooms *(right)*. By September the blooms become a colorful cluster of red berries *(right)* that are allegedly edible.

AVALANCHE LILY *(Erythronium montanum)*. Days after the snow melts, millions of these curling white lilies erupt along the Timberline Trail *(above and right)*, an avalanche of white wildflowers. After just a week or two, however, the delicate blooms vanish like the snow they seem to love.

BEARGRASS *(Zerophyllum tenax)*. This plant resembles a giant bunchgrass, but every two or three years it reveals itself as a lily, sprouting hillsides of 3-foot-tall flower clusters. Native Americans wove baskets from its leaves, and bears sometimes dig up the succulent roots for food.

PAINTBRUSH *(Castilleja sp.)*. Paintbrush splashes red and orange across timberline meadows in August. The actual flowers, however, are green nectar tubes hidden amongst the showy sepals *(left)* to reward hummingbirds for pollinating it. Often parasitic, paintbrush saps the roots of nearby flowers—notably blue lupine *(background)*.

HIKE 13 McNeil Point

Easy (around Bald Mountain)
2.2-mile loop   400 feet elevation gain
Open June through early November
Use: hikers
Map: Mount Hood Wilderness

Difficult (to pond below McNeil Point)
6.8 mile round trip   1640 feet elevation gain

Wildflowers, tumbling brooks, and craggy mountain vistas lend alpine splendor to this ridge on Mt. Hood's northwest shoulder. An easy loop circles Bald Mountain to a postcard view of Mt. Hood. But for real alpine drama, climb the Timberline Trail to a pond reflecting massive McNeil Point.

The Top Spur Trail starts in a patch of blue huckleberries (ripe in August), and climbs through a forest of hemlock and Douglas fir. Look for bunchberry, carpeting the ground with white blooms

Beargrass blooms around a tarn on the Timberline Trail below McNeil Point.

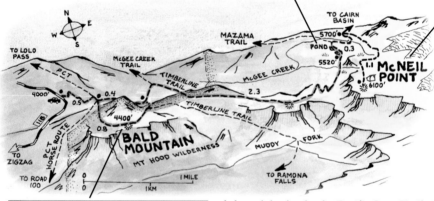

Mt. Hood from the Timberline Trail at Bald Mountain.

in June and red berries in fall. After 0.5 mile turn right on the Pacific Crest Trail for 60 yards to a big, 4-way trail junction that can be confusing. Go uphill to the right on the Timberline Trail. Don't go left, and don't take the Pacific Crest Trail to the far right.

The correct path emerges from the woods after 0.3 mile onto the steep, meadowed face of Bald Mountain, with views ahead to Mt. Hood and west to the distant Willamette Valley. After 0.4 mile through these meadows, watch carefully for the unmarked loop trail around Bald Mountain. When the trail reenters the woods after the second, smaller meadow, continue 100 yards to a fork in a draw. If you reach a stock gate to block horses you've gone too far.

Then take an unmarked left-hand fork over a ridge 100 yards to an unsigned

The McNeil Point shelter was one of four built by the Civilian Conservation Corps around Mount Hood in the 1930s.

junction with another section of the Timberline Trail.

For the easy loop, turn left here to return to the car. If you'd like a longer hike, turn right. If you turn right on this portion of the Timberline Trail (heading clockwise around Mt. Hood this time), you'll climb up a ridgecrest with wind-dwarfed firs, summer-blooming beargrass, and mountain views.

After 1.9 miles the trail switchbacks four times up a steep wildflower meadow. Then you'll pass a cascading, mossy creek and a trail fork at a (sometimes dry) pond amidst a display of early August wildflowers. From the pond, sharp eyes can spot the McNeil

Point shelter high on the ridge above.

If you're backpacking, be sure to camp in the woods out of sight and not on the fragile meadows or near the shore. Bring a lightweight backpacking stove, because campfires are banned within 500 feet of the shelter and are discouraged anywhere near timberline.

Marmots live in timberline rockslides around Mount Hood and whistle when alarmed.

Adventurers who want to continue to McNeil Point's shelter should keep right at all junctions, following the Timberline Trail another 0.3 mile past the pond. Then turn right at a "McNeil Point" pointer and follow a trail up a ridgecrest. The path traverses to the right across a rockslide or snowfield and climbs 1.1 mile to the 10-foot-square stone shelter, built in the 1930s by the CCC and later named to honor Portland newspaperman Fred McNeil (1893-1958). Return as you came.

Getting There

Turn north off Highway 26 at the Zigzag store (42 miles east of Portland) onto East Lolo Pass Road. After 4.2 miles fork right onto paved Road 1825. After 0.7 mile, just before a bridge, go straight on unsigned, one-lane paved Road 1828. Continue 5.6 miles and fork to the right on gravel Road 118 for 1.5 miles to the Topspur Trailhead. A $5 Northwest Forest parking pass is required.

HIKE 14   Cooper Spur

Moderate (to the shelter)
3-mile loop   1000 feet elevation gain
Open mid-July to mid-October
Use: hikers
Map: Mount Hood Wilderness

The highest hiking trail on Mt. Hood switchbacks up Cooper Spur's cindery shoulder. From this vertiginous perch, peaks from Mt. Rainier to the Three Sisters dot the horizon. Below, the Eliot Glacier is a splintered river of ice.

Park at Cloud Cap's restroom, walk across a primitive campground 200 feet to a message board, and go steeply uphill to the left on the Timberline Trail. After 0.2 mile fork left, following the Timberline Trail up into a bouldery gully. After another mile

The Eliot Glacier writhes below the Cooper Spur Trail.

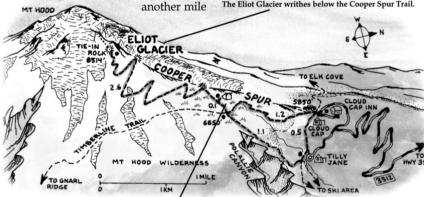

The Cooper Spur shelter dates to the 1930s.

you'll climb to a 4-way trail crossing in a field of blue lupine. Turn right 200 yards to find the stone shelter.

If you're up for a tougher 8.2-mile hike, continue up past the shelter on a well-graded trail 2.6 miles to Tie-in Rock, where climbers rope up.

To complete the loop, hike down from the Cooper Spur shelter and go straight at the Timberline Trail junction for 1.1 mile to a junction near a windowless 1924 cookhouse. Turn left, passing the historic Tilly Jane Guard Station and climbing gradually half a mile to your car.

Getting There

Drive Highway 35 around Mt. Hood to the Cooper Spur Ski Area turnoff between mileposts 73 and 74. Head west on Cooper Spur Road for 2.3 miles to Cooper Spur Junction and turn left onto Cloud Cap Road for 1.5 paved miles. Then continue straight on a slow, bumpy, one-lane gravel road for 8.2 miles. At a T-shaped junction, turn right toward Cloud Cap 0.6 mile to a restroom on the right. A $5-per-car Northwest Forest Pass is required.

WHERE TO STAY

Campgrounds *(map pp62-63)*

	Campsites	Water	Showers	Flush Toilet	Fee
9 ALPINE. A mile below Timberline Lodge, this small, handy camp is popular with climbers but suffers from traffic noise. Open July to Oct.	16	●			$$
3 CAMP CREEK. This forested USFS campground on the Barlow Trail route is near milepost 50 of Highway 26. Reservations: 877-444-6777.	25	●		●	$$
1 GREEN CANYON. On the Salmon River amid old-growth, this quiet USFS camp accesses a riverside trail. Open May through September.	15				$$
6 LOST CREEK. Near Ramona Falls *(see p74)*, this lovely, quiet forest camp has an all-accessible creekside trail. Open May through September.	16	●			$$
7 LOST LAKE. At a lake with a spectacular Mount Hood view *(see p68)*, this large campground also offers Adirondack-style group shelters and primitive cabins with propane lights for $50-100. Reserve cabins at 541-386-6366. Open May 10 to mid-October.	125	●			$$
4 McNEIL. On the road to Ramona Falls *(see p74)*, this sunny Forest Service campground is open from May through September.	34				$$
11 NOTTINGHAM. Opened in 2002, this quiet campground borders the whitewater East Fork Hood River. Near milepost 70 of Highway 35.	23				$$
5 RILEY HORSE CAMP. This equestrian camp on the road to Ramona Falls *(see p74)* accesses horse trails. Open May through September.	14	●			$$
12 SHERWOOD. Wedged beside the whitewater East Fork Hood River (near milepost 72 of Highway 35), this USFS camp has a footbridge to the Tamanawas Falls trail. Open all year.	14	●			$$
8 STILL CREEK. This dark, wooded camp across Highway 26 from Government Camp is open mid-June through September.	27	●			$$
2 TOLLGATE At a Barlow Trail tollgate, this 1930s camp 2.5 miles east of Zigzag on Highway 26 is open mid-May through September.	15	●			$$
10 TRILLIUM LAKE. With a spectacular Mount Hood view *(see p66)*, this lakeshore camp is open June through September.	57	●			$$

◁ Trillium Lake.

B&Bs and Quaint Hotels *(map pp62-63)*

	Rooms	Private bath	Cont. breakfast	Full breakfast	Rate range
1 BRIGHTWOOD GUESTHOUSE. On the historic Barlow Trail at 64725 E. Barlow Trail, Brightwood, OR 97011, this quiet, flower-filled 1930s bed & breakfast house sleeps four. Info: 888-503-5783 or *www.mounthoodbnb.com*.	1	●		●	$126 -145
3 FALCON'S CREST INN. Handy for skiing, this three-story bed & breakfast inn occupies a glass-fronted 1983 Cascadian chalet across from a brewpub at 87287 Government Camp Loop Highway, Government Camp, OR 97028. Info: 800-624-7384 or *www.falconscrest.com*.	5	●		●	$115- 179
2 OLD WELCHES INN. In the original 1890 Welches Hotel on the Salmon River, this bed & breakfast inn is at 26401 E. Welches Road, Welches, OR 97067. Info: 503-622-3754 or *www.mthoodlodging.com*.	5	3		●	$96- 162
4 TIMBERLINE LODGE. This grand 1937 hotel *(see p70)* at 6000 feet elevation on Mount Hood has individually designed rooms, spectacular views, a heated pool, and Jacuzzi. Info: 800-547-1406 or *www.timberlinelodge.com*.	70	60			$85- 250

Timberline Lodge room. ▷

North Coast

Craggy capes, quiet beaches, and bustling resort towns alternate along the shore.

As a vacation getaway, the Oregon Coast might be said to date to 1806, when explorers Lewis and Clark set up camp on a Seaside beach and hiked across a scenic headland nearby, admiring the spectacular view.

Today the North Coast has become a popular weekend retreat from Portland and the cities of the Willamette Valley, an hour's drive to the east.

Still, vast stretches of this coastline remain remarkably quiet, isolated by dense rainforests that descend from the Coast Range's ridges to the edge of the beach itself.

The picturesque headlands and islands that give this shore its distinctive charm are relics of monumental basalt lava flows that originated in Eastern Oregon 10 to 17 million years ago. The rock floods poured down the Columbia River to the sea, gradually pushing the river north. When the Coast Range later rose, erosion left the tough basalt in the old river channels exposed as capes from Astoria to Newport.

The Oregon Coast's 260 miles of beaches are entirely open to the public, but visitors should note a few rules and tips:

Do not build fires in driftwood piles, remove tidepool animals, or disturb seals or birds.

Although surfing is possible with a wetsuit, don't expect to swim otherwise, because the Alaska Current leaves the water chilly year-round and can create a dangerous undertow.

The tide rises and falls about eight feet twice a day, but large "sneaker waves" can surprise beach walkers at any time.

◁ **Harts Cove** *(see p100-101).* △ **Sunset from Newport's Nye Beach** *(see p104).*

Exploring the
NORTH COAST

After driving an hour across the Coast Range from Portland or the Willamette Valley, your first glimpse of the Pacific Ocean is likely to be between motel signs and billboards in Seaside or Lincoln City — but just beyond these busy vacation centers you'll discover long stretches of quiet beaches, parks, and headlands. Inland, rainforest paths lead past giant trees to hidden waterfalls and viewpoints.

Astoria

The oldest permanent American settlement in the West, Astoria is packed with historic charm: Victorian homes, museums, and an antique trolley that offers rides along the waterfront *(see p84)*.

Ecola State Park

Postcards of the Oregon Coast often wear photos from this park on the cliff-edged capes of Tillamook Head *(see p91)*. The easiest place to size up the 1000-foot-tall headland is from the popular beach at Seaside *(at left, and on p90)*, a resort town with a carnival atmosphere.

Newport

This romantic port features two world-class aquariums, two historic lighthouses, and a bustling bayfront *(see pp103-04)*. There's plenty of room for guests, too; Newport has more oceanview hotel rooms than any other city between San Francisco and Seattle.

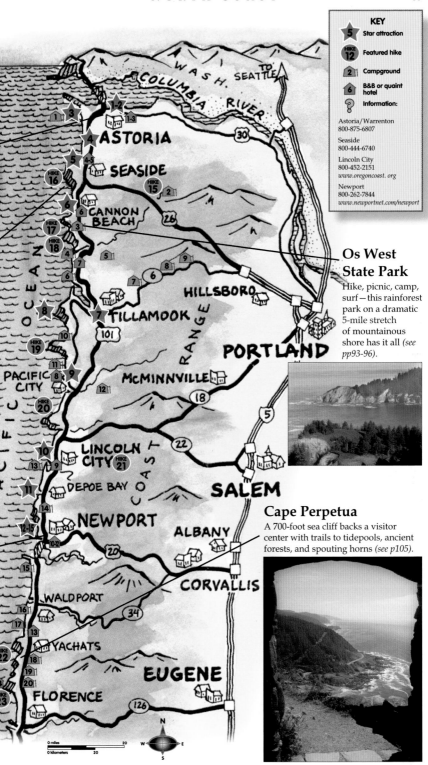

KEY

5 Star attraction

HIKE 12 Featured hike

2 Campground

6 B&B or quaint hotel

? Information:

Astoria/Warrenton
800-875-6807

Seaside
800-444-6740

Lincoln City
800-452-2151
www.oregoncoast.org

Newport
800-262-7844
www.newportnet.com/newport

Os West State Park

Hike, picnic, camp, surf—this rainforest park on a dramatic 5-mile stretch of mountainous shore has it all *(see pp93-96)*.

Cape Perpetua

A 700-foot sea cliff backs a visitor center with trails to tidepools, ancient forests, and spouting horns *(see p105)*.

Astoria

From the barnacled piers of cannery docks to the painted gingerbread of Victorian mansions, this picturesque city on the Columbia River wears its history with a salty pride. A 2.3-mile walking tour samples the old town's sights.

Start your visit at the first-class Columbia River Maritime Museum, on

The gingerbread porch of a Victorian house in Astoria's historic district was built by the blind son of Captain Flavel with material gleaned from the broomstick factory where he worked.

The Astoria-Megler Bridge across the Columbia River arches above the Finnish community's Suomi Hall.

the riverfront. In front of the museum you'll pass a trolley stop for "Old 300," a restored 1913 San Antonio streetcar that passes about every 45 minutes in summer (weekdays 3-9pm, weekends noon-9pm), as well as Friday through Sunday in fall, and on non-stormy weekends in winter. For $1 you can ride as long as you like on the 2.8-mile track

along Astoria's waterfront.

A promenade also follows the trolley route, so you can either walk or ride the first 0.7 mile of the recommended loop tour, heading west past docks, shops, offices, restaurants, and fish-packing plants to Sixth Street. Here detour briefly to the right to climb a viewing platform on a pier beside the river's main shipping channel.

Then head inland a block on 6th Street, turn left beside busy Highway 30, and keep straight on quiet Astor Street three blocks. At 10th Street turn right two blocks to Astoria's business district, turn right on Commercial two blocks to the county courthouse, and turn left on 8th Street to the Flavel House, a museum in a sumptuous Queen Anne-style mansion built by a Columbia River bar pilot. Stop

The lightship *Columbia* served for decades as a floating lighthouse at the mouth of the Columbia River. Now it's docked at the Columbia River Maritime Musem. Admission to the museum inclues a boarding pass to the old ship.

here to buy a $3.50 brochure describing 64 historic buildings along the next mile of the walking tour's route. Or simply follow the zigzagging route on the map below, admiring the elegant churches and ornate homes, several of which have been converted to bed & breakfast inns. A few blocks before returning to your car at the riverfront museum you'll pass a replica stockade tower built on the the site of the original Fort Astoria, where the city began in 1811.

A replica of Fort Astoria stands at 15th and Exchange streets.

exhibits feature shipwrecks, fishing, and early exploration. Admission includes a boarding pass to the adjacent lightship *Columbia* that served as a floating light-house at

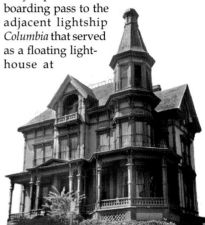
Captain George Flavel built this turreted, Queen Anne-style mansion at 441 8th Street in 1885. Restored as an elegant museum, it's open daily from 10am to 5pm for a small fee.

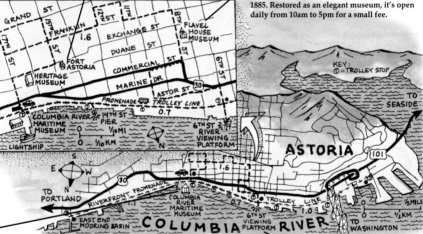

GETTING THERE: Start at the Columbia River Maritime Museum, on Highway 30 at 17th Street, 1.5 miles west of the Highway 101 bridge across the Columbia River.

2 Columbia River Maritime Museum

Open daily 9:30-5pm. Adults $8, seniors $7, children ages 6-17 $4.

On Astoria's riverfront promenade at 6th Street a viewing platform overlooks the river's main shipping channel. Shops nearby offer coffee drinks and ice cream.

In this first-rate interpretive center you can spin the wheel of a replica steamboat pilothouse, walk the bridge of a World War II destroyer, or watch the rotating prisms of a lighthouse's lens. Other

the river's entrance until 1979.

GETTING THERE: Drive Highway 30 to 17th Street in Astoria, 1.5 miles west of the Highway 101 bridge across the Columbia River.

3 Fort Stevens

Day use: open all year; $3 parking permit.
Military museum: open 10am-6pm daily from
May through September and 10am-4pm
daily the rest of the year; $3 parking fee.

Once a military reservation guarding the mouth of the Columbia River, this 11-square-mile state park has the largest campground in Oregon—and many other attractions as well:

A viewing platform overlooks the Columbia River's South Jetty, a good place to watch birds and waves.

fort's history. You can visit concrete bunkers and gun batteries nearby for free. Civil War reenactments, blacksmithing demonstrations, and tours in a 1950s Army truck take place in summer.

▶ Battery Russell, a visitable bunker that saw service from 1904 to 1944.

GETTING THERE: Drive Highway 101 south of Astoria 4 miles (or north of Seaside 9 miles) turn west at a sign for Fort Stevens State Park, and follow park signs.

Park at the Military Museum to explore bunkers and gun batteries that date to the Civil War.

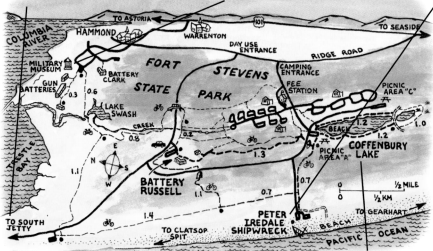

▶ A broad beach with the rusting remains of the *Peter Iredale* shipwreck.

▶ A popular picnic area beside swimmable Coffenbury Lake.

▶ A viewing platform overlooking the Columbia River's South Jetty. Bird-watching blinds are nearby.

▶ Five miles of hiking paths and 7 miles of paved bicycle paths through the area's flat coastal forest.

▶ A military museum displaying uniforms, armaments, and photos of the

The picnic area at Coffenbury Lake is a popular place to swim because the water is much warmer than the ocean.

The *Peter Iredale* missed the Columbia River entrance in 1906. Its skeletal hull has been a beach attraction ever since.

⭐4 Fort Clatsop

Open daily 9am-5pm (9am-6pm in summer).
Admission is $3 per adult ($5 in summer).

The log stockade where explorers Lewis and Clark spent the rainy winter of 1805-06 is gone, but a new replica on the site captures the spirit of those early years.

Admission to this part of the Lewis & Clark National & State Historical Parks includes a slide show in an extensive interpretive center. In summer, rangers in frontier garb demonstrate sewing moccasins, splitting shakes, dipping candles, and carving dugout canoes.

GETTING THERE: Drive Highway 101 south of Astoria 4 miles and follow signs.

Lewis and Clark named their log stockade Fort Clatsop after the local Indian tribe. This 1955 replica burned in 2005 and was replaced by a more accurate replica in 2006.

A statue at Seaside's Turnaround *(see p90)* honors Meriwether Lewis and William Clark, who led the Corps of Discovery to Oregon in 1805.

LEWIS AND CLARK

Sent by President Jefferson to scout and claim the Oregon Country, Lewis and Clark's Corps of Discovery canoed down the Columbia River in late 1805. They camped for ten days across the river from present-day Astoria to reconnoiter. Then they voted to build winter quarters on a slough 6 miles south of Astoria where the hunting was better.

Their journals include complaints that rain fell on all but twelve of the 106 dreary days they spent in Fort Clatsop's 50-foot-square log stockade.

Clark also grumbled that their diet lacked salt and fat. He led a trip to Seaside's beach and boiled seawater to obtain a quart of salt a day. Then he hiked to Cannon Beach to get blubber from a stranded whale. With these provisions, the explorers left Fort Clatsop early in 1806 and returned east.

HIKE 15 Saddle Mountain

Difficult
5.2 miles round trip   1620 feet elevation gain
Open all year, but avoid in winter storms
Use: hikers
Map: Saddle Mountain (USGS)

A lava flow filled a valley here 15 million years ago. When the Coast Range later rose, erosion exposed the hard basalt lava as Saddle Mountain.

Highest point in northwest Oregon, this saddle-shaped peak commands a panorama from the ocean to Mount St. Helens. The climb is especially popular in May and June, when wildflowers fill the mountain's meadows with the richest floral display in the Coast Range.

The path starts in a forest of alder and salmonberry. Flowers line the trail in spring: candyflower, bleeding hearts, fringecup, trilliums, wild lily-of-the-valley, and fairy bells. Old 8-foot stumps recall 1920s logging and 1930s fires.

After 0.2 mile a side trail to the right leads 0.2 mile to a rock outcrop with the park's best view of the mountain itself.

Continuing on the main trail, you'll switchback steeply up 1.1 mile to a narrow spine of rock running up the mountain like a stone wall. This basalt dike is part of the same lava flow that formed the rest of the mountain. Here, however, the weight of the flow extruded molten lava down into cracks in the ground. Exposed by erosion, the dike now resembles a stack of cordwood.

Another half mile's climb brings you to wildflower meadows with paintbrush, iris, larkspur, aster, and phlox. At the 2.2-mile mark you'll cross a saddle

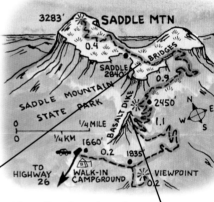

with a dizzying view down to your car.

Cables anchored along the final 0.4-mile pitch help you climb the steep slope to the railed summit. The panorama includes Astoria's bridge and half a dozen Cascade snowpeaks.

A dike shows the hexagonal fractures typical of basalt.

Bridges cross fragile meadows with the most spectacular wildflower displays of the Coast Range.

Getting There

Drive Highway 26 west of Portland 66 miles (or east of Seaside 10 miles). Turn at a state park sign near milepost 10 and follow a winding, one-lane paved road uphill 7 miles.

WILDFLOWERS OF THE COAST

The rhododendrons and azaleas that gardeners elsewhere carefully cultivate grow wild along the Oregon Coast. Some alpine flowers live in windswept headland meadows, while woodland blooms grow in the shadowy rainforest just inland.

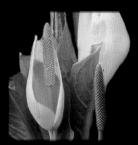

SKUNK CABBAGE (Lysichiton americanum). Pollinated by flies, this swamp bloom smells putrid.

SEA FIG (Mesembryanthemum chilense). The sea fig stores water in its fleshy leaves to survive in sand.

RHODODENDRON (Rhododendron macrophyllum) blooms in May and can grow 20 feet tall.

WESTERN AZALEA (Rhododendron occidentale) blooms in May along the Southern Oregon Coast.

COW PARSNIP (Heracleum lanatum). This giant-leaved plant stands up to 8 feet tall in summer meadows.

SALAL (Gaultheria shallon). Salal covers coastal headlands with dense bushes. It has edible blue berries.

FOXGLOVE (Digitalis purpurea). Showy 5-foot foxglove stalks spangle sunny summer hillsides.

SOURGRASS (Oxalis oregana). The shamrock-shaped leaves carpet forests and taste tart when chewed.

SALMONBERRY (Rubus spectabilis). Hummingbirds rely on nectar from salmonberry's April flowers.

SALMONBERRY (Rubus spectabilis). This slightly stickery rainforest shrub has edible berries in July.

CANDYFLOWER (Claytonia sibirica). Common by woodland creeks and trails, candyflower is edible.

See and be seen on the Promenade, a 1.6-mile walkway along Seaside's beach.

 5   # Seaside

Founded as a tourist goal in 1873 by railroad king Ben Holladay, Seaside revels in its carnival mood. Arcades and snack shops line the **"Million-Dollar Walk,"** the section of Broadway between Highway 101 and the beach.

Seaside pivots at the **Turnaround**, a circular plaza overlooking the busy beach's volleyball courts, kites, and lifeguard chairs. Extending on either side is the **Promenade**, a paved walkway between the grassy foredunes and the town. If you like, stroll two blocks north to the **Seaside Aquarium**, a 1937 tourist draw boasting a "hideous octopus."

For a free tour of the city, hop on board **Seaside's streetcar**. The rubber-tired trolley loops from Avenue U to 12th Avenue in summer from 9:30am to 10pm, absolutely free.

Explore the Necanicum River from **Quatat Marine Park.** Between First and A Avenues, the park has picnic tables, paved paths, and a boat dock. Canoe, kayak, paddleboat, and "bumper boat" rentals are nearby.

For a look at the past, visit the **Seaside Museum and Historical Society** at 570 Necanicum Drive. Hours are noon-3pm daily in winter. In summer it's open Sunday noon-3pm, otherwise 10am-4pm. The $3 admission (students $1) includes a visit next door to one of Seaside's original beach cottages, fully restored.

GETTING THERE: Drive Highway 26 west of Portland 74 miles and turn north 5 miles on Highway 101.

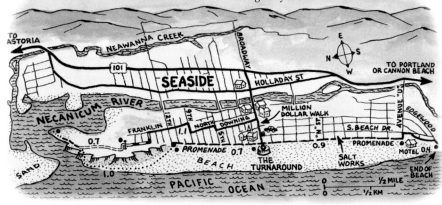

HIKE 16 Ecola State Park

Moderate (to World War II bunker)
3.9-mile loop   900 feet elevation gain
Open all year   Use: hikers
Map: Tillamook Head (USGS)

Difficult (shuttle across headland)
6.1 miles one way   1350 feet elevation gain

Tillamook Head's jagged cliffs rise 1000 feet from the ocean. When the Lewis and Clark expedition crossed this headland in 1806, Clark marveled that a viewpoint along the way was "the grandest and most pleasing prospect which my eyes ever surveyed."

To see it for yourself, visit Ecola State Park. Even the trailhead in the Indian Beach picnic area has a such a great view that it's often used on postcards.

The trail up Tillamook Head starts as an old gated road on the right-hand side of the parking turnaround. After 100 yards keep left at a fork and climb, steeply at times, through old-growth spruce and alder woods. Wear boots,

Kids love to play with "waterdogs," the rough-skinned newts that crawl the forest floor of the Coast Range after rains, but because the newt's skin is poisonous, children should wash their hands after picking one up.

as there are a few slippery spots.

After 1.6 miles turn left at a trail crossing near a primitive camping area for

TILLAMOOK ROCK LIGHTHOUSE

Oregon's strangest lighthouse stands atop Tillamook Rock, an island crag one mile off the shore of Tillamook Head, between Seaside and Cannon Beach.

Engineers had originally wanted to build the light on the mainland, but because Tillamook Head is 1000 feet high and often hidden by fog, they decided in 1878 to mount the beacon on this 121-foot island instead.

It proved to be a difficult place to build anything. The first surveyor who landed was swept away by a wave and drowned. The next builder ferried workers to the island by suspending them

from pulleys and zinging them across the sea on a cable strung from a ship.

It took seven months to dynamite a flat spot, and another seven months to build the tower. When it was done, gigantic storms off the North Pacific routinely broke lantern windows 144 feet above sea level. In 1935 the Coast Guard replaced the light with a whistling buoy, and in 1954 they sold the island at auction. Now it's owned by Eternity At Sea, a funeral business that helicopters urns to the island, carrying the cremated remains of people who want to be buried in a lighthouse when they die.

Crews who staffed the lighthouse on Tillamook Rock between 1881 and 1934 dubbed it "Terrible Tilly."

backpackers. In another 0.2 mile you'll find a dark, 6-room concrete bunker that housed a radar installation in World War II. Just beyond is a cliff-edge viewpoint, breathtakingly high above a rugged rock beach. A mile to sea is Tillamook Rock, a bleak island with a lighthouse.

If you're ready to return on the loop to your car, simply walk back from the viewpoint to the trail crossing and go straight on a well-graded abandoned road 1.6 miles downhill to the Indian Beach parking lot.

If you'd prefer to continue across Tillamook Head, turn left at the trail crossing. The trail climbs and dips for 2.6 miles, passing some excellent views north (including the one Clark liked), before switchbacking down through the forest 1.7 miles to a parking area at the end of Sunset Boulevard.

To find this northern trailhead, drive

A trailside sign identifies "Clark's Point of View," possibly the spot that inspired explorer William Clark.

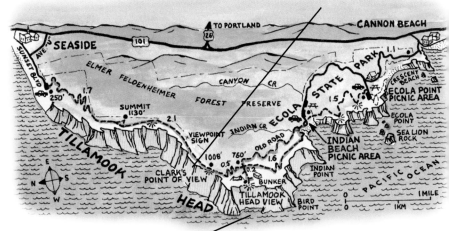

The islands below Tillamook Head — and the headland itself — are remnants of a massive 15-million-year-old Columbia River basalt lava flow that began near Idaho.

Highway 101 to Seaside's southernmost traffic signal, turn west on Avenue U for two blocks and turn left on Edgewood (which becomes Sunset) for 1.2 miles to road's end.

Getting There

From Highway 101, take the north exit for Cannon Beach and follow Ecola State Park signs, keeping right for 2 miles to the park's entrance booth. Pay a $3-per-car parking fee here. Then turn right for 1.5 miles to the Indian Beach picnic area.

Cannon Beach

This arts-oriented village on one of Oregon's most beautiful beaches is grappling with its own popularity — and seems to be winning. The area was named for a cannon that washed ashore from a shipwrecked war sloop.

Today, clusters of tasteful shops and boutiques fill the small, busy downtown. **Sandcastle Day** draws crowds to watch spectacular sand sculptures being built — and swallowed by the tide — each year on a Saturday in early June. The community **Coaster Theater**, downtown at 108 North Hemlock Street, stages plays Friday and Saturday at 8pm from February to December.

Haystack Rock, a massive 235-foot island in Cannon Beach's surf, is off-limits as a refuge for seabirds, but the tidepools at its base are fun to explore.

GETTING THERE: From Portland or Seaside, take Highway 101 to the first Cannon Beach exit (also signed for Ecola State Park) and keep left for 0.7 mile to a city parking lot by the information center on Second Street.

HIKE 17 Os West State Park

Easy (to Short Sand Beach)
1.2 miles round trip   100 feet elevation gain
Open all year   Use: hikers
Map: Arch Cape (USGS)

Moderate (to Cape Falcon)
5 miles round trip   300 feet elevation gain

This park honors Oswald West, the clever Oregon governor who, in 1913, had the state's beaches declared public highways to help assure that the beaches would never fall into private developers' hands. Today an easy walk through the park leads to Short Sand Beach's dramatic cove, one of the treasures preserved by his policy. If you'd like to camp, wheelbarrows are provided to wheel your gear a quarter mile to a campground in an old-growth rainforest beside the beach. For a longer hike, take the Oregon Coast Trail to views at the tip of Cape Falcon.

From the day-use parking lot on Highway 101, the trail follows Short Sand Creek down through a old-growth rainforest of mossy alder, hemlock, red

TSUNAMIS ON THE COAST

Never in written history has the Oregon Coast suffered a major earthquake or a devastating tsunami (tidal wave). So why do so many beaches have warning signs?

In the 1990s scientists realized that earthquake pressure gradually builds up off Oregon's coast as the North American continent slowly arches westward across the Pacific seafloor. Then the ground suddenly drops, causing a massive quake and tsunami every 300 to 500 years.

Excavators found one clue to this violent past: repeated layers of tsunami debris in estuary soils many miles inland. Another tipoff was the

TSUNAMI EVACUATION ROUTE

Tsunami signs direct people to the nearest high ground in case of an alert.

stumps of a drowned forest exposed at low tide at many North Coast beaches. Ring counts of the trees show they all died at once in 1700.

The earthquakes are about ten times more powerful than the 1906 San Francisco temblor, and launch a tsunami as much as 100 feet tall.

Although it has been more than 300 years since the last great coastal earthquake, the next one might not occur for several centuries. On any given day the risk posed by snoozing on the beach is statistically no greater than the risk of driving a car.

cedar, and spruce. Douglas squirrels scold from the 6-foot-thick trunks. Salal, salmonberry, and three varieties of ferns line the path.

After 0.3 mile ignore a left-hand fork to the campground. Continue 200 yards to the Oregon Coast Trail, a junction marked by a large post.

For the short hike, turn left and follow "Beach Access" pointers for 0.2 mile to Short Sand Beach. On the way you'll cross a dramatic 70-foot suspension footbridge over Necarney Creek and finally hop across driftwood logs to the secluded strand.

Short Sand Beach is popular for surfing—but wet suits are a must.

If Cape Falcon's your goal, backtrack 0.2 mile from Short Sand Beach to the big junction where you first met the Oregon

Getting There

Drive Highway 101 south of Seaside 18 miles (or north of Tillamook 30 miles) to a small wooden "Oswald West State Park" sign marking the day-use parking lot. It's on the east side of the highway, a bit south of milepost 39. Park at the far left end of the lot and take a paved path under the highway bridge.

Coast Trail. This time head north, cross through a picnic area, and keep left at an unmarked fork. This path has a few muddy spots where it winds through the woods. Then it heads out the cape, gaining views of Neahkahnie Mountain.

Finally you'll reach a junction in a field of wind-trimmed salal bushes. For the Cape Falcon viewpoint, turn left on a 0.2-mile spur trail that becomes increasingly panoramic and rugged before petering out near the headland's tip.

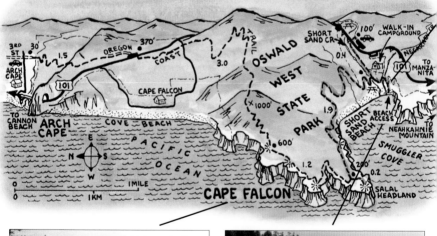

A 12-mile segment of the Oregon Coast Trail traverses the park, passing viewpoints on Cape Falcon.

Short Sand Beach is isolated by the cliffs of Smuggler Cove, named for pirates who once sought shelter here.

A footbridge across Necarney Creek leads from Oswald West's campground to Short Sand Beach.

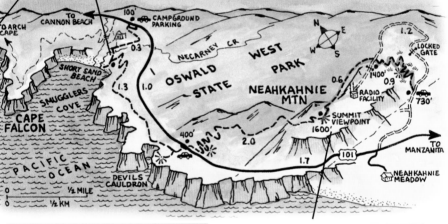

HIKE 18

Neahkahnie Mountain

Moderate
3 miles round trip   900 feet elevation gain
Open all year   Use: hikers
Map: Nehalem (USGS)

Neahkahnie Mountain juts 1600 feet above the beach. Indians thought it a viewpoint fit for gods, and named it with the words *Ne* ("place of") and *Ekahni* ("supreme deity"). White men shroud the peak with legend as well. Treasure seekers sift the beach at the mountain's base, spurred by tales of gold buried by sailors from a shipwrecked Spanish galleon. The discovery here of a strangely inscribed

Neahkahnie Mountain overlooks the Nehalem Spit.

Rising 1600 feet above the ocean, Neahkahnie Mountain has a stunning view—and has inspired several legends.

block of beeswax, possibly of Spanish origin, adds to the speculation.

From the trailhead, steep switchbacks lead up through meadows 0.9 mile to a ridgetop junction. Continue straight on a path that contours 0.6 mile around the wooded back of the mountain before emerging at the summit, a stunning viewpoint in a steep meadow.

Getting There

Drive Highway 101 south of Seaside 20 miles (or north of Tillamook 28 miles) to a brown hiker-symbol sign opposite the Neah-Kah-Nie subdivision, between mileposts 41 and 42. Turn east on gravel 0.4 mile and park at a wide spot. At the far end of this small pullout look for a gray post on the left where the trail begins.

 7   ## Tillamook

Five rivers meander across dairy pastureland to Tillamook, an area touted as the "land of cheese, trees, and ocean breeze." When local dairymen in the 1880s tired of having their butter spoil before it reached Portland and San Francisco, they built their own sailing ship and started making cheddar cheese. Today the **Tillamook Cheese**

factory, 2 miles north of Tillamook on Highway 101, offers a free self-guiding tour and a gift shop. Daily hours are 8am to 8pm in summer and 8am to 6pm in winter. The **Blue Heron French Cheese Company**, a mile farther south on Highway 101, keeps the same hours but features camembert and brie.

Twenty stories tall and nearly a quarter mile long, the 1942 blimp hangar near Tillamook is the largest clear-span wooden building in the world.

Navy blimps from an enormous Tillamook hangar prowled the coast for Japanese submarines during World War II. Three miles south of Tillamook off Highway 101, the hangar now houses a collection of fighter planes in a **World War II aircraft museum,** open daily from 10am to 5pm for an admission fee.

Tillamook's **Pioneer Museum**, in a restored 1905 county courthouse, features a blacksmith shop, a pioneer house, and an operating steam-powered donkey logging engine. The museum at 2106 Second Street is open daily from 8am to 5pm for a small admission fee.

Tillamook dairy cow.

Munson Creek Falls is the Coast Range's tallest.

Sunday hours are 12noon to 5pm.

Nearby, a quarter-mile path leads to the tallest waterfall in the Coast Range, 266-foot **Munson Creek Falls**. To find this lovely three-tiered cascade, drive 8 miles south of Tillamook on Highway 101 and follow signs.

GETTING THERE: From Portland, head west on Highway 26 and follow "Tillamook" signs 77 miles.

8 Cape Meares

The park is open year-round. The lighthouse opens for free tours 11am-4pm daily from April through October.

An 1890 lighthouse, a bluff-top picnic area, and the odd-limbed Octopus Tree are the top attractions in this park on the Three Capes Loop west of Tillamook. The headland's name honors British Captain John Meares, who built a fur-trading fort in Nootka, Alaska and sailed south in 1788 questing for the great river of the Northwest. He overlooked the Columbia and turned back here.

Although Sitka spruce trees can grow 200 feet tall, the winds on Cape Meares trimmed this spruce's top so often that it became the many-limbed "Octopus Tree."

From the parking turnaround, follow a wide paved path straight ahead 0.2 mile to the lighthouse. To the south, the view extends past Three Arch Rocks to Cape Lookout. To the north, the view includes Pyramid Rock and (closer to shore) Pillar Rock, crowded with hundreds of black-and-white nesting murres in May and June.

Return to your car, cross the parking lot, and walk past the restroom to find the short, wide path to the Octopus Tree, a 12-foot-thick spruce with big, odd limbs. For a longer stroll, walk halfway around the tree to find a smaller path that continues half a mile to the highway, passing several viewpoints.

GETTING THERE: Drive west from Tillamook 10 miles (or north from Pacific City 26 miles) following "Three Capes Scenic Route" signs, and take the Cape Meares State Park entrance road 0.6 mile to a turnaround.

Cape Meares' spectacularly prismed one-ton lighthouse lens was hand ground in Paris in 1887.

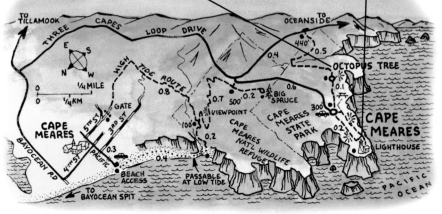

HIKE 19
Cape Lookout

Moderate
5 miles round trip   400 feet elevation gain
Open all year   Use: hikers
Map: Sand Lake (USGS)

Hang gliders sail from a cliff near Cape Lookout toward the Netarts sand spit.

Cape Lookout State Park stretches from a massive, cliff-edged headland to the tip of the 5-mile-long Netarts sand spit, with a popular picnic area and campground in between.

For the best views, hike out Cape Lookout itself. Like an unfinished dike to Hawaii, this narrow, cliff-edged cape juts 2 miles straight out into the Pacific Ocean. Wear boots, because the trail has a few muddy spots.

From the end of the trailhead parking lot take the left-hand path and keep straight at a junction 100 yards beyond.

Cape Lookout juts so far to sea that its tip leaves a white wake in the ocean current.

The dense forest of gnarled old spruce and hemlock trees shelters ferns, salal, salmonberry, and tiny white candyflower.

The first view to the south, after 0.6 mile, is just above the site where a B-17 bomber crashed into the cape's 800-foot cliffs on a foggy day in 1943.

At the tip of the cape, paintbrush, yarrow, and fireweed bloom on a clifftop meadow 400 feet above the waves. A red buoy moans offshore. Bring binoculars to watch for gray whales here from December to June. Up to 20,000 migrate from Alaska to Mexico each year, with as many as 30 passing this cape in an hour.

Getting There

From downtown Tillamook, head west on 3rd Street and follow signs for Cape Lookout State Park 13 miles. Continue past the campground turnoff 2.7 miles to the trailhead turnoff on the right.

9 Pacific City

Best known for its dory fishing fleet, Pacific City offers broad beaches, dunes, a quiet bay, and a scenic headland, all conveniently close to the shops and popular brewpub of this coastal village.

Start at the Cape Kiwanda parking lot. Fishermen here launch dories directly through the waves each morning and zoom back ashore in mid-day.

A short walk takes you to the foot of the wave-sculpted yellow sandstone cape. Explore the tidepools along its base or climb short trails to viewpoints atop surf-smashed cliffs. Do not venture onto the slippery slopes beyond the viewpoints.

To explore Nestucca Spit, return to your car and drive a mile back toward Pacific City. Just before the bridge,

A shop by the beach rents recumbent tricycles.

jog right onto Sunset Drive and continue 0.8 mile to the road's end in Bob Straub State Park. Climb across a grassy foredune and stroll the wide beach 2.3 miles to the mouth of Nestucca Bay. The park bans horses and camping.

GETTING THERE: Drive Highway 101 north of Lincoln City 18 miles (or south of Tillamook 25 miles) and turn west on the Three Capes Scenic Route for 2.7 miles. In the center of Pacific City, turn left for 2 blocks across a river bridge, and then turn right for a mile to the Cape Kiwanda parking lot on the left.

Pacific City's Haystack Rock, larger than the similarly shaped Haystack Rock at Cannon Beach, serves as a natural breakwater for the local dory fleet.

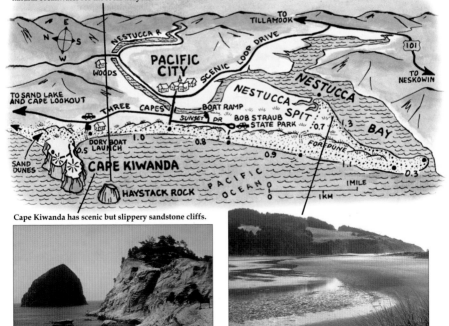

Cape Kiwanda has scenic but slippery sandstone cliffs.

Hike around the edge of Nestucca Spit to look for birds and seals on the shore of Nestucca Bay.

HIKE 20   Cascade Head

Difficult (Nature Conservancy trail)
4.2 miles round trip   1200 feet elevation gain
Open all year   Use: hikers
Map: Neskowin (USGS)

Difficult (to Harts Cove)
5.4 miles round trip   900 feet elevation gain
Open July 16 through December 31

When developers threatened Cascade Head's panoramic, blufftop wildflower meadows in the 1960s, fans rallied to donate the fragile area to the non-profit Nature Conservancy. Ironically, the impact of up to 10,000 visitors a year now threatens the meadows' ecology.

Flower picking, hunting, camping, fires, bicycles, and dogs have been

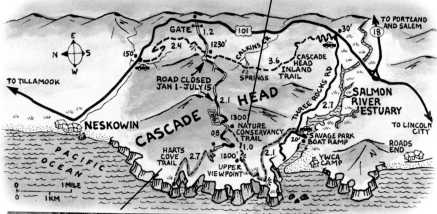

The Nature Conservancy trail through the Cascade Head's meadows has a sweeping view of the Salmon River estuary.

Cascade Head won its name when sailors noticed a waterfall pouring directly into the sea at Harts Cove.

banned. The upper trailhead and the trail to Harts Cove are closed six months of the year to protect threatened Oregon silverspot butterfly caterpillars in the headland meadows. If you hike here, please *stay on the trail.* Even spreading out a picnic may inadvertently trample the violets that feed the rare caterpillars.

From the Savage Park boat ramp, the Nature Conservancy trail climbs through a forest of large, gnarled spruce for 1.5

Sea lions bark from the recesses of Harts Cove.

10 Lincoln City

The longest town on the Oregon Coast, Lincoln City formed when five coastal communities voted to consolidate in 1964. Today the city's biggest draws are the Siletz tribe's flashy Chinook Winds casino at the north edge of town on 40th Street and the massive factory outlet shopping complex in the middle of town at 14th Street.

Also in the middle of town, the shortest river in the world flows a mere 200 yards from Devils Lake to the sea.

Taft, at the southern end of Lincoln City, has a dock beside Siletz Bay and a beach where you can watch seals.

miles to a meadow with a breathtaking view across the Salmon River estuary. Then the path steepens and climbs 0.6 mile to an upper viewpoint, a good turnaround spot.

If you'd prefer the less crowded path to Harts Cove, return to Highway 101 and drive 3 miles north. Just before a crest, turn left on gravel Cascade Head Road (Road 1861) for 4.1 miles to its end. From here a trail switchbacks down through a young hemlock forest 0.7 mile to a footbridge over pretty Cliff Creek. Next the path contours amid 6-foot-thick Sitka spruce and hemlock giants. At the 2.5-mile mark you'll enter the headland's scenic meadow. Take the leftmost of several paths down the grassy bluff to find a cliff-edge viewpoint overlooking Harts Cove and Chitwood Creek's waterfall.

The state wayside at the Highway 101 bridge over the D River provides access to a busy — and reliably windy — beach. One of the world's largest kite festivals is held here each year on a fall weekend, bolstering Lincoln City's claim to be "Kite Capital of the World."

For seal watching and family beach fun, head for the Siletz Bay dock in Lincoln City's Taft district, at the south end of town on South 51st Street.

GETTING THERE: Drive 82 miles southwest of Portland or 52 miles west of Salem.

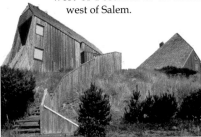

Houses on the Salishan Spit south of Lincoln City have daring angles — and a daring perch on shifting sand.

Getting There

For the Nature Conservancy trail, drive Highway 101 north 1 mile from the interchange where highways 101 and 18 join (just north of Lincoln City). Then turn left on Three Rocks Road for 1.6 miles and turn left into the Savage Park boat ramp parking area.

HIKE 21 — Drift Creek Falls

Easy
3 miles round trip   340 feet elevation gain
Open all year   Use: hikers
Map: Devils Lake (USGS)

This well-graded path descends through the woods to a dramatic, 150-foot suspension footbridge beside a 75-foot waterfall.

Passable even for strollers and wheelchairs, the packed gravel trail descends through a second-growth Douglas fir forest with sword ferns, red huckleberries, vine maple, and salal bushes. In early spring, look for big white trilliums and tiny white sourgrass blooming here.

The swaying 150-foot suspension footbridge above Drift Drift Falls doesn't feel safe, but it is anchored well.

After a mile the trail crosses a 20-foot-wide creek amid alders. At the 1.3-mile mark the trail spans Drift Creek's sudden, curving canyon on a dizzying suspension footbridge. Continue on a steeper path 0.2 mile down to the base of the waterfall, where a ribbon of spray spills into a misty pool.

Getting There

From Portland or Salem, take Highway 18 toward the Coast. After passing Rose Lodge and milepost 5 (short of Highway 101 by 5 miles), turn left onto paved Bear Creek Road for 9 miles. This road, often narrow and occasionally gravel, becomes Road 17 by the time you reach the trailhead. If you don't have the required $5-per-car parking permit, you can buy one here.

⭐ 11 — Depoe Bay

In picturesque Depoe Bay, whale watching boats thread their way through a rock channel to the sea. At high tide a spouting horn nearby sprays saltwater across Highway 101, so don't park where the road is wet. Among the row of gift shops lining the highway you'll find a branch of the Oregon Coast Aquarium museum store and the Siletz Tribal Smokehouse, featuring smoked fish. Down at the bay's docks, a small Coast Guard station with 44-foot ships is open to visitors Monday through Saturday from 4pm-8pm and Sunday 1pm-8pm.

Smallest natural harbor in the world, Depoe Bay has its own Coast Guard station.

GETTING THERE: Drive Highway 101 south of Lincoln City 9 miles or north of Newport 13 miles.

12 Yaquina Head

$5 per car entrance fee. Interpretive center open daily 10am-4pm.

Inside Oregon's tallest lighthouse, built in 1873, narrow spiral stairs lead visitors up to a dizzying view. The lighthouse's scenic cape, Yaquina Head, was preserved in 1980 when Congress bought the headland from a gravel company that had planned to quarry it to sea level.

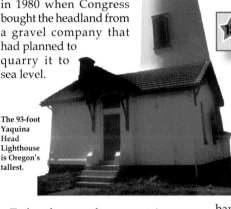

The 93-foot Yaquina Head Lighthouse is Oregon's tallest.

Today the cape features an interpretive center, stairs to an unusual beach of black cobbles, and a tidepool loop trail through a portion of the old quarry.

A viewpoint beside the lighthouse overlooks islands teeming with cormorants, murres, tufted puffins, and seals. Whale watching is excellent here too.

For an 0.8-mile hike from the lighthouse parking area, climb a switchbacking path up through the wildflowers of Salal Hill to a bird's-eye view of the entire cape.

GETTING THERE: Drive Highway 101 north of Newport 3 miles and turn left.

Short trails through a former gravel quarry on Yaquina Head reveal how tidepool life is colonizing the area.

Newport's fishing fleet docks along the bayfront.

13 Newport

This historic coastal town has lighthouses, a quaint bayfront, and two world-class aquariums (*see p104*).

In the old streets along **Newport's bayfront** you'll find upscale shops and restaurants rubbing shoulders with fish canneries, whale watching tour offices, and commercial tourist attractions like the Wax Works. At the west end of the bayfront, near Newport's bridge, an active **Coast Guard station** offers free daily tours from 1pm to 4pm. At the east end are the Embarcadero docks, where you can charter a boat or rent crab pots.

Newport's historic bayfront teems with chowder restaurants, pubs, fish canneries, and art galleries.

Art galleries and romantic beachfront hotels cluster near Third and Coast streets in Newport's historic **Nye Beach district**. The Newport Visual Arts Center at 239 NW Beach Drive hosts juried art exhibits; it's free, and open daily in summer from noon to 4pm (otherwise 11am to 3pm).

Newport's Nye Beach district, one of Oregon's first beach resorts, still attracts sand castle builders.

14 Oregon Coast Aquarium

Open daily 9am-6pm in summer; otherwise 10am-5pm. Adults $12, seniors $10, $7 for children age 4-13.

This modern aquarium features a transparent underwater tunnel surrounded by sharks and deep-sea fish. Other areas exhibit playful sea otters, curious seals, and chattering sea birds. Indoors are hands-on exhibits.

Jellyfish pulse in special tanks.

GETTING THERE: Follow signs from the south end of Newport's Yaquina Bay Bridge.

Sea lions at the aquarium. ▷

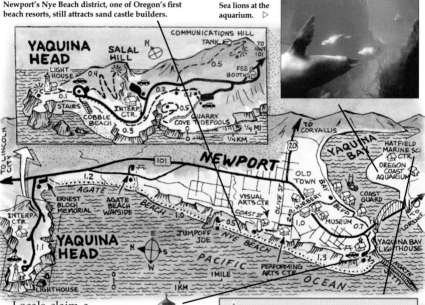

Locals claim a ghost haunts the 1871 **Yaquina Bay Lighthouse**, a building that stood empty for decades. Restored as a free museum, it's open daily from 11am to 5pm. Follow signs from the north end of the Yaquina Bay bridge.

A ghost may haunt the Yaquina Bay Lighthouse, Newport's oldest building.

GETTING THERE: Drive Highway 20 west of Corvallis 54 miles to Newport.

15 OSU Hatfield Marine Science Center

Open daily 10am-5pm in summer; otherwise 10am-4pm. Admission by suggested donation.

This scientific research center's computerized displays explain tsunamis, weather forecasting, and salmon recovery plans. You'll also find carefully labeled exhibits of Oregon marine species, including an octopus lurking in a tank by the door.

GETTING THERE: Follow signs from the south end of Newport's Yaquina Bay Bridge.

Cape Perpetua

HIKE 22

Easy (4 short walks)
3.3 miles in all   100 feet elevation gain
Open all year   Use: hikers
Map: Yachats (USGS)

Where Cape Perpetua confronts the sea, Highway 101 clings to a 700-foot cliff. Nearby are short walks to viewpoints, tidepools, and giant trees.

Explorer Captain Cook named this cape in 1778 while seeking a Northwest Passage to England. Start your own

From a 1933 stone shelter atop Cape Perpetua, the view extends across a lava shore riddled with tidepools.

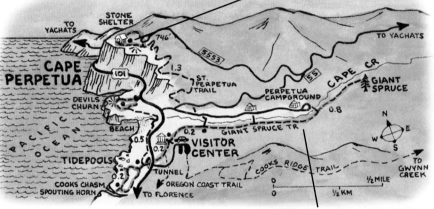

exploration at the Cape Perpetua Visitor Center, where you'll find interpretive displays and helpful staff. Then try these scenic short walks:

▶ From the visitor center's front door, follow a "Tidepools" pointer to a paved trail that tunnels below Highway 101. Keep left on a loop that visits tidepools, a spouting horn, and an Indian mound.

Tidepool starfish.

▶ From the visitor center, follow a "Giant Spruce" pointer and keep right at all junctions for a mile. The path traces a creek to a tree 15 feet in diameter.

▶ From the Devils Churn parking area (north of the visitor center 0.3 mile) walk a very short loop down to a frothing, collapsed sea cave.

▶ Drive Highway 101 north of the visitor center 0.2 mile, turn right on a

The Giant Spruce Trail follows Cape Creek inland.

paved road, and keep left for 2 miles to the top of Cape Perpetua, where a 0.2-mile loop trail leads to a 1933 stone shelter with an unmatched view.

Getting There

Drive Highway 101 south of Newport 28 miles (or north of Florence 23 miles) to the Cape Perpetua Visitor Center between mileposts 168 and 169. Expect a $5-per-car parking fee.

Highway 101 travelers often photograph Heceta Head without knowing that a trail leads to the lighthouse itself.

HIKE 23 Heceta Head

Easy
1 mile round trip　　　200 feet elevation gain
Open all year　　　Use: hikers
Map: Heceta Head (USGS)

An easy trail climbs to Oregon's most photographed lighthouse from a state picnic area at the Devils Elbow, a scenic cove that confounded early mariners with devilish currents. Heceta Head (pronounced huh-SEE-tuh) honors Bruno de Heceta, the Portuguese captain of a Spanish ship, who first sighted the cape in 1775. The beacon here first shone in 1894, using a 2-ton array of prism lenses that is still in service.

The lighthouse trail starts at the far end of the parking lot and climbs 0.3 mile through salal meadows and spruce groves to an old road. To the right is the Heceta Light Station, a white clapboard, 1893 duplex that once housed the two assistant light keepers. Still allegedly haunted by a young woman named Rue, the building is now a bed and breakfast inn.

From the Heceta Light Station, walk

The trailhead picnic area is framed by the graceful 220-foot arch of the 1933 Cape Creek Bridge.

left along the old road 0.2 mile to the lighthouse. When it's open (noon to 5pm Monday through Thursday and 11am to 6pm Friday through Sunday), volunteers lead visitors up the tower's 58 steps to see the lens rotating on its ball bearing track. Even if you don't climb the tower, bring binoculars to watch the antics of the 7000 long-necked, black Brandt's cormorants that roost April through August on the rocks below the railed yard.

In service since 1894, the original Fresnel lens still shines from the Heceta Head Lighthouse.　▷

Getting There

Drive Highway 101 north of Florence 12 miles or south of Yachats 15 miles. Just north of a tunnel, turn downhill into the Heceta Head Lighthouse Viewpoint (alias Devils Elbow State Park). Expect a $3 parking fee.

WHERE TO STAY

Campgrounds *(map p83)*

	Campsites	Water	Showers	Flush Toilet	Fee
[6] BARVIEW JETTY COUNTY PARK. This park's grassy hill sites beside Tillamook Bay have good birdwatching. Off Highway 101 north of Tillamook 11 miles. Reservations 503-322-3477.	249	●	●	●	$$
[16] BEACHSIDE STATE PARK. Between Highway 101 and a broad beach 3 miles south of Waldport. Two yurts ($29). Res: 541-563-3220. Open Mar.-Oct.	70	●	●	●	$$
[14] BEVERLY BEACH STATE PARK. From this large campground, walk under a Highway 101 bridge to a broad, windy beach. North of Newport 7 miles, this park has 21 yurts ($29). Reservations 800-452-5687.	256	●	●	●	$$
[10] CAPE LOOKOUT STATE PARK. On a sand spit between the ocean and Netarts Bay, this popular park has birdwatching, hiking, and 13 rentable yurts ($29). Reservations 800-452-5687.	215	●	●	●	$$
[18] CAPE PERPETUA. Often overlooked, this campgorund is within walking distance of tidepools, old-growth forests, trails, and views. Open late May through September. Reservations 877-444-6777.	38	●		●	$$
[13] DEVILS LAKE STATE PARK. Within walking distance of Lincoln City's restaurants and beaches, this park has a boat ramp for canoers. Ten yurts are available at $29. Reservations 800-452-5687.	83	●	●	●	$$
[8] ELK CREEK WALK-IN. These quiet sites on the Wilson River are near milepost 28 of Highway 6. Open May-October.	15	●			$
[1] FORT STEVENS STATE PARK. Largest campground in Oregon, this park has visitable artillery bunkers, 15 yurts (for $29), bike paths to broad beaches, and more *(see pp86-87).* Reservations 800-452-5687.	519	●	●	●	$$
[9] GALES CREEK. Where the 1933 Tillamook Burn began, this quiet woodsy camp has trails nearby. Open May through October.	23	●			$
[12] HEBO LAKE. On the forested shore of a small lake, this camp is open mid-April to mid-November. From Highway 101 at Hebo, take Highway 22 west 0.3 mile and turn left on Forest Road 14 for 5 miles.	15	●			$
[7] JONES CREEK. Spacious, private campsites on the Wilson River are open Memorial Day to early October. Near milepost 24 of Highway 6.	38	●			$
[4] NEHALEM BAY STATE PARK. On a 3-mile sand peninsula with a broad ocean beach, this park has 18 yurts ($29) and 17 primitive horse campsites with corrals. Reservations 800-452-5687. Drive Highway 101 south of Seaside 22 miles or north of Tillamook 26 miles to milepost 44.	267	●	●	●	$$
[5] NEHALEM FALLS. By a river cascade, this camp is open Memorial Day to early October. Drive Highway 101 north of Tillamook 22 miles. Near Nehalem take Highway 53 east 1.3 miles, turn right on Miami River Road 1 mile, and turn left on Foss Road 7 miles.	18	●			$
[3] OSWALD WEST STATE PARK. Wheelbarrows let you cart gear 0.2 mile to this rainforest camp beside Short Sand Beach *(see p93).* Open Mar.-Oct.	30	●		●	$$
[19] ROCK CREEK. Stroll 0.2 mile from this creekside camp to a quiet ocean beach. Drive Highway 101 north of Florence 16 miles. Open May-Oct.	15	●		●	$$
[2] SADDLE MOUNTAIN STATE PARK. This small trailhead camp is open March through October *(see p88).*	10	●			$
[15] SOUTH BEACH STATE PARK. In the beachfront dunes beside Newport's South Jetty, this park has trails and 27 yurts (for $29). Drive Highway 101 south of Newport 2 miles. Reservations 800-452-5687.	228	●	●	●	$$
[17] TILLICUM BEACH STATE PARK. Between Highway 101 and a broad beach south of Waldport 5 miles. Open all year. Res: 877-444-6777.	60	●		●	$$
[20] WASHBURNE STATE PARK. Trails lead 0.3 mile to the beach or 3 miles to Heceta Head *(see p106)* from this camp amid salal. Two yurts ($29). Drive Highway 101 north of Florence 14 miles to milepost 176.	65	●	●	●	$$
[11] WEBB PARK. Beside Pacific City's Cape Kiwanda *(see p99),* this quiet county park is relatively undeveloped. Reservations 503-322-3477.	30	●	●	●	$$

WHERE TO STAY

B&Bs and Quaint Hotels (map p83)

	Rooms	Private bath	Cont. breakfast	Full breakfast	Rate range
4 **10TH AVENUE BED & BREAKFAST.** Walk to the beach in one minute from this 1908 home with an ocean view, at 125 10th Avenue, Seaside, OR 97138. Info: 800-745-2378 or www.10aveinn.com.	3	●		●	$99-160
9 **AN EXCEPTIONAL PLACE.** This modern bed & breakfast inn is on the Siletz bayfront of the charming Taft district at 1213 SW 52nd Court, Lincoln City, OR 97367. Info: 541-994-4920 or www.anexceptionalbandb.com.	3	●		●	$99-149
7 **THE ARBORS BED & BREAKFAST.** Afternoon tea is served in this oceanview 1922 English cottage, near shops and the beach at 78 Idaho Avenue, Manzanita, OR 97130. Info: 888-664-9587.	2	●		●	$99-110
6 **CANNON BEACH HOTEL.** Originally a loggers' boardinghouse, this remodeled 1914 European-style hotel is half a block from the beach and a variety of upscale shops at 1116 S. Hemlock Street, Cannon Beach, OR 97110. Info: 800-238-4107 or www.cannonbeachhotel.com.	9	●	●		$100-230
1 **CLEMENTINE'S BED & BREAKFAST.** This 1888 Italianate Victorian mansion in Astoria's historic downtown district (at 847 Exchange Street, Astoria, OR 97103) has gardens and a Columbia River view. Pets OK. Info: 800-521-6801 or www.clementines-bb.com.	5	●		●	$80-160
8 **EAGLE'S VIEW.** On 4 acres overlooking Nestucca Bay, 3 of the rooms in this bed & breakfast inn have Jacuzzis. Located at 37975 Brooten Road, Pacific City, OR 97135. Info: 888-846-3292 or www.eaglesviewbb.com.	5	●		●	$120-150
2 **FRANKLIN STREET BED & BREAKFAST.** In a 1900 Victorian at 1140 Franklin Avenue, Astoria, OR 97103, this inn is four blocks from Astoria's riverfront promenade. Info: 800-448-1098 or www.franklin-st-station-bb.com.	6	●		●	$80-135
10 **GREEN GABLES BED & BREAKFAST.** A charming bookstore and bakery share this Victorian-style, turreted 1981 house in the Nye Beach district two blocks from the ocean at 156 SW Coast Street, Newport, OR 97365. Info: 800-515-9065 or www.greengablesbb.com.	2	●		●	$85-125
14 **HECETA LIGHT STATION.** Allegedly haunted by a ghost named Rue, this 1890s lighthouse keeper's duplex beside the Heceta Head lighthouse (see p106) serves as a fabulously scenic bed & breakfast inn. Info: 866-547-3696 or www.hecetalighthouse.com. ◁ The Heceta Light Station.	6	4		●	$133-251
12 **NEWPORT BELLE BED & BREAKFAST.** This sternwheel riverboat stays moored at H Dock of Newport's South Beach Marina, near the Yaquina Bay Bridge. Info: 800-348-1922 or www.newportbelle.com.	5	●		●	$125-145
3 **ROSE RIVER INN.** In a 1910 home within walking distance of downtown Astoria (1510 Franklin Avenue, Astoria, OR 97103) this bed & breakfast has a Finnish sauna in its river suite. Info: 888-876-0028 or www.roseriverinn.com.	4	●		●	$90-150
5 **SEASIDE OCEANFRONT INN.** This modern beachside hotel at 581 S. Promenade, Seaside, OR 97138 decorates its rooms with whimsical themes from bubbles to rock & roll. Info: 800-772-7766 or www.theseasideinn.com.	15	●		●	$90-305
13 **SERENITY BED & BREAKFAST.** A European ambiance reigns at this inn on 10 acres by the Yachats River (5985 Yachats River Road), where host Baerbl serves a full German breakfast. Info: 541-547-3813.	3	●		●	$110-150
11 **SYLVIA BEACH HOTEL.** Restored with a literary theme, this 1913 hotel at Nye Beach (267 NW Cliff Street, Newport, OR 97365) offers rooms decorated for Dr. Seuss, Mark Twain, Agatha Christie, and Edgar Allen Poe. Info: 888-795-8422 or www.sylviabeachhotel.com. ▷	20	●		●	$68-178

SOUTH COAST

Hidden beaches, massive capes, and vast sand dunes highlight this unspoiled shore.

On Southern Oregon's wild and scenic shore you really can find coves where there are no footprints in the sand.

Because this coastline lies just out of day-trip range from Portland and Northern California, the beaches remain uncrowded and the coastal villages are quiet.

Hidden here are the nation's largest coastal dunes — sand hills 400 feet tall along 45 miles of lonely beach. To the south, cape after cape juts into the Pacific, with tidepool reefs, sandy coves, and islands with nesting sea birds.

This scenery did not impress early white explorers to the Pacific Northwest, sailors venturing north from California in search of treasure. The first such visitor, a Spanish pilot named Ferrelo, could not even land in 1544 because of torrential rainstorms. A second explorer, Sir Francis Drake of England, complained in 1577 that the coast was beset by "vile, thicke, and stinking fogges."

After a reconnaisance voyage by the Spanish captain Sebastian Viscaino in 1603 confirmed that the coast had no navigable harbors — and that the local Indians did not even know what gold was — no white explorers visited the state for 170 years. Ironically, prospectors in the 1850s found gold dust in the area's black sand beaches. Later settlers shipped timber, butter, cheese, and cranberries to markets in San Francisco and Portland.

Today, visitors to Oregon's unspoiled South Coast discover that the area's scenery and solitude are its true treasures.

◁ **The Coquille River Lighthouse at Bandon** *(see p124).*　△ **Harris Beach State Park at Brookings** *(see p132).*

Exploring the
SOUTH COAST

Tourists who merely drive Highway 101 along the South Coast are missing a lot. To be sure, the car-window views are spectacular between Port Orford and Brookings, where the route hugs beaches and cliffs. But to really explore this area, detour to the dramatic coastal parks at Shore Acres, window-shop in the Old Towns of Florence and Bandon, and hike through the Oregon Dunes or Boardman State Park.

Florence

By the 1936 Siuslaw River Bridge, quaint shops pack this fishing port's Old Town *(see p114)*. Ocean beaches are a mile to the west in a landscape of shifting dunes.

Oregon Dunes

With 400-foot dunes and 36 virtually unbroken miles of beach, the Oregon Dunes National Recreation Area is a perfect place to run barefoot along a dune, slide down a sand chute, or look for sand dollars on a quiet beach. A good first stop is the Oregon Dunes Visitor Center in Reedsport at the junction of highways 101 and 38. But for a closer look, hike into the sand at the Oregon Dunes Overlook *(see pp118-19)*. If you're camping, try Honeyman State Park *(see p116)*.

KEY	
⭐ **5**	Star attraction
🅗 **12**	Featured hike
2 🏕	Campground
6	B&B or quaint hotel
❓	Information:

Florence
800-524-4864
www.florencechamber.com

Coos Bay
800-824-8486
www.ucinet.com/~bacc

Bandon
541-347-9616

Brookings
800-535-9469
www.brookings-harbor.com

Boardman State Park

The coastline north of Brookings is a spectacular parade of islands, coves, and capes. Both Highway 101 and the Oregon Coast Trail trace the 12.6-mile length of the narrow park that preserves this scenic shore *(see pp130-31)*.

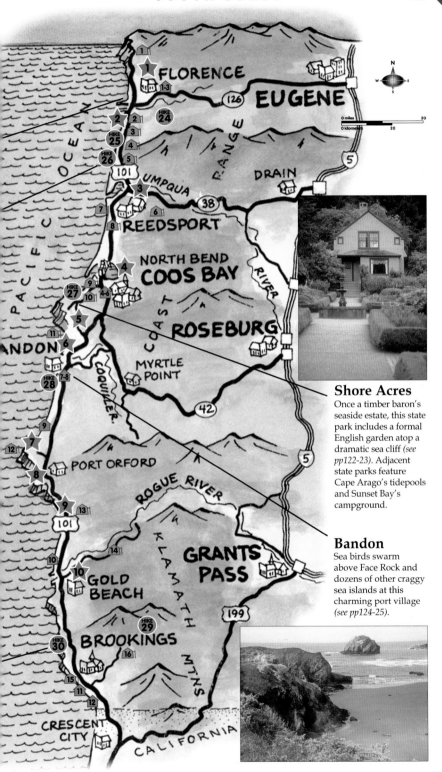

Shore Acres
Once a timber baron's seaside estate, this state park includes a formal English garden atop a dramatic sea cliff (see pp122-23). Adjacent state parks feature Cape Arago's tidepools and Sunset Bay's campground.

Bandon
Sea birds swarm above Face Rock and dozens of other craggy sea islands at this charming port village (see pp124-25).

Florence

Founded in 1893, this delightful river-front district between Highway 101 and the docks at the Port of Siuslaw is home to 36 boutiques and a dozen eateries. Parking can be tight on weekends. Start your exploration afoot at the gazebo and fishing dock in the cute pocket park at Laurel and Bay streets. Shops line the waterfront in both directions. First explore under the arched 1936 Siuslaw River Bridge to the west. Then walk back to the wharf at Mo's chowder restaurant and continue along a boardwalk to the end of the marina.

GETTING THERE: From Highway 101 in Florence, follow "Old Town" signs east four blocks to the riverfront.

Shops line the streets of Florence's bayfront Old Town.

Sweet Creek Falls

Easy
2.2 miles round trip   350 feet elevation gain
Open all year   Use: hikers, horses, bicycles
Map: Goodwin Peak (USGS)

Catwalks have been bolted to the cliffs of this Coast Range gorge as part of a dramatic trail to a dozen small water-falls. Visit in April or May to see wood-land wildflowers, including big white trilliums and rare pink fawn lilies.

The valley here was settled in 1879 by the Zarah T. Sweets, a family of Oregon Trail pioneers. The modern trail incorporates portions of an early wagon road.

Catwalks lead through Sweet Creek's inner gorge.

From the Homestead Trailhead, the graveled path heads upstream past a split, 10-foot waterfall. Later, the trail hugs a cliff through a canyon full of punchbowl-shaped falls. Four-foot-thick Douglas fir trees tower above the creekside alder and bigleaf maple.

After 0.7 mile a path from a second trailhead joins on the left. Continue upstream 0.4 mile to a cliff-edged plunge pool at the base of 20-foot Sweet Creek Falls. A spur trail switchbacks up 150 yards to a viewpoint of an upper falls in a thundering slot.

If you'd like to explore the valley's upper reaches, hike back to your car and drive the paved road 1.3 miles beyond the Homestead Trailhead. Just after a bridge, park at the Wagon Road Trail-head on the left. Across the road, a path heads downstream 0.8 mile to a different viewpoint of Sweet Creek Falls.

A nearby 0.6-mile trail to Beaver Creek Falls is also nice, and very quiet. From the Wagon Road Trailhead, walk across the road's bridge to find a Sweet Creek Trail sign on the right. This portion of the path heads upstream to the base of a fan-shaped waterfall where Beaver Creek and Sweet Creek merge.

Getting There

Drive Highway 126 to the Siuslaw River Bridge in Mapleton (15 miles east of Florence or 46 miles west of Eugene). Cross the bridge from town and immediately turn west on Sweet Creek Road for 10.2 paved miles. Then take a paved turnoff to the right to the Homestead Trailhead turnaround.

After half a mile the Sweet Creek Trail passes a ledge-shaped waterfall.

Sweet Creek Falls.

IS THAT MUSHROOM EDIBLE?

Western Oregon's rainforests sprout each fall with hundreds of varieties of mushrooms—so many, in fact, that the Forest Service has begun regulating professional mushroom hunters. Several communities hold annual mushroom festivals.

Unfortunately there are no simple rules to separate the few edible species from those that are deadly poisonous or simply unsavory. Sample wild fungi only if you're with an expert with a detailed guide.

◁ Edible but strange-looking, morels appear in spring, particularly after a fire.

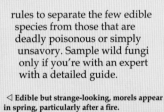

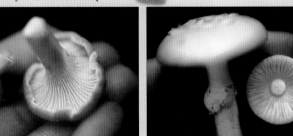

GOLDEN CHANTERELLE (*Cantharellus cibarius*) is common and delicious—peppery when raw and firm when cooked. Orange ribs run down onto its stem.

PANTHER AMANITA (*Amanita pantherina*) is deadly poisonous and very common. Note that the papery white gills under its cap are not attached to the stem.

2 Honeyman Park

Kids slide down sand dunes straight into swimmable Cleawox Lake at this extremely popular park.

Open year round, the park's 381-site campground usually fills early on summer afternoons. Reservations are particularly handy if you'd like to rent one of the ten yurt cabins *(see p132)*.

Parking is free at the two day-use areas east of Highway 101 on forest-rimmed Woahink Lake, where a boat ramp caters largely to waterskiers. Expect a $3-per-car fee at the two Cleawox Lake picnic areas west of Highway 101, but this is where you'll find the dunes. There's also a historic 1930s store by a swimming beach where paddleboats are available for rent in summer.

Woodsy trails connect the picnic areas but hikers generally prefer to explore the trailless dunescape to the west. Few venture beyond the tree islands to the ocean, however, because this zone is dominated by off-highway vehicles (OHVs).

GETTING THERE: Drive Highway 101 south of Florence 3 miles or north of Reedsport 18 miles.

Dunes surround a "tree island" at Honeyman Park.

At Cleawox Lake you can rent paddleboats, swim at a picnic area, or slide down a dune straight into the water.

HIKE 25 Siltcoos River

Easy
2.6-mile loop   50 feet elevation gain
Open all year   Use: hikers, horses, bicycles
Map: Oregon Dunes (USFS)

An easy trail with some of the best birdwatching in Oregon follows this lazy river as it loops from the forest to a quiet beach.

From the Stagecoach Trailhead, hike left on the Waxmyrtle Beach Trail between the Siltcoos River and the road 0.2 mile, turn right across a campground entrance bridge, and then turn right again on a riverside trail.

stork-like birds standing stilt-legged in the river shallows are great egrets (if white) or great blue herons (if gray).

The trail leaves the shore pine woods, joins an abandoned sandy road, and follows it to the beach. Turn right 0.2 mile to the river mouth. The dry-sand-

Fish-hunting osprey nest in riverside snags.

and-driftwood zone near the river is off limits from March 15 to September 15 because snowy plovers lay their eggs there then. These rare birds resemble sandpipers but have a white shoulder yoke and search for

Deep and lazy until it reaches its estuary, the Siltcoos River fans out calf-deep across the beach.

Look here for kingfishers perched on branches above the water. These robin-sized birds with oversized heads dive suddenly into the water to spear fish.

Ignoring left-hand spur trails from Waxmyrtle Campground, you'll climb along a bluff edge overlooking the estuary. If a black-and-white hawk-like bird cruises past, it's probably an osprey. The

food in dry sand rather than near the waves. A 1994 survey found only 60 snowy plovers on the Oregon Coast, but they now seem to be increasing.

You can return as you came, of course, but to make a loop, take off your shoes and wade calf-deep across the river where it fans out across the beach. Then hike 0.6 mile north along the beach, head inland following footprints across the start of the grassy foredune, cross the day-use parking lot, and follow the paved road 0.6 mile to your car.

Getting There

Drive Highway 101 south of Florence 8 miles (or north of Reedsport 13 miles) to the Siltcoos Recreation Area turnoff at milepost 198, and take the road 0.9 mile to the Stagecoach Trailhead on the left. Expect a $3-per-car fee if you don't have a Northwest Forest Pass.

HIKE 26 Oregon Dunes

Easy (to the ocean)
2.2 miles round trip   150 feet elevation gain
Open all year   Use: hikers
Map: Oregon Dunes (USFS)

Moderate (to Tahkenitch Creek)
4.8-mile loop   250 feet elevation gain

Visitors who simply photograph the view from the Oregon Dunes Overlook are missing the best scenery in this sea-front Sahara. It's just over a mile from the overlook's picnic area to a remote, windswept beach. Even better is a 4.8-mile loop hike to beautiful Tahkenitch Creek, through dunes and tree islands.

From the parking area's turnaround,

Shells of razor clams, scallops and sand dollars litter the beach.

After 1.7 miles, turn inland at a brown hiker-symbol sign atop the foredune. This path touches a bend of lazy Tahkenitch Creek, curves left across a

The Oregon Dunes Overlook's all-accessible platform.

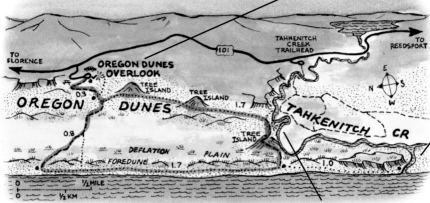

take a paved path to the right. This trail switchbacks 0.3 mile down through the forest into the dunes themselves.

Sand dollar.

Once in the open sand, head toward the roar of the ocean, first following posts in the dunes and then a trail across the deflation plain. Crest the foredune and head left along a remote, windswept stretch of beach. Seals peer from the surf. Pipers and gulls run along the waves' edge.

Getting There

Drive Highway 101 south of Florence 10 miles (or north of Reedsport 11 miles) to a turnoff between mileposts 200 and 201. Expect a $5 parking fee.

Sand dunes shoulder Tahkenitch Creek aside.

willow marsh full of driftwood, and climbs around the edge of a tree island. After another view of Tahkenitch Creek the trail vanishes into open dunes. Head straight across the sand to find posts marking the route along the left side of two more tree islands back to your car.

The lower part of Tahkenitch Creek's estuary is off-limits in summer to protect endangered shore birds.

3 Umpqua Discovery Center

Open daily 9am-5pm daily in summer, otherwise 10am-4pm. Adults $8, kids age 6-15 $4.

This modern interpretive center on Reedsport's old riverfront features the Umpqua River's ecology and history. Walk-through exhibits simulate the sights and sounds of an Indian village, a logging camp, a 19th-century waterfront dock, a one-room schoolhouse, and an old-time barbershop.

GETTING THERE: From Highway 101 in Reedsport, turn east on Highway 38 for half a mile and follow signs.

Reedsport's Umpqua Discovery Center.

Active dunes move slowly inland, burying forests.

THE LAST OF THE DUNES

Along most of the Oregon Coast, bluffs block the prevailing west winds from blowing beach sand inland. But in the lowlands of the Oregon Dunes, wave after wave of wind-driven dunes have marched ashore. Each onslaught buries forests before gradually petering out and sprouting forests of its own.

Man accidentally changed the dunes' traditional cycle by introducing European beachgrass to stabilize sand near railroads in 1910. The stubborn grass spread along the beach, creating a 30-foot-tall foredune. Because this grassy dike stops sand from blowing off the beach, the inland dunes have been cut off from their supply of sand.

The last dunes still marching eastward are expected to disappear within a century. Already they have left behind a broad deflation plain, a marshy area regrowing with brush and trees, between the ocean and the dying dunes.

European beachgrass has created a foredune barrier.

The mile-long McCullough Bridge across Coos Bay opened in 1936, the largest of the many graceful coastal bridges designed by luminary Oregon highway engineer Conde B. McCullough.

★ 4   Coos Bay

Although Coos Bay and North Bend grew side by side in Oregon's "Bay Area," the coast's largest metropolitan center, the two rival timber towns long refused to merge.

From the downtown Coos Bay visitor center, cross Highway 101 to stroll the **Coos Bay waterfront boardwalk**. Tugboats, yachts, and huge ocean-going freighters tie up at the deep-water port here. The **Coast Guard patrol boat** *Orcas* docks at the north end of the boardwalk. When the ship's not at sea, it's open to visitors weekdays 3pm to 6pm and weekends 10am to 4pm.

The city of Coos Bay spent its first 70 years known as Marshfield. From 1891 to 1944 the town's news appeared weekly in the 4-page *Marshfield Sun*. The newspaper's ancient printing press, typecases, and equipment remain in working order in the **Marshfield Sun Printing Museum**, open Tuesday through Saturday from 1pm to 4pm throughout summer, at Coos Bay's Front Street and Highway 101, north of the visitor center eight blocks.

The city of **North Bend** was founded by the Simpsons—a dynasty of shipbuild-

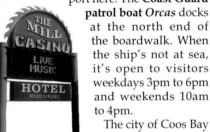

North Bend's old sawmill now houses an Indian casino.

ers and timber barons whose posh seaside summer estate has been preserved as Shore Acres State Park. During the Depression, North Bend was reduced to paying its public employees with myrtlewood tokens. Prosperity began to return in 1936 with the construction of the graceful, mile-long **McCullough Bridge** across Coos Bay. In the same year, North Bend built a steel **entry arch** across Highway 101 that remains a source of civic pride.

Beside North Bend's entry arch, the artifacts and displays in the **Coos County Historical Museum** are open from 10am to 4pm Tuesday through Saturday ($2 admission over age 12).

At the south edge of North Bend's bayfront, the Coquille Indian tribe has converted an abandoned sawmill into the **Mill Casino,** a resort with slot machines, bingo, three 24-hour restaurants, and a hotel.

GETTING THERE: Start at the visitor center at Highway 101 and Commercial Avenue in the middle of Coos Bay.

Tugboats on Coos Bay's waterfront help ships dock.

South Slough Estuarine Reserve

5

Open 8:30am-4:30pm daily. Free.

This first-rate interpretive center explains the importance of the tidal salt marshes that snake into the forested hills along South Slough, an arm of Coos Bay.

Take a look at the center's displays, then hike a pleasant trail a mile down to the slough's breached dikes to see wildlife first-hand.

GETTING THERE: From Highway 101 in Coos Bay, follow signs 9 miles west to Charleston. Just before that harbor town, turn left on Seven Devils Road for 4.3 miles to the reserve's entrance road.

Pilings line a breached dike along South Slough.

Harbor seals rest at the tip of Siletz Bay's sand spit.

SEAL OR SEA LION?

Most likely that dog-like shape you've spotted in the surf is a **harbor seal**. About 5 feet long and weighing up to 300 pounds, they like to lounge on sand spits near river mouths.

Steller sea lions are ruddier and three times as large. Look for them at Newport's docks and on offshore rocks.

Elephant seals are ten times larger, but breed only near Cape Arago (see p123). With a trunk-like snout and a roar heard for a mile, males can be 21 feet long and weigh over 7000 pounds.

Federal laws protect marine mammals from harassment, so don't approach too closely—even if you see an "abandoned" seal pup on the beach. It's just resting while its mother hunts for food.

BIRDS OF THE OREGON COAST

Because birds must nest on land, thousands of sea birds flock to rocky islands and headlands each summer. Watch them at Yaquina Head (p103), Shore Acres (p123), or Coquille Point (p125).

BROWN PELICAN. With gigantic 7-foot wingspans, rows of pelicans cruise past jetties, flying low.

OYSTERCATCHER. This bird struts about tidepool rocks, prying open mussels with its long red bill.

TUFTED PUFFIN. This 15-inch sea bird lands on islands and tall sea cliffs to nest in dirt tunnels.

COMMON MURRE. Like skinny penguins, thousands of murres crowd sea rocks to guard their eggs.

RHINOCEROS AUKLET. Look for this puffin relative swimming near headlands on summer evenings.

HIKE 27 — Shore Acres

Easy (to Simpson Cove)
0.6 miles round trip   80 feet elevation gain
Open all year   Use: hikers
Map: Cape Arago (USGS)

Moderate (to Cape Arago)
4.6-mile loop   550 feet elevation gain

Breakers crash against the tilted sandstone cliffs of Cape Arago's rugged coast. Sea lions bark from offshore reefs. Wavelets lap the beaches of hidden coves. If this seems an unlikely backdrop for a formal English garden, welcome to the surprises of Shore Acres State Park, one of three adjacent parks on this cape.

If you only have time for a whirlwind tour, it's possible to drive to viewpoints and picnic areas at each of the three parks, but to explore this unusual coastline thoroughly, you'll need to hike at least a portion of the trail between Sunset Bay and Cape Arago. Note that dogs are not allowed outside of cars in Shore Acres State Park.

From the oceanfront lawns at the far end of Shore Acres' parking area, walk to the observation building overlooking the sea cliffs. The waves below are slowly leveling the yellow sandstone's tilted strata, creating weirdly stepped reefs in the process. The plateau you're standing on was similarly leveled by waves thousands of years ago before the coastline here rose.

Turn left along the cliff edge for a hundred yards and veer left to find the entrance to the fabulous formal gardens that remain from the 1906 estate of timber baron Louis Simpson. Explore the pathways here until you reach the Japanese garden at the far end.

Then follow the sound of surf through a gate to the paved path along the oceanfront. Turn left to descend to Simpson Cove. This hidden bay's charming beach makes a good turnaround point for hikers with children.

If you're interested in a more substantial hike, hop the cove's inlet creek, take an unpaved path up a forested gully 300 yards to a T-shaped trail junction, and turn left to the park's paved road. Look on the far side of the road for a "Cape Arago Pack Trail" sign.

Follow this path uphill through a coastal rainforest of fir, spruce, waxmyrtle, and alder for 0.3 mile. Briefly explore a fork to the right to find a roofless 4-room concrete bunker, a military observation post from World War II.

The mansion that once dominated Shore Acres has burned, but the formal gardens and gardener's cottage remain.

Then continue 0.9 mile along a wooded ridge to a marked fork. Take the right-hand path downhill 0.9 mile to a gravel road and turn left 0.1 mile to Cape Arago's paved road.

To return to your car on a loop, you'll have to turn right along the park's paved

A heron sculpture perches in the park's Japanese garden.

A trail over Cape Arago tunnels through the rainforest.

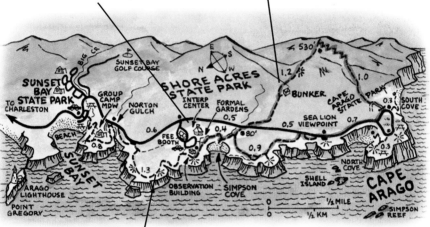

Waves crash against the shore's tilted sandstone cliffs.

road for 0.7 mile, but traffic is light and the views are good. Beyond a sea lion viewpoint 100 feet, look for a trail post. The path that begins here touches the paved road only once on its 1.2-mile route back to your car.

Getting There

From Highway 101 in Coos Bay, follow signs 9 miles to Charleston, and then continue straight 4 miles. A mile past Sunset Bay State Park, turn right into the Shore Acres entrance and pay a $3 parking fee at the entry booth.

6 Coquille River Lighthouse

Open 10am-4pm daily in summer. Free.

HIKE
28   **Bandon**

Easy   *(refer to map on facing page)*
3.3-mile loop   100 feet elevation gain
Open all year   Use: hikers
Map: Bandon (USGS)

This picturesque lighthouse was built in 1896, nearly rammed by a schooner in 1906, replaced by an automated beacon in 1939, and restored in 1978 after years of neglect. Nostalgia buffs added a small solar-powered light in 1991. In summer, when the small museum and gift shop inside are open, volunteers lead tours up the tower stairs.

The road to the lighthouse passes through **Bullards Beach State Park,** where you'll find riverside picnic lawns, a boat ramp, and a 207-site campground. In a forest behind overgrown dunes, the camp is sheltered from the beach's north winds. The map below shows some exploration opportunies.

GETTING THERE: Drive Highway 101 north of Bandon 3 miles (or south of Coos Bay 21 miles), turn west into Bullards Beach State Park, and keep left for 3 miles.

Bandon's Old Town is remarkably quaint, considering that it burned to the ground in both 1914 and 1936. Start this hike through Bandon by strolling around the Old Town's three main blocks of gift shops, boutiques, and galleries.

Then set off toward the ocean, following First Street along the riverfront. This street curves left at a 1939 Coast Guard building that is now used for offices. Shortly afterward turn right on narrow Jetty Road to the South Jetty.

The jetty was built in 1906 to stem a rash of shipwrecks on the Coquille River bar. When the *Oliver Olson* rammed the jetty so hard in 1953 that the ship couldn't be pulled free, the South Jetty was extended by building right over the ship's hull. Now sailors complain that

the uneven lengths of the river's two jetties make the bar more treacherous than ever.

From the jetty, turn left along the ocean beach. To sea, Table Rock's flat top swarms with seagulls, cormorants, and murres. Bring binoculars to spot the red-beaked puffins that arrive in April. They nest in tunnels up to 30 feet long that they dig in the sides of the island's dirt top. To protect easily frightened seabirds, climbing and tidepooling are

The Coquille River Lighthouse was built on a small rock island that sanded in to become part of the mainland.

banned on all Bandon's islands and sea stacks—even those easily accessible at low tide.

After a mile on the beach you'll cross a sandy gap between Coquille Point and Elephant Rock, a huge island shaped like a big-eared elephant with sea caves for eyes. For the short loop, climb a staircase on the far side of Coquille Point to Beach Loop Drive and follow this street left 1 mile, ignoring the street's frequent name

Getting There

Turn off Highway 101 through an archway proclaiming "Welcome to Old Town Bandon," drive a block to the riverfront, and turn left a block to a big parking area beside the boat basin.

changes. Finally turn left on Edison Street to return to your car.

For a longer loop, continue 0.9 mile along the beach to the far side of Grave Point, climb a staircase, and keep left on Beach Loop Drive.

Bandon's port is small, but a century ago it had the largest fleet between San Francisco and Astoria.

A Coquille tribal legend says that Face Rock is Ewauna, an Indian maiden forever gazing at the North Star.

A historic Coast Guard building from 1939 is now used for offices.

Bring binoculars to watch seagulls, cormorants, and murres swarming above the islands off Coquille Point.

7 Cape Blanco State Park

Oregon's westernmost point, Cape Blanco juts more than a mile to sea. Spanish sea explorers named it *Cabo Blanco* ("White Cape") in 1602. A scenic but often windy state park encompasses the entire cape, including an 1870 lighthouse that's open for summer tours, a 64-site campground that's open year round, miles of trails, and a Victorian home restored as a museum.

Start your exploration at the tip of the cape. When the gate to the lighthouse compound is open (10am to 3pm Thursday through Monday from

a meadow of wind-matted salal bushes and white yarrow for 0.3 mile to the cape's secluded north beach.

Next, drive back a mile on the park's entrance road and turn left at a sign for the Hughes House

Irish immigrants Patrick and Jane Hughes built this elegant Victorian farmhouse in 1898. Now it's a museum.

The lighthouse's beacon still shines.

April through October), you can drive out to the lighthouse itself and tour the tower.

Whether or not the lighthouse gate is open, park at a pullout beside the gate for some exploration afoot. A post just beyond the gate on the right marks the Oregon Coast Trail. This path descends through

The Oregon Coast Trail crosses the neck of the headland.

Museum. Down the road 0.2 mile, stop to see this elegantly restored 1898 ranch house (open April to October from 10am to 3:30pm Thursday through Monday).

GETTING THERE: Drive 4 miles north of Port Orford on Highway 101, turn west at a Cape Blanco State Park sign, and drive straight for 5 miles to a parking area at the lighthouse gate.

A crane hoists fishing boats to safety atop Port Orford's dock for the night. Humbug Mountain is on the horizon.

GETTING THERE: Drive Highway 101 to milepost 301 for the Port Orford Heads turnoff; continue south half a mile to the Battle Rock parking area.

Picturesque Battle Rock, on the beach at downtown Port Orford, was the scene of a bloody skirmish in 1851.

Port Orford

Westernmost city in the lower 48 states, Port Orford overlooks a sheltered cove with a natural ocean harbor that has attracted settlers since 1851.

Pull into a parking lot beside Highway 101 at the south edge of downtown to visit **Battle Rock**, a rock island on Port Orford's beach. In 1851, nine white settlers huddled here for 15 days, killing Indians with cannon fire before escaping by night.

Next, drive or walk west 0.5 mile to **Port Orford's harbor dock**. Each afternoon a crane hoists the fishing fleet, boat by boat, from the ocean for storage atop the dock for the night.

Then drive half a mile north on Highway 101 to 9th Street and follow signs west a mile to **Port Orford Heads State Park**. The 1934 Coast Guard lifeboat station on this scenic headland closed in 1970, but volunteers have opened a free museum in the barracks (open 10am to 3:30pm Thursday to Monday from April through October). A network of short trails explores the headland's fabulously scenic meadows.

Humbug Mountain State Park

Highway 101 detours inland around this remote 1761-foot mountain that fronts the sea with cliffs on three sides. In a glen beside the highway you'll find a handy 108-site campground *(see p132)* that's open all year. A short path from the campground leads under a Highway 101 bridge to a pocket beach at the foot of the Mountain's ocean cliffs.

For a more difficult hike with great ocean views, tackle a 5.5-mile loop through old-growth woods to the mountain's summit. Start at a "Humbug Mountain Trail Parking" sign on Highway 101 a quarter mile north of the campground entrance.

GETTING THERE: Drive Highway 101 south of Port Orford 6 miles or north of Gold Beach 21 miles.

Scenic Humbug Mountain won its name when an inept explorer led an 1851 expedition here in search of gold.

10 Gold Beach

Miners sluiced Gold Beach's sand in the 1850s for gold flakes washed from the Klamath Mountains by the Rogue River. Today the Rogue is prized for different treasures — whitewater, wilderness, and wildlife.

Explore the river either by hiking the Rogue River Trail *(see pp222-24)*, by driving the 35-mile paved road from the Gold Beach bridge to the hamlet of Agness, or by taking a jet boat ride.

Jet boat on the Rogue.

Two fleets of 50-seat **jet boats** whisk tourists from Gold Beach into the Rogue's wilderness. Loudspeakers announce herons, seals, and deer. Stops at rustic lodges allow passengers to buy buffet meals. The 64- to 104-mile tours cost about $30 to $80 and leave Gold Beach at about 8am and 2:30pm from May 1 to October 31. Rogue River Mail Boats (800-458-3511) dock upstream from the north end of Gold Beach's bridge, while their rivals, Jerry's Rogue Jets (800-451-3645),

A scenic bridge spans the Rogue River at Gold Beach.

dock downstream from the bridge's south end, beside a free museum of Rogue River memorabilia.

GETTING THERE: Jet boat offices are on either end of the Highway 101 Rogue River Bridge in Gold Beach. To drive upriver, take Jerrys Flat Road at the bridge's south end.

HIKE 29 Vulcan Lake

Moderate
2.8 miles round trip   730 feet elevation gain
Open May through November   Use: hikers
Map: Kalmiopsis Wilderness (USFS)

Stark red ridges, shimmering green lakes, and the strange plants of the Klamath Mountains highlight this corner of the remote Kalmiopsis Wilderness. It's also an interesting place to see the rejuvenating effects of the 2002 Biscuit Fire, the biggest Oregon blaze in a century. Here the fire left most trees intact, instead clearing out underbrush to make room for wildflowers.

Knobcone pine cone.

After a few yards on the trail, turn

The Rogue River twists through a wilderness canyon.

Vulcan Lake from Vulcan Peak, before the 2002 fire.

Kalmiopsis leachiana, the rare azalea-like shrub that gave the Kalmiopsis Wilderness its name, grows on Dry Butte two miles north of Vulcan Lake.

rock. Only a few pines and cedars have gained a foothold. If you're backpacking, bring a stove and build no campfire.

To find another lake nearby, backtrack 200 yards from Vulcan Lake to a rock cairn, turn right, and keep to the right on a faint downhill path. After 0.2 mile you'll reach Little Vulcan Lake's shore, ringed with carnivorous pitcher plants that trap insects.

Pitcher plants trap insects for fertilizer.

right on a path that switchbacks up through wind-twisted Jeffrey pine. After a mile you'll reach a rocky pass with sweeping views. The trail then angles down 0.4 mile to Vulcan Lake, a magical place where red bedrock curves into deep green water.

During the Ice Age this basin was a cirque—the birthplace of a glacier—and the immense weight of moving ice shaped the rounded, scratched bed-

Getting There

From the Highway 101 bridge in Brookings, take North Bank Road 8 miles and continue straight on one-lane Road 1376 another 8 miles to a T-junction just beyond the South Fork Chetco Bridge. Then, following Kalmiopsis Wilderness signs, turn right on gravel Road 1909 for 13.4 miles (keeping right when in doubt) to a fork where signs point left for Vulcan Lake and right for Vulcan Peak. Keep left for 1.7 miles very rough miles to a trailhead at road's end. A $5-per-car Northwest Forest Pass is required here.

Vulcan Lake after the Biscuit Fire of 2002, the largest Oregon wildfire in a century.

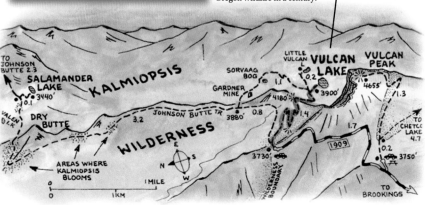

HIKE 30 Boardman Park

Easy (six short viewpoint walks)
3.2 miles altogether   300 feet elevation gain
Open all year   Use: hikers
Map: Mack Point (USGS)

Boardman State Park's coast is a spectacular parade of islands, coves, and capes. Most travelers simply take in the views as they drive through. A few hike the entire route on a 12.6-mile section of the Oregon Coast Trail. A good compromise is to park your car at half a dozen stops along Highway 101 for a series of short walks to the best viewpoints.

The northernmost of these recommended stops is the Arch Rock Picnic Area, between mileposts 344 and 345. Park here and stroll the paved, 0.2-mile path around the rim of the picnic area's bluff. Waves crash against seabird-dotted islands on all sides of the cape.

Next drive south 1.2 miles to a pull-

The North Island Viewpoint overlooks China Beach.

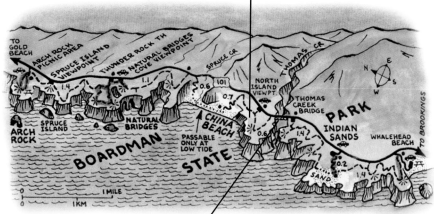

The 345-foot-tall Highway 101 span across Thomas Creek's gorge is Oregon's tallest bridge.

out near milepost 346 marked "Natural Bridges Cove Viewpoint." Trails leave from both the left- and right-hand edges of this parking area. First take the left-hand trail 100 feet to a viewpoint of the cove below, where the sea boils through two archways into a collapsed former cave. Then return to the car and take the right-hand trail along the cove's rim to discover a 0.7-mile loop with more views. This route crosses the Thunder Cove Viewpoint pullout, continues into the woods, and then forks left to start the loop itself.

For the third short hike, drive south another 2.5 miles to Indian Sands Viewpoint. From the left side of the parking lot's entrance, a 0.2-mile trail descends through forest to an unusual area of sand dunes perched above a rocky shore.

Next drive 0.7 mile south and take the Whalehead Beach turnoff down to a picnic area beside a gorgeous, secluded beach. Offshore is Whalehead Island, where waves send up a spout-like plume of sea spray when the tide is just right. Hop across Whalehead Creek and explore the beach as far as you like.

For the fifth viewpoint hike, return to your car, drive 0.3 mile back uphill to the junction with Highway 101, and park by a trail sign on the left. Take this path 0.2 mile out along a meadowy cape to a breathtaking viewpoint overlooking Whalehead Island.

Conclude your exploration of Boardman State Park 3 miles farther south. Near milepost 352 of Highway 101,

Purple lupine blooms on the bluffs near Cape Ferrelo.

Whalehead Island "spouts" when waves hit it just right.

turn off to the Cape Ferrelo Viewpoint. From the parking area, walk 0.5 mile out through grassy wildflower meadows to the cape's panoramic tip.

Getting There

The Arch Rock trailhead is 12 miles north of Brookings on Highway 101 (or 18 miles south of Gold Beach). The Cape Ferrelo trailhead is 4 miles north of Brookings on Highway 101 (or 26 miles south of Gold Beach).

WHERE TO STAY

Campgrounds *(map p113)*

	Campsites	Water	Showers	Flush Toilet	Fee
9 BASTENDORFF BEACH. On a beach with surfing, this county campground near Shore Acres State Park has two cabins (reservations: 541-396-3121 x354). From Coos Bay, drive west past Charleston 2 miles.	81	●	●	●	$$
11 BULLARDS BEACH. On the Coquille River near an ocean beach and lighthouse *(see p124)*, this state park has 13 yurts that rent for $29. Drive Highway 101 north of Bandon 3 miles. Reservations: 800-452-5687.	185	●	●	●	$$
12 CAPE BLANCO. Salal and shore pine hedges serve as campsite windbreaks at this spectacular state park cape with a lighthouse *(see p126)*. Four cabins rent for $35 (reservations: 800-452-5687).	64	●	●	●	$$
4 CARTER LAKE. At this wooded Forest Service camp you can canoe a small lake, slide down giant dunes, or hike 0.9 mile to the ocean. Open mid-May through September, south of Florence 9 miles on Highway 101.	23	●		●	$$
15 HARRIS BEACH. From the wooded campsites of this state park, paths lead to beaches with craggy islands where sea birds wheel. Drive Highway 101 north of Brookings 1 mile. Six yurts rent for $29 (reservations: 800-452-5687).	149	●	●	●	$$
2 HONEYMAN. Oregon's busiest state park campground *(see p116)* has dunes, lakes, forests, and 10 rental yurts ($29). Drive Highway 101 south of Florence 3 miles. Reservations: 800-452-5687.	357	●	●	●	$$
13 HUMBUG MOUNTAIN. From this handy state park campground a short path leads to a remote beach and a long path leads to a mountain viewpoint (see p127). Drive Highway 101 south of Port Orford 6 miles.	99	●	●	●	$$
16 LOEB. On the Chetco River near a redwood grove, this state park has 3 rental cabins for $35 (reservations: 800-452-5687). From the Highway 101 bridge in Brookings, take North Bank Rd. inland 7.3 miles.	48	●	●	●	$$
6 LOON LAKE. This 2-mile-long lake has swimming, boating, and a trail to a waterfall. From Reedsport take Highway 38 inland 13.5 miles and turn south 7.5 miles. Open late May-Oct. Res: 541-756-0100 or *www.reserveusa.com*.	53	●	●	●	$$
14 QUOSATANA. This Forest Service camp is on the bank of the Rogue River by a gravel bar. From the Highway 101 bridge in Gold Beach, take Jerrys Flat Road inland 13 miles.	42	●		●	$
10 SUNSET BAY. Beside a charming ocean cove with swimming and tidepools, this state park campground has 8 yurts ($29). Drive as to Shore Acres *(see pp122)*. Reservations: 800-452-5687.	131	●	●	●	$$
1 SUTTON. Where Sutton Creek winds through sand dunes and forest, this Forest Service camp has lovely trails, but you have to wade the creek to reach the beach. Drive Highway 101 north of Florence 6 miles.	80	●		●	$$
5 TAHKENITCH. Scenic trails from this wooded Forest Service camp lead 0.6 miles to huge dunes or 1.9 miles to the beach. Open mid-May to Labor Day. Drive Highway 101 south of Florence 13 miles.	34	●		●	$$
8 TUGMAN. Swimming, fishing, and waterskiing are popular on sinuous Eel Lake, where this state park has a campground with 13 yurts ($29). South of Reedsport 8 miles on Highway 101. Reservations: 800-452-5687.	100	●	●	●	$$
7 UMPQUA LIGHTHOUSE. Near a lighthouse, this state park has trails that circle Lake Marie and lead to gigantic sand dunes. Two cabins ($35) and 8 yurts ($29-66). Reservations: 800-452-5687. Drive Highway 101 south of Reedsport 6 miles and follow signs.	44	●	●	●	$$
3 WAXMYRTLE. This Forest Service camp on the Siltcoos River *(see p117)* has a 1-mile trail through dunes to the beach. Open late May to Labor Day.	55	●		●	$$

Harris Beach State Park. ▷

WHERE TO STAY

B&Bs and Quaint Hotels (map p113)

	Rooms	Private bath	Cont. breakfast	Full breakfast	Rate range
8 BANDON OCEAN GUESTHOUSE. Birdwatching is excellent at this contemporary bed & breakfast inn 2 miles south of Bandon at 200 Beach Street, Bandon, OR 97411, two minutes from the beach. Some rooms have spa tubs or fireplaces. Info: 888-335-1076 or www.beach-street.com.	6	●		●	$100-180
4 BLACKBERRY INN. Remarkably inexpensive, this renovated 1903 bed & breakfast in downtown Coos Bay offers a continental breakfast on nice china. 843 Central Avenue, Coos Bay, OR 97420. Info: 800-500-4657 or www.myblackberryinn.com.	3	1	●		$35-65
1 BLUE HERON INN. Overlooking the Siuslaw River, this 1940s ranch-style bed & breakfast inn is east of Florence 2.5 miles at 6563 Highway 126, Florence, OR 97439. Info: 800-997-7780 or www.blue-heroninn.com.	6	●		●	$75-140
11 BY THE SEA. Near Harris Beach State Park, this contemporary bed & breakfast inn has fireplaces in every room. At 1545 Beach Avenue, Brookings, OR 97415, the inn faces a rocky cove with islands. Info: 877-469-4692 or www.brookingsbythesea.com.	3	●		●	$98-150
2 DRIFTWOOD SHORES. Florence's only beachfront hotel is practical rather than quaint. Every room has an ocean view and a patio or deck. Most have a full kitchen. Info: 800-422-5091 or www.driftwoodshores.com.	128	●			$87-299
3 EDWIN K. In a 1914 Craftsman-style home overlooking the Siuslaw River, this bed & breakfast inn is in Florence's Old Town at 1155 Bay Street, Florence, OR 97439. Info: 800-833-9465 or www.edwink.com.	6	●		●	$115-170
9 FLORAS LAKE. Beside a lakeside windsurfing park, just across a dune from the ocean, this 1991 bed & breakfast inn at 92870 Boice Cope Road, Langlois, OR 97450 is open February through October. Drive Highway 101 south of Bandon 16 miles and turn west on Floras Lake Road. Info: 541-348-2573 or www.floraslake.com.	4	●		●	$135-155

Oregon Dunes. ▷

	Rooms	Private bath	Cont. breakfast	Full breakfast	Rate range
7 LIGHTHOUSE. Between Bandon's Old Town and the beach, this 1980 bed & breakfast inn at 650 Jetty Road SW, Bandon, OR 97411 overlooks the Coquille River and a historic lighthouse. Info: 541-347-9316 or www.lighthouselodging.com.	5	●		●	$130-225
12 LOWDEN'S BEACHFRONT BED & BREAKFAST. Where the Winchuck River meets the Pacific, the rooms in this inn (14626 Wollam Road, Brookings, OR 97415) each have a private entry, views, beach access, and fireplace. Info: 800-453-4768 or www.beachfrontbb.com.	2	●		●	$99-139
5 OLD TOWER HOUSE. Rooms have antiques and claw-foot bathtubs in this 1893 Victorian home converted to a bed & breakfast inn overlooking Coos Bay at 476 Newmark Avenue, Coos Bay, OR 97420. One rental cottage is nearby. Info: 541-888-6058 or www.oldtowerhouse.com.	3	2		●	$85-125
10 ROGUE REEF INN. In a contemporary oceanfront home with a private path to the beach, this bed & breakfast is 1 mile north of the Rogue River's mouth. Info: 877-234-7333 or www.roguereef.com.	4	●		●	$120-150
6 THIS OLDE HOUSE. Built in 1885 by the family of an English lord, this antique-filled bed & breakfast inn overlooks the boats at Coos Bay's waterfront at 202 Alder Avenue, Coos Bay, OR 97420. Info: 541-267-5224 or www.bnbweb.com/thisoldehouse.html.	4	●		●	$97-175

VALLEY & FOOTHILLS

Beyond the broad Willamette Valley lie the forested canyons of the Cascade foothills.

Thirty miles wide and a hundred miles long, the broad, fertile Willamette Valley was the prize that lured pioneer settlers in covered wagons west across the dangerous Oregon Trail in the mid 1800s.

The valley is so flat and fertile because gigantic Ice Age floods from Montana repeatedly filled the basin with silty water hundreds of feet deep 12,000 years ago. Later, native tribes burned off the valley's forests to improve hunting.

The resulting grassland was so easy to farm that early settlers sometimes sowed wheat one year and harvested it three years in a row without replowing.

Salem, Corvallis, Eugene, and other cities grew along the Willamette River, linked by steamboats and then trains.

The Cascade Range to the east has long been a barrier to transportation — and not merely because of the dozen spectacular snowpeaks along the range's crest. The 1500 Oregon Trail pioneers of the Lost Wagon Train, for example, attempted a shortcut west to Eugene in 1853. They managed to hew a path past the snowpeaks but abandoned their wagons in dismay when they saw that sixty miles of steep, forested canyons still lay between them and the Willamette Valley.

Even today, only a few paved highways traverse these densely forested Cascade foothills, following raging whitewater rivers past waterfalls. Although decades of clearcut logging have left their mark, giant stands of ancient trees remain, especially in protected Wilderness Areas.

◁ **South Falls in Silver Falls State Park** *(see pp140-41).*   △ **Fifth Street Market in Eugene** *(see p151).*

Exploring the
VALLEY & FOOTHILLS

Interstate 5 and half a dozen daily Amtrak trains link the state's three largest cities, Portland, Salem, and Eugene. But you'll need to explore side roads to see the Willamette Valley's vineyards, farms, parks, covered bridges, and villages. For a wilder getaway, take a day trip into the Cascade Range's foothills for a hike to a primitive hot springs, across a wildflower meadow, or through an old-growth forest to a waterfall.

Silver Falls

A spectacular loop trail in this large, woodsy state park passes ten waterfalls, five of them over 100 feet tall (*see pp140-41*).

Salem

The State Capitol, built in 1938 with a surprisingly modern look, is not the only attraction in Salem. Riverfront Park on the Willamette has an elaborate carousel, a riverboat, and a discovery center for kids. The historic downtown includes large stores linked by sky bridges. And the Mission Mill Museum features a working, water-powered woolen mill (*see pp144-45*).

McKenzie River

Half a dozen lava flows from the Cascade Range have tortured this charming whitewater river over the past 6000 years, damming it at Clear Lake, squeezing it into a gorge at Koosah Falls (*at left*), and burying it altogether at the dry riverbed above turquoise Tamolitch Pool. Short hikes through old-growth forest explore the riverside sights (*see pp154-55*).

Eugene

Home to the University of Oregon, Eugene has a counter-culture flair, with coffee shops, brewpubs, laid-back festivals, and more bridges across the Willamette River for bicycles than for cars. Rent a bike to tour miles of riverside paths (*at right*). Hop a shuttle bus to ride from Fifth Street's upscale craft shops to the university's art museum (*see pp150-53*).

The glassy Willamette River slides past Willamette Mission State Park, site of an 1834 missionary outpost.

HIKE 31 Willamette Mission

Easy

2.7-mile loop	No elevation gain
Open all year	Use: hikers, horses, bikes
Map: Mission Bottom (USGS)	

This riverside walk through Willamette Mission State Park not only visits the world's largest cottonwood tree and the site of a historic 1834 settlement, it also includes a free ferry ride across the Willamette River and back.

Start at the Filbert Grove Day Use Area—a picnic area set in an old hazelnut orchard. Some years the trees still produce a bumper crop of nuts that you can gather for free in autumn. From the restrooms at the far

World's largest cottonwood tree.

end of the parking loop, follow a path 0.2 mile to the riverbank and turn right on a paved bike path for a mile to the Wheatland Ferry.

This is the oldest ferry landing in Oregon, dating to 1844 when mules winched a log barge across the river with ropes. The present steel vessel uses an overhead cable and electric engines. Pedestrians ride free, but car drivers pay 50 cents. The ferry runs from 6am to 9:45pm every day except Christmas and Thanksgiving—but it closes for about 30 days each winter due to high water or repairs.

The gravelly shore beside the landing is perfect for skipping rocks and watching the river. Children delight in find-

Pedestrians ride free on the Wheatland Ferry.

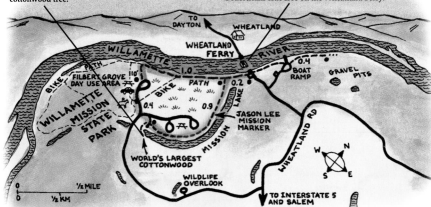

ing tadpoles, frogs, and crawdads here. Look in the wet sand for the palm-sized tracks of great blue herons and the little hand-shaped tracks of raccoons.

To return on a loop, hike 300 yards back from the landing on the bike path and turn left onto a broad trail. This path soon follows the shore of marshy Mission Lake. Before a flood changed the course of the Willamette River in 1861, this lake was the main channel.

A trailside monument describes the mission built on the old riverbank by Methodist minister Jason Lee in 1834. In 1840, weary of the river's floods, Lee moved operations to Chemeketa (now Salem), where he founded the Oregon Institute, which became Willamette University.

After passing the monument, the trail enters a picnic lawn in an old walnut orchard. Keep left at all junctions for half a mile to the trail's end at a road. A

sign here points out the world's largest black cottonwood—155 feet tall and over 26 feet in circumference. Walk along the road to return to your car, turning left at the first stop sign and right at the next.

Evergreen Aviation Museum

Open 9am-5pm daily. Adults $11, veterans and seniors $10, children age 6-18 $7.

Wider than a football field, the world's largest airplane dominates this McMinnville museum. Built of birch plywood, the unbelievably huge "Spruce Goose" actually flew for one minute in 1947.

GETTING THERE: From Interstate 5 south of Portland, take exit 294 and drive Highway 99W toward McMinnville 30 miles. Then follow "Ocean Beaches" signs on Highway 18 for 5 miles.

The "Spruce Goose," the largest airplane ever built, dwarfs dozens of other historic aircraft at the museum.

OREGON VINEYARDS

Oregon had few vineyards before 1970, but now they carpet Willamette Valley hillsides, particularly between McMinnville and Salem.

Robust red Oregon pinot noir wines can demand over $100 a bottle.

One key to this sudden success is the fact that Oregon's latitude and climate match those of France. Unlike California, Oregon's dry summers and crisp autumns generate distinctive vintages.

Oregon has won an international reputation for pinot noir, pinot gris, and chardonnay wines.

Several dozen vineyards have tasting rooms open daily from 11am to 5pm. For directions, check *www.oregonwine-country.org*, or simply drive along Highway 99W from Portland to Eugene and watch for signs.

Vineyards drape slopes of the Willamette Valley.

HIKE 32 Silver Falls

Moderate
5.2-mile loop   500 feet elevation gain
Open all year   Use: hikers
Map: Drake Crossing (USGS)

The popular trail through Silver Falls State Park's forested canyons visits ten spectacular waterfalls, five more than 100 feet high. The path even leads through mossy caverns *behind* the falls' shimmering silver curtains.

This loop is suitable for families with beginning hikers, because side trails provide shortcuts back to the car, trimming the distance to just 2.4 or even 0.7 miles. The park is usually snow-free even in mid-winter. Dogs, however, are not allowed on the trail.

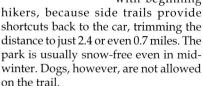
Silver Falls Lodge.

From the Picnic Area C parking lot, follow a broad path downstream a few hundred yards to historic Silver Falls Lodge, built by Civilian Conservation Corps crews in 1940. After inspecting this rustic stone-and-log building, continue a few hundred yards to an overlook of 177-foot South Falls. From here take a paved trail to the right. Then

At Middle North Falls, you've completed slightly more than half of the recommended 5.2-mile loop.

switchback down into the canyon and behind South Falls.

All waterfalls in the park spill over 15-million-year-old Columbia River basalt. As the lava slowly cooled, it sometimes fractured to form the honeycomb of columns visible on cliff edges. Circular indentations in the ceilings of the misty caverns behind the falls are *tree wells*, formed when the lava flows hardened around burning trees. The churning of

A stuntman canoed off 177-foot South Falls in 1928 for a paying audience. He survived, but was seriously hurt.

Silver Creek gouged the soft soil from beneath the harder lava, leaving these caverns and casts.

A few hundred yards beyond South Falls is a junction at a scenic footbridge. Don't cross the bridge unless you're truly tired, because that route merely returns to the car. Instead take the unpaved path along the creek. This path eventually switchbacks down and behind Lower South Falls' broad, 93-foot cascade. Beyond Lower South Falls the trail forks again. If you're wearing down, you can turn right and climb the steepish ridge trail to the canyon rim and parking lot, for a total trip length of 2.4 miles.

If you're ready for a longer hike continue straight, heading up the north fork of Silver Creek to 30-foot Lower North Falls. At a footbridge just above the falls, take a 250-yard side trail to admire tall, thin Double Falls. Then continue on the main trail past Drake and Middle North Falls to the Winter Falls trail junction.

At this point, turn right for the recommended loop. This path climbs to a parking area above Winter Falls. From there, keep right on a 1.6-mile return trail through the woods to the South Falls area, the lodge, and your car.

The loop crosses a bridge above Middle North Falls.

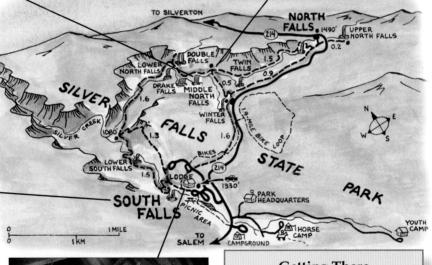

Silver Falls Lodge was built in 1940 by the same architect and interior designer that created Timberline Lodge.

Getting There

From Interstate 5 exist 253 in Salem, drive 10 miles east on North Santiam Highway 22, turn left at a sign for Silver Falls Park, and follow Highway 214 for 16 miles to the park entrance sign at South Falls. (Coming from the north, exit Interstate 5 at Woodburn and follow Highway 214 southeast through Silverton 30 miles.) In the South Falls parking complex, follow signs to Picnic Area C, and park at the far end of the lot. A special $3 parking fee is charged throughout the park.

HIKE 33 Bagby Hot Springs

Easy

3 miles round trip   200 feet elevation gain
Open all year   Use: hikers, horses
Map: Bull of the Woods Wilderness (USFS)

Hollowed-out cedar logs serve as 8-foot-long bathtubs at this rustic, free hot springs. Even if you don't plan to soak, the trail here is a delight, through a towering old-growth forest. Expect crowds on weekends and in summer.

Remember the area's rules: no unleashed dogs, no music, no baths longer than an hour, and no soap. Swimsuits are rare.

If you keep right at the log cabin, you'll follow the Bagby Trail through a picnic meadow. After 0.2 mile, a spur descends to eight riverside campsites. Next the Bagby Trail passes 50-foot Shower Creek Falls—a cascade some people use for a cold shower after their hot bath.

To fill a tub, unplug a bunghole to divert scalding water from a trough behind the wall. To adjust the temperature, use one of the plastic buckets to dip cold water from a vat outside.

The trail to Bagby Hot Springs is wheelchair-accessible to the second bridge.

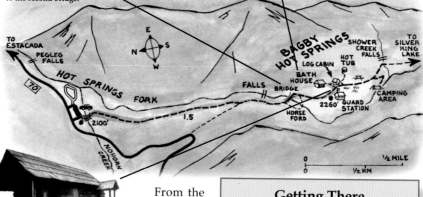

A log cabin houses the hot springs' old guard station.

From the parking area, the trail crosses Nohorn Creek on a footbridge and launches into the woods. After 1.5 miles you'll reach a signboard at the hot springs. To the left is the bathhouse, with long benches outside for the waiting line. The original house burned in 1979 when bathers carelessly used candles for light. The rebuilt structure includes five private rooms and an annex with four more tubs.

Getting There

To find Bagby Hot Springs from Interstate 205 near Oregon City, take exit 12 and follow signs east 18 miles to Estacada. Go straight, continuing 26 miles on Highway 224 to the bridge at Ripplebrook. Then, following signs for Bagby Hot Springs, keep straight on paved Road 46 for 3.6 miles, turn right onto paved Road 63 for 3.5 miles, and turn right onto paved Road 70 for 6 miles to the trailhead parking lot on the left, where a Northwest Forest Pass is required ($5 per car per day). Leave no valuables in your car, as this area has a history of theft.

Flower displays spiral out from the Rose Petal Fountain.

2 Oregon Garden

Open 10am-6pm in summer (winter 10am-4pm). Adults $8, seniors $7, children age 8-17 $6; prices are lower in winter.

A showcase of the Willamette Valley's nursery industry, this 64-acre garden in Silverton includes waterfalls, flowerbeds, rock gardens, and wetlands. Walk the looping pathways or

The only Frank Lloyd Wright building open to the public in the Northwest, the Gordon House was designed in 1957 to be affordable for an average family.

ride a free tram on a guided tour.

Don't miss the **Gordon House**, just below the Oregon Garden's main parking area. Designed by architect Frank Lloyd Wright in 1957, this strangely modern, angular home was moved here from its original location on the Willamette River in 2001. Inside tours are available daily from 10am to 5pm. A self-guided tour of the first floor runs $2, while a guided tour of the entire house is $5.

GETTING THERE: Drive Interstate 5 north of Salem to Keizer exit 260 and follow signs 13 miles east to the garden entrance on Main Street at the south edge of Silverton.

Carriagehouse at the Old Aurora Colony Museum. The museum is open Tuesday-Saturday 10am-4pm and Sunday noon-4pm (except in January) for $4.50.

3 Aurora

The "antique capital of Oregon" with 23 antique shops, this charming village was founded in 1856 as a utopian commune by a fundamentalist sect of Germans.

GETTING THERE: Drive Interstate 5 south of Portland 22 miles to exit 278 and go 2 miles east.

COVERED BRIDGES

COVERED BRIDGE TOUR ROUTE NEXT•LEFT

Tour routes visit covered bridges near Albany and Cottage Grove.

Dozens of covered bridges remain on Willamette Valley backroads from the early 20th century.

The scenic spans were not built merely so horse-and-buggy drivers could escape the rain. A 1909 study showed that Western Oregon's wet climate caused uncovered wooden bridges to rot in just seven years.

A typical covered bridge cost $4000 to build in 1920. The construction crew was expected to fell trees on the spot, cut their own lumber, split

their own roof shakes, and fish for their dinners.

Five visitable bridges remain on backroads east of Albany and another cluster of six surround Cottage Grove, south of Eugene 18 miles.

The Gilkey covered bridge dates to 1939.

4 Salem

Founded by missionaries and dominated by government offices, Salem struggles with a reputation as a staid burg. But there's actually a lot to do here.

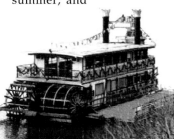

A gold-plated pioneer statue tops the Capitol.

The riverfront has been revitalized with family attractions, historic downtown buildings have been linked with a dozen sky bridges for shoppers, and three downtown museums have been opened in park settings.

Start at the **State Capitol**, built with daringly modern lines in 1938. Inside, free tours of the building leave on the hour from 9am to 4pm (except noon) during summer, and

Continue down State Street 3 blocks to Riverfront Park. A top attraction here is **Salem's Riverfront Carousel,** with 42 hand-carved horses. Rides are only

The Elsinore Theatre, a 1926 Tudor Gothic movie palace, has been restored as a performing arts center.

The *Willamette Queen* docks at Salem's riverfront for day trips and dinner cruises.

free tours up to the dome's gold pioneer statue leave every half hour.

The back door of the Capitol faces State Street and **Willamette University**. If you like, stroll through the campus to watch ducks at the mill race or to visit the **Hallie Ford Museum of Art.**

Heading downtown along State Street you'll pass the spectacular white wooden spire of the **First Methodist Church**. A block beyond, detour briefly left on High Street to look inside the 1926 **Elsinore Theatre**, a palatial movie house with stained glass windows and gothic tracery. Restored as a performing arts center, it has a 1924 Wurlitzer organ.

Rides cost $1.25 on the hand-carved and hand-painted horses of the Riverfront Carousel.

The Mission Mill Museum includes a functioning 1889 woolen mill powered by a mill race among oak-shaded lawns.

$1.25. Hours are 10am-7pm in summer and 10am-6pm in winter (but then it opens an hour late on Sundays and closes later on Fridays and Saturdays).

Nearby is the **Willamette Queen Riverboat,** a paddlewheeler that offers luncheon cruises from noon to 1pm Tuesday through Saturday for $15. Call 503-371-1103 for reservations and other cruise offerings.

The 1841 home of Methodist missionary Jason Lee, at the Mission Mill Museum, is Oregon's oldest frame building.

The First Methodist Church is on Church Street, of course.

Three blocks downriver, take the kids to **A.C. Gilbert's Discovery Village,** a hands-on museum named for Salem's famous inventor of children's toys.

Hours are 10am-5pm Monday through Saturday and noon-5pm Sunday. General admission (ages 3-59) runs $5.50.

Fourteen historic buildings — including a working, water-powered woolen mill, are clustered at the **Mission Mill Museum** (1313 Mill Street SE), open 10am-5pm Monday through Saturday. Admission is $7 for adults and $4 for children age 6 to 18.

Complete your visit with a stroll through 100-acre **Bush Park,** where you can tour the **Bush House,** an 1878 Victorian mansion, and **Deepwood,** an 1894 Queen Anne home amid English gardens.

GETTING THERE: From Interstate 5, take the third Salem exit (#253), follow Mission Street west 2 miles, and veer right onto 12th Street. The Mission Mill Museum is 3 blocks ahead on the right. If you're headed for the State Capitol, continue another 3 blocks on 12th Street and turn left on Court Street.

Oldest college west of the Mississippi, Willamette University began as a missionary school in 1841.

HIKE 34   Opal Creek

Moderate
7.1-mile loop   200 feet elevation gain
Open all year   Use: hikers
Maps: Battle Ax, Elkhorn (USGS)

Opal Creek's ancient forest, on the edge of the Bull of the Woods Wilderness, was thrust to fame in the 1980s by controversy over Forest Service logging proposals. National television crews and thousands of visitors hiked to Jawbone Flats' rustic mining camp and scrambled over a rugged "bear trail" to view the endangered old-growth groves towering above this creek's green pools.

An old-growth red cedar tree 12 feet in diameter.

Chicken-of-the-woods, a brightly colored fungus.

By the time Opal Creek finally won Wilderness protection in 1998 an improved path had been built to make the area more hiker-friendly. The new trail shortcuts from the Little North Santiam River to Opal Creek, making possible a loop trip to Opal Pool's gorge and Jawbone Flats.

The hiking trail begins as a gated road. Residents of Jawbone Flats are allowed to drive this dirt track; others must park and walk. The pleasantly primitive road crosses Gold Creek on a 60-foot-high bridge, skirts dramatic cliffs above the

After 2 miles the trail passes Sawmill Falls, with a deep but chilly swimming hole on the Little North Santiam River.

Little North Santiam River, and winds through an old-growth grove as impressive as any found farther upstream.

At the 2-mile mark, stop to inspect the rusting machinery of Merten Mill on the right. The mill operated briefly during the Depression, using winches from the battleship *USS Oregon,* but folded after two of the mill's lumber trucks fell off the narrow canyon road. Now a camping area for backpackers, the mill site has one small empty building that can serve as emergency shelter. A short

Jawbone Flats is a well-preserved 1929 mining camp.

Mossy Opal Creek tumbles out of a trailless canyon.

side trail behind the building leads to Sawmill Falls, a 30-foot cascade pouring into a deep green pool ideal for a chilly swim.

The road forks 0.2 mile beyond Merten Mill. Turn right, cross the river, and turn left onto the Mike Kopetsky/Opal Creek Trail. The path follows the Little North Santiam River a mile and crosses a forested bench to a junction beside Opal

Pool's scenic gorge.

To return on a loop, turn left, cross a bridge, and keep left on an old mining road that leads through Jawbone Flats, a well-preserved collection of 27 buildings dating from 1929-1932. Jawbone Flats has been donated to the Friends of Opal Creek as an old-growth study center. Respect the residents' privacy by staying on the road.

Getting There

From Interstate 5 exit 253 in Salem, drive on North Santiam Highway 22 for 23 miles to Mehama's second flashing yellow light. Opposite the Swiss Village Restaurant, turn left on Little North Fork Road for 15 paved miles and an additional 1.3 miles of gravel. At a fork, veer left on Road 2209 past the sign "Road Closed 6 Miles Ahead." Then drive 6 miles to the locked gate. A Northwest Forest Pass is required to park here. The pass costs $5 per day or $30 per season.

HIKE 35 Iron Mountain

Moderate (to lookout)
1.6 miles round trip   700 feet elevation gain
Open early June through October   Use: hikers
Map: Harter Mountain (USGS)

Difficult (Loop via Cone Peak)
6.8-mile loop   1900 feet elevation gain

Iron Mountain's lookout building is one of the Cascade foothills' most popular hiking goals, but most people hike to it the hard way, from the bottom of the mountain. To cut the work in half, drive instead to a shortcut used by the lookout staffers.

This shorter route still shows off the spectacular plant life that has made Iron Mountain famous. The peak hosts a total of 17 different types of trees, more than any other area in Oregon.

Sharp-shinned hawk.

From the small gravel parking area, keep uphill at all trail junctions to climb to the lookout tower. The trail switch-

backs up into a natural rock garden of early-summer wildflowers, including fuzzy cat's ears, purple larkspur, yellow stonecrop, red paintbrush, and pink penstemon.

After 0.8 mile you'll reach the flat-roofed lookout building, perched on a cliff of red volcanic rock. To the east, all the major Cascade peaks are visible from Mount Hood to Diamond Peak.

Be careful near the summit cliffs. The original lookout building blew off in a 1977 windstorm. In 1990, a staffer fell to his death here. No one knows whether he slipped, was pushed, or jumped.

For an alternate route back to your car, take a trail that circles the mountain. Simply keep right at junctions on the way down. You'll traverse the wildflower meadows of Cone Peak and descend to Highway 20. Cross the road and keep right on the Tombstone Nature Trail for 0.6 mile to Tombstone Pass. Cross a parking area and follow the Santiam Wagon Trail 0.3 mile to a junction. Then turn right on the Iron Mountain Trail, recross the highway, and climb a mile back to your car.

The lush wildflower displays on Cone Peak sprout from improbably thin-soiled, rocky slopes in June and July.

Getting There

From Interstate 5 exit 233 in Albany, drive Highway 20 east 62 miles. Ignore signs for the Iron Mountain Trailhead—the start of a longer trail. Instead, at a junction near milepost 62 (a mile west of Tombstone Pass), turn left onto gravel Road 035 for 2.8 miles to its end at a less-used trailhead. A Northwest Forest Pass is required to park here. The pass costs $5 per day or $30 per season.

WILDFLOWERS OF THE VALLEY & FOOTHILLS

For the many Oregonians who live in the Willamette Valley, these are among the most common wildflowers near home, from the lowland fields of the valley (on the left of this page) to the dense forests of the Cascade foothills (on the right).

SHOOTING STAR (*Dodecatheon jeffreyi*). Early in summer, shooting stars carpet wet fields and slopes.

FAIRY BELLS (*Disporum hookeri*). This lily of moist woodlands later develops pairs of orange berries.

QUEEN ANNE'S LACE (*Daucus carota*). This ancestor of the garden carrot blooms in valley fields.

OREGON GRAPE (*Berberis nervosa*). Oregon's state flower has holly-like leaves and blue berries.

BLEEDING HEART (*Dicentra formosa*). Look near woodland creeks for these pink hearts.

CAMAS (*Camassia quamash*). The roots of this valley wetland flower were an important Indian food.

NOOTKA ROSE (*Rosa nutkana*). This elegant wild rose loves valley hedgerows and open oak woods.

LARGE SOLOMONSEAL (*Maianthemum racemosum*). White plumes lean across forest paths.

FIREWEED (*Epilobium angustifolium*). After a fire, this plant crowds slopes with tall pink spires.

PEARLY EVERLASTING (*Anaphalis margaritacea*). Try this roadside bloom in dried floral arrangements.

FAIRY SLIPPER (*Calypso bulbosa*). This lovely 6-inch orchid haunts the mossy floor of old-growth forests.

4 Eugene

The architecture of this university town is a mostly modern grab bag, but Eugene wins hearts for its picturesque setting along the whitewater Willamette River—and for its artsy, alternative ambiance. Dreadlocked hippies, tuxedoed

The Hult Center for the Performing Arts has resident symphony, ballet, theater, and opera companies.

The DeFazio suspension footbridge is one of five Willamette River spans off-limits to cars, linking a dozen miles of scenic riverside bike paths.

the city's bus mall. Take a look at the library's entry sculpture (a statue of city founder Eugene Skinner), the central spiral staircase, and the reading rooms' two-story stained glass windows.

Then zigzag two blocks northeast to downtown's center, a plaza at **Broadway and Willamette streets** where you'll find

Pillars honor the seasons at downtown's center, Broadway and Willamette.

symphony-goers, and burly loggers all seem to fit right in. At times the city revels in its zaniness, electing a Slug Queen, for example, to reign over the Eugene Celebration each September.

Start your tour—preferably on foot or on bicycle—at the downtown **Eugene Public Library**, across the street from

ceramic sculptures representing the four seasons.

Next zigzag two more blocks northeast to the **Park Blocks** at 8th and Oak, where you'll find a fountain with a sculpture of a school of salmon. On Saturdays from April to mid-November, the Park Blocks come alive with **Saturday Market,** a free-wheeling counter-culture crafts market

Saturday Market fills downtown's Park Blocks with a laid-back carnival of local crafts, art, food, and music.

where you can buy everything from tofu burritos to tie-dyed underwear.

Return to Willamette Street and head north a block to the **Hult Center**, a performing arts center with a dramatically pillared glass lobby and a basement art venue, the Jacobs Gallery.

Continue another block up Willamette and turn right on Fifth Avenue two blocks to the **Fifth Street Public Market**, a former warehouse converted to a labyrinth of upscale shops, galleries, crafts booths, and eateries.

Go to Fourth Avenue, turn right, and cross the Willamette River on the **DeFazio Bike Bridge**, an elegant suspension span. On the far shore you'll enter **Alton Baker Park**, where stepping stones lead to an island in a duck pond. A four-foot yellow globe nearby represents the sun. It's part of a vast **scale model of the solar system**. Planets are located at appropriate distances along the Ruth Bascom Southbank Bike Path all the way to pea-sized Pluto, on a pedestal 3.5 miles to the west.

A Saturday Market toy honors the U of O mascot, a duck.

To continue your Eugene tour, however, head east (upriver) along the Northbank Bike Path for 0.8 mile, recross the Willamette on the Autzen footbridge, and continue straight to the **University of Oregon**'s park-like campus.

Turn right on 13th Avenue, closed to cars in the campus area. On the right you'll spot the towers of **Deady Hall,** the university's oldest building. Then detour left through a grassy quadrangle to the **U of O Museum of Art**, an ornate brick building with an extensive collection from the Far East.

Continue west down 13th Avenue to the end of campus, where coffeeshops, pubs, and eateries cluster. Although you could walk a mile back downtown, it's easier to catch a bus. At the edge of

A park-like campus setting surrounds the University of Oregon's oldest building, 1876 Deady Hall.

The University of Oregon's Jordan Schnitzer Museum of Art has a courtyard koi pond, an upscale cafe, and impressive exhibits of Chinese and Korean art—including a Qing dynasty throne and a 6-foot jade pagoda. The museum is open Thursday-Sunday 11am-5pm and Wednesday 11am-8pm. Adult admission is $5.

campus, a bus station on the right has a stop for the **Breeze**, a handy shuttle that loops to downtown and the Valley River Center shopping mall every fifteen minutes, Monday through Saturday, for a 50-cent fare.

GETTING THERE: From Interstate 5, take Eugene exit 194b, follow "City Center" signs 2 miles to Sixth Avenue, follow this street west

5 blocks, and turn left on Charnelton Street 4 blocks to the library.

6   Brownsville

Settled in 1846, this historic town (population 1440) has been used by Hollywood as a movie set. Stroll 3 blocks of antique shops and cafes in downtown. Then visit the free Linn County Historical Museum (open Monday-Saturday 11am-4pm, Sunday 1-5pm) and the 1881 Moyer House (open Saturday 11am-4pm and Sunday 1-5pm).

Railcars at Linn museum.

GETTING THERE: Drive Interstate 5 north of Eugene 22 miles to exit 216 and go east 4 miles.

Next to Eugene's bus transit mall, the downtown public library opened in 2003 with a central spiral staircase and a talking book-return conveyor belt.

Brownsville's Moyer House, an 1881 Italianate home.

7 Corvallis

Home to **Oregon State University** and electronics giant Hewlett-Packard, this small but literate city claims the highest per capita use of computers and libraries in the nation.

Start at the elegant 1889 **Benton County Courthouse** and head two blocks west on

Benton Hall is the oldest building on the Oregon State University campus, dating to 1887.

The Benton County Courthouse cost $70,000 in 1889. Two of the three commissioners who authorized the sum were voted out before it opened. Now it's the oldest Oregon courthouse still used for its original purpose.

Monroe Street to the Willamette River. On your right, the white brick **Majestic Theatre** is a 1913 vaudeville house converted to a civic performing arts center.

Turn right along the river through **Riverfront Park**, a half-mile promenade with picnic lawns, outdoor cafes, and shops.

GETTING THERE: From Interstate 5, take Corvallis exit 228 and drive west 9 miles. Just beyond the Willamette River bridge to downtown, turn left a block on Fourth Street to the courthouse.

HOT SPRINGS OF THE WESTERN CASCADES

The volcanic furnaces of the Cascade Range fire several hot springs and warm seeps in the canyonlands to the west. Here are three of the hottest and most visitable of these infrequent natural spas.

▶**Belknap Hot Springs**. This commercial resort pipes water on a bridge across the McKenzie River to a 102° F swimming pool that's open daily 9am-8pm for a $4.50/hour fee. The woodsy, riverside resort also offers lodge rooms, cabins, and campsites (*see p157*). From Eugene, drive McKenzie Highway 126 east 55 miles. Beyond McKenzie Bridge 6 miles, turn left on Belknap Springs Road.

▶**Terwilliger (Cougar) Hot Springs.** A heavily used half-mile path ($5 per person, closed after dark) leads to a

series of natural hot spring pools in a shady forest canyon—a hippie hangout where swimsuits are rare. Drive McKenzie Highway 126 east of Eugene 40 miles. Beyond Blue River 4 miles, at a Cougar Reservoir pointer, turn right on Aufderheide Drive 19 for 7.5 miles.

▶**McCredie Hot Springs**. Instead of hippies, expect truck drivers at this free, natural hot springs pool wedged between icy Salt Creek and busy Highway 58. From Interstate 5 exit 186 south of Eugene, drive Willamette Highway 58 east 45 miles. Near milepost 45 (beyond Oakridge 9.5 miles), look for an unmarked gravel parking lot on the right, opposite a sign for McCredie Station Road. A 200-yard path leads to the 25-foot-wide pool.

HIKE 36   McKenzie River

Easy (Sahalie Falls)
2.6-mile loop   400 feet elevation gain
Open May through November
Use: hikers, bicycles
Map: Clear Lake (USGS)

Difficult (entire trail)
26.5 miles one way   1800 feet elevation gain

Here's a quick introduction to Oregon's roaring rivers, waterfalls, and old-growth forests: a loop trail around the McKenzie River's two grandest waterfalls.

The hike starts at 100-foot-tall Sahalie Falls, a raging cataract that pounds the river into rainbowed mist. Then the route descends past 70-foot Koosah Falls and returns on the river's far shore through forests of 6-foot-thick Douglas fir and droopy-limbed red cedar. This part of the loop follows the McKenzie River Trail, a 26.5-mile path that extends from Clear Lake to McKenzie Bridge.

From the Sahalie Falls parking lot, walk 100 yards down to the railed viewpoint of the falls. In Chinook jargon, the old trade language of Northwest Indians, *sahalie* meant "top," "upper," "sky," and "heaven." *Sahalie Tyee* (heaven chief) was the pioneer missionaries' translation for God. Natives pronounced the word *saghalie*, accenting the first syllable and using a guttural *gh*.

The McKenzie River vanishes into a lava flow, tumbles over an eerily dry, phantom "waterfall," and then reemerges from Tamolitch Pool, a turquoise lake.

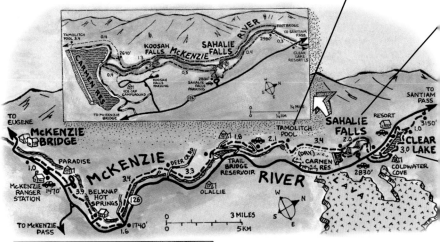

Whitewater rafters and kayakers often float the swift, cold McKenzie River below the impassable waterfalls.

Start the loop by heading left from the viewpoint, following a "Waterfall Trail" pointer downstream. The river churns through continuous whitewater for half a mile before leaping off another cliff at Koosah Falls (*photo p136*). The word *koosah* also meant sky or heaven in Chinook. Notice the massive springs emerging from the lava cliff near the base of the falls.

Over the past 6000 years, half a dozen basalt flows from the High Cascades have tortured the McKenzie River, dam-

At Sahalie Falls the McKenzie River thunders over the 100-foot lip of an old lava flow.

ming it at Clear Lake, squeezing it into a gorge here, and burying it altogether on the dry riverbed near Tamolitch Pool.

Keep right at all junctions after Koosah Falls. In another 0.4 mile you'll meet a gravel road beside Carmen Reservoir. Follow the road right 150 yards to a trail sign, take the path into the woods 100 yards, and turn right on the McKenzie River Trail. This route heads upstream past even better

River otter.

viewpoints of Koosah and Sahalie Falls. After 1.3 miles, cross the river on a footbridge and turn right for 0.4 mile to your car.

If you'd like to sample other portions of the McKenzie River Trail, try the 5.5-mile loop around Clear Lake or the 2.1-mile section from Road 655 near Trailbridge Reservoir to Tamolitch Pool.

A lava flow dammed the McKenzie River 3000 years ago, creating Clear Lake—a pool so clear and cold that ghostly tree snags are still visible 100 feet deep. Rent a rowboat at the old-timey Clear Lake Resort to see them.

Getting There

From Interstate 5 exit 194a in Eugene, drive McKenzie Highway 126 east 68 miles. Beyond McKenzie Bridge 19 miles, near milepost 5, pull into the large, well-marked Sahalie Falls parking area.

WHERE TO STAY

Campgrounds *(map p137)*

	Campsites	Water	Showers	Flush Toilet	Fee
15 BLACK CANYON. Amid alders along the Middle Fork Willamette River, this overlooked camp always has room. Drive Highway 58 east of Interstate 5 for 30 miles (or west of Oakridge 6 miles). Open April through September.	72	●		●	$$
7 CASCADIA. Swim in the South Santiam River or hike 0.7 mile to Lower Soda Falls at this state park on the site of an 1895 soda springs spa. Open May through September. East of Sweet Home 14 miles on Highway 20.	25	●		●	$$
1 CHAMPOEG. Oregon government began at this Willamette riverbank meadow in 1843. The state park here has a log cabin museum, six rentable cabins ($35) and six yurts ($29). Take Donald exit 278 of Interstate 5 (south of Portland 20 miles) and follow signs. Reservations: 800-452-5687.	85	●	●	●	$$
10 COLDWATER COVE. On beautiful Clear Lake (no motors), this Forest Service camp accesses the McKenzie River Trail *(see pp 154-55)*. Open late May to early October. Reservations: 877-444-6777.	35	●			$$
13 DELTA. Amid old-growth fir on the McKenzie River, this Forest Service camp is open April to late October. Drive Highway 126 east of Springfield 45 miles and turn right toward Cougar Reservoir 0.2 mile.	38	●		●	$$
6 DETROIT LAKE. Noisy, crowded, and immensely popular, this state park by a reservoir is the place to grill, swim, or waterski. Open March to late November. West of Detroit 2 miles on Highway 22. Reservations: 800-452-5687.	311	●	●	●	$$
14 FRENCH PETE. Giant trees line a bouldery creek at this Forest Service camp near a hot springs and Three Sisters Wilderness trails. Drive to Terwilliger Hot Springs *(see p153)* and continue 2.5 paved miles. Open May-Oct.	17	●			$$
9 HOUSE ROCK. Pioneers on the Santiam Wagon Road once camped beneath this house-sized boulder. Now a Forest Service camp beside the South Santiam River has paths to the rock and a waterfall. Open May to October. Drive Highway 20 east of Sweet Home 25 miles to a pointer between mileposts 53 and 54.	17	●			$
2 INDIAN HENRY. A quiet camp on the Clackamas River, with trails nearby. From Estacada, drive Highway 224 upriver 21 miles and follow signs. Open late May to early September. Reservations: 877-444-6777.	86	●		●	$$
11 LIMBERLOST. Eerily quiet in the shadows of giant trees, this camp on Lost Creek is open May to mid-September. From Highway 126 near McKenzie Bridge, take old McKenzie Pass Highway 242 east 1.5 miles.	12				$
12 PARADISE. Giant cedars line the rushing McKenzie River *(see pp154-55)* at this Forest Service camp east of McKenzie Bridge 3.5 miles on Highway 126. Open mid-May to mid-October. Reservations: 877-444-6777.	64	●		●	$$
3 RIVERSIDE. In big woods along the Clackamas River Trail, this camp is open mid-May to late September. From Estacada, take Highway 224 upriver 26 miles and continue 2.5 miles on Road 46. Reservations: 877-444-6777.	37	●			$
5 SHADY COVE. This quiet, primitive camp on the swimmable Little North Santiam River is close to Opal Creek's trailhead. Drive as to Opal Creek *(see p147)*, but at the final fork, keep right on Road 2207 for 2 miles.	13				$
4 SILVER FALLS. This waterfall-packed state park *(see pp140-41)* has a campground with 14 rentable cabins ($35). Reservations: 800-452-5687.	93	●	●	●	$$
8 TROUT CREEK. On the South Santiam River, this Forest Service camp has a historic shelter and trails into the Menagerie Wilderness. Open May to October. Drive Highway 20 east of Sweet Home 19 miles.	24	●			$

Footbridge at House Rock. ▷

WHERE TO STAY

B&Bs and Quaint Hotels (map p137)

		Rooms	Private bath	Cont. breakfast	Full breakfast	Rate range
12	**BELKNAP HOT SPRINGS.** Although this old-time resort has been commercialized, it retains a fabulous setting on the McKenzie River with a hot riverside swimming pool (see pp153-54). Seven cabins (pets OK in two) rent for $55-400. Info: 541-822-3512 or www.belknaphotsprings.com.	18	●	●		$85-185
3	**BOOKMARK.** Walk to the Capitol from this 1915 arts-and-crafts bungalow, restored with a large library and player piano. Located at 975 D Street NE (on Capitol Street), Salem, OR 97301. Info: 503-399-2013.	2			●	$60-70
6	**CAMPBELL HOUSE.** In downtown Eugene's historic district, this elegant 1892 mansion is decorated with antiques and four-poster beds. Rooms have themes such as golf, fishing, and gardening. At 252 Pearl Street, Eugene, OR 97401. Info: 800-264-2519 or www.campbellhouse.com.	19	●		●	$92-349
4	**A CREEKSIDE GARDEN INN.** This 1938 Colonial bed & breakfast offers movies and popcorn nightly, with murder mysteries on weekends. On scenic Mill Creek, it's within walking distance of the Capitol at 333 Wyatt Court NE, Salem, OR 97301. Info: 800-949-0837 or www.salembandb.com.	5	4		●	$65-100
7	**EXCELSIOR INN.** Attached to an upscale Italian restaurant and bistro, this modern European-style inn is two blocks from the University of Oregon and eight blocks from downtown at 754 E. 13th Avenue, Eugene, OR 97401. Info: 800-321-6963 or www.excelsiorinn.com.	14	●		●	$99-225
11	**HOLIDAY FARM RESORT.** Herbert Hoover slept in this riverside 1910 stage coach stop at 54455 McKenzie River Drive, Blue River, OR 97413. The resort now offers 2 rental houses that sleep 2-8 and 11 cottages, most with kitchenettes and fireplaces. Info: 800-823-3715 or www.holidayfarmresort.com.	13	●			$140-250
1	**HOTEL OREGON.** Ride an elevator to the funky, panoramic rooftop bar of this four-story 1905 hotel, artistically restored by the popular McMenamin's brewpub chain in downtown McMinnville at 310 NE Evans Street, McMinnville, OR 97128. Info: 888-472-8427 or www.hoteloregon.com.	42	8			$50-110
2	**MAGNOLIA COTTAGE.** Between the Oregon Garden (see p143) and historic Silverton's charming downtown, this 1938 gabled English bed & breakfast inn also offers a bungalow for $100. At 504 W. Main Street, Silverton, OR 97381. Info: 503-873-6712 or www.magnoliacottage.com.	2	●		●	$60-100
8	**McGARRY HOUSE.** This 1939 cottage one block from the University of Oregon became a bed & breakfast in 1994. Located at 856 E. 19th Avenue, Eugene, OR 97401. Info: 800-953-9921 or www.mcgarryhouse.com.	2	●		●	$85-95
9	**THE OVAL DOOR.** Walk to downtown Eugene from this bed & breakfast inn at 988 Lawrence Street, Eugene, OR 97401. Built in 1980, the inn has farmhouse styling with a wraparound porch, a library, and rooms with wildflower themes. Info: 800-882-3160 or www.ovaldoor.com.	5	●		●	$85-195
10	**THE SECRET GARDEN.** Once a sorority, this 1918 gabled mansion one block from the University of Oregon now serves as a bed & breakfast inn with garden artwork and a hot tub in a hidden nook. At 1910 University Street, Eugene, OR 97403. Info: 888-484-6755 or www.secretgardenbbinn.com.	10	●		●	$115-245
5	**TRAIN HOUSE INN.** Reserve a corner tower room in this 1886 Queen Anne mansion, built by pioneer Samuel Train with an octagonal pavilion and wraparound porch in Albany's historic downtown (206 7th Avenue SW). Info: 541-791-5281 or www.trainhouseinn.com.	5	●		●	$90-110
13	**WESTFIR LODGE.** Across a covered bridge on a whitewater fork of the Willamette River, this 1925 lumber company office has been remodeled as a bed & breakfast inn. Turn off Highway 58 at Oakridge to 47365 First Street, Westfir, OR 97492. Info: 541-782-3103 or www.westfirlodge.com.	8	●		●	$60-90

The Secret Garden. ▷

CENTRAL OREGON

Sun and snowpeaks are top draws in the state's recreational heartland.

Days begin and end in Central Oregon with a rosy glow on the snow-capped summits of the High Cascades. With names like the Three Sisters, Three Fingered Jack, and Mount Bachelor, these volcanic peaks sound like family. Even Mount Jefferson is on a first-name basis with most locals, going by the friendlier handle, "Jeff."

The Cascades roared to life 33 million years ago. As the range grew it blocked Western Oregon's rainclouds, bringing sun to the eastern half of the state.

The snowpeaks capping the range are relatively young volcanic additions, only a few million years old. Some, like Three Fingered Jack, are glacier-scoured plugs, extinct for 100,000 years. Others, like Broken Top and the Newberry Caldera, are the ruins of mountains destroyed long ago by cataclysmic explosions a la Mount St. Helens. South Sister is still very much alive, bulging an inch a year.

Visitors are often astonished to find Central Oregon strewn with volcanic momentos — miles of lava beds, hundreds of cinder cones, fields of lava "bombs," and uncounted lava tube caves where basalt flows drained.

But 1300 years have passed since the area's last lava eruption. Today, Central Oregon's mountains are treated with the sentimental familiarity of old family friends. To join the cameraderie, share a picnic in an alpine wildflower meadow with Jeff, plan a ski date with Mount Bachelor, or relax on the deck of a Deschutes River cabin, raising a glass to toast the beautiful Three Sisters.

◁ **Mount Jefferson and Jefferson Park in April.**   △ **James Creek Shelter in the Three Sisters Wilderness.**

Exploring
CENTRAL OREGON

Bend serves as the hub of Central Oregon's sunny recreation lands, but popularity is threatening to drown this charming Western town with traffic jams and strip malls. Escape to a lakeside meadow high in the Mount Jefferson Wilderness, a gushing spring in a pine forest beside the Metolius River, or a clifftop surrounded by the Three Sisters. In winter, when the Cascade peaks parade in dress whites, inspect them by ski, snowshoe, or snowboard.

Mount Jefferson

Oregon's second tallest peak dominates a 22-mile-long wilderness with alpine lakes, meadows, buttes, and forests *(see pp162-69)*.

The Three Sisters

Like scoops in the world's largest sundae, these three 10,000-foot snowpeaks are served up as the centerpiece of the state's most visited wilderness. For a roadside look at the area's highlights, drive the switchbacking old highway from Sisters across the lava fields of McKenzie Pass *(see p176)* or motor from Bend up the Cascade Lakes Highway to the trailheads for Green Lakes and South Sister *(see pp181-85)*.

Bend

The glassy Deschutes River slides past park lawns in this rapidly growing city. Downtown has upscale shops, brew pubs, and restaurants, but retains its small-town air *(see p186)*. Pine forests and sagebrush steppes begin just south of town. Look here for the world-class High Desert Museum and a variety of explorable volcanic oddities: Lava River Cave, the Lava Cast Forest, and Lava Butte *(see p187-88)*.

Winter

From Thanksgiving to May, when snowdrifts up to 20 feet deep drape the High Cascades, the recreation season is at its hottest at Mount Bachelor, Santiam Pass, and Willamette Pass *(see p177)*. Ride the developed ski areas' lifts for a downhill rush, or break quieter trails to a dozen free, rustic Forest Service shelters in the woods. *(At right: the Maiden Peak Shelter, 5 miles by trail from Willamette Pass.)*

MT JEFFERSON

TO PORTLAND
TO THE DALLES

TO SALEM

HIKE 37

HIKE 38

THREE-FINGERED JACK

RANGE

METOLIUS RIVER

26

1

2

1

3

MADRAS

22

SANTIAM PASS

HIKE 39

HIKE 40

97

HIKE 42

TO ALBANY

20

2-5

5

7

HIKE 41

SISTERS

126

TO PRINEVILLE

6

BLACK BUTTE RANCH

1

4

126

TO EUGENE

126

McKENZIE PASS

242

2-4

8

REDMOND

9

6

11

BEND

HIKE 43

10

HIKE 44

RIVER

5-7

7

THREE SISTERS

HIKE 46

HIKE 45

HWY

8

9

20

TO BURNS

12

13-14

MT BACHELOR

8

9

10

15-16

SUNRIVER

CASCADE

CASCADE LAKES

DESCHUTES

11

NEWBERRY CALDERA

21

22

LA PINE

17

12

18-20

27

26

9

25

HIKE 47

24

97

TO EUGENE

WILLAMETTE PASS

58

23

CRESCENT

TO KLAMATH FALLS

N
W   E
S

Bend
800-905-2363
www.bendchamber.org

Deschutes National Forest
1645 Highway 20 E, Bend
OR 97701, 541-383-5300
www.fs.fed.us/r6/centraloregon

KEY

5 — Star attraction

HIKE 12 — Featured hike

2 — Campground

6 — B&B or quaint hotel

? — Information:

0 miles   20
0 kilometers   20

HIKE 37 Jefferson Park

Difficult
10.2 miles round trip   1800 feet elevation gain
Open mid-July to mid-October
Use: hikers, horses
Map: Mt. Jefferson (Geo-Graphics)

Mount Jefferson is the most difficult Oregon peak to climb because of the long hike in, the large elevation gain, and the 400-foot summit spire of crumbly lava.

Oregon's second tallest mountain rises like a wall from the lake-dotted wildflower meadows of Jefferson Park. The view of Mount Jefferson is so impressive and the meadows are so delightful to explore that the area shows signs of overuse.

The gray jay or "camp robber" boldly swoops to picnic tables for food scraps. Don't feed them! Human food can hurt wild animals.

On August weekends hundreds of people roam this corner of the wilderness. Some of the lakeshores, once green with vegetation, are closed for restoration. Wilderness rangers enforce restric-

The Clark's nutcracker uses its bill to open whitebark pine nuts near timberline.

tions: campfires are banned throughout the area and camping within 250 feet of the lakes is permitted only at approved sites marked with an embedded post.

To visit this alpine treasure without damaging it or fighting crowds, do not come on August weekends. Wait for the clear, crisp weather of September—or come in late July, when the wildflowers (and, alas, the mosquitoes) are at their peak. Or visit only on a day trip. If you insist on backpacking, bring a stove and seek out one of the remote, forested corners of the park

for your camp.

From the parking area, the well-graded trail starts in an old-growth Douglas fir forest. Gradually you'll switchback up into a higher-elevation forest of true firs and beargrass. After 1.5 miles, turn right at a trail junction on a ridgecrest.

Breathtaking views of Mount Jefferson open up as the path climbs east along the ridge. At the 3.9-mile mark, a footbridge crosses Whitewater Creek in a meadow with shooting star, larkspur, and bleeding heart. At the Pacific Crest

Wildflowers bloom in Jefferson Park in late July and August, but the park is perhaps prettier—and less crowded, and less prone to mosquitoes—in September when the leaves of huckleberry bushes turn scarlet.

Views of Mount Jefferson open up as you hike along the Sentinel Hills toward Jefferson Park.

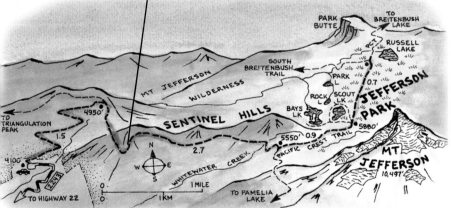

Trail junction, turn left.

For the next 0.9 mile the trailside meadows become larger and prettier until the path reaches Jefferson Park—a vast plateau of heather, red paintbrush, lupine, and clumps of wind-gnarled mountain hemlock. Here, unfortunately, a confusion of trails proliferate—left to Bays Lake, right to the head of White-water Creek. To follow the PCT, keep straight to the first glimpse of Scout Lake, then veer right.

One way to explore the area is to follow the PCT 0.7 mile across the park to large Russell Lake and return cross-country, either south through the heather or southwest to find the hidden lakes. Though chilly, these sandy-bot-tomed pools are among Oregon's most beautiful spots for a quick swim.

Getting There

From exit 253 of Interstate 5 in Salem, drive 61 miles east on North Santiam Highway 22. Between mileposts 60 and 61 (beyond Detroit 10 miles), turn left on Whitewater Road 2243. Follow this gravel route 7.4 miles to its end at a large parking area. Especially if you're leaving your car here overnight, leave no valuables inside and leave doors unlocked to discourage car clouters, an occasional problem here. A Northwest Forest Pass is required to park here. The pass costs $5 per day or $30 per season.

HIKE 38   Pamelia Lake

Moderate
4.4 miles round trip   790 feet elevation gain
Open mid-July to mid-October
Use: hikers, horses
Map: Mt. Jefferson (Geo-Graphics)

The popular trail to Pamelia Lake has something for everyone: an easy creek-side forest stroll for the novice hiker, a lake with a mountain reflection for the meditative, and an optional, strenuous viewpoint climb for the go-getters.

Pamelia Lake's water level drops in late summer because its underground outlet continues to drain.

What's the catch? Only that the trail is so popular. To limit crowds, the Forest Service requires that trail users headed for Pamelia Lake pick up a special permit in advance at the Detroit Ranger Station. Call them at 503-854-3366 for information. Note that permits are issued to a limited number of groups for each day, so plan ahead if you want a weekend reservation. Camping at the lake is allowed only

Raccoons are occasional night visitors.

at approved sites marked by posts.

The wide Pamelia Lake Trail begins in an enchanting forest so thickly carpeted with moss that fallen trees and rocks soon become mere lumps in the green cushion. Trilliums and rhododendrons bloom profusely along the way in May and June. Vine maple and huckleberry turn scarlet in fall. In all seasons, noisy Pamelia Creek accompanies the trail with little whitewater scenes.

Your first glimpse of the lake comes at a trail junction. Signs here point right to Grizzly Peak and left to the Pacific Crest Trail. For the time being, ignore both pointers and go straight ahead to inspect the lakeshore.

The lake formed after the Ice Age when a rockslide pinched off a steep valley left by a retreating glacier. Since the lake's outlet mostly seeps underground through the old rockslide, the water level varies seasonally. By summer, expect a reservoir-like beach. Walk to the right around the lakeshore for a noble view of Mount Jefferson.

To hike to a grander viewpoint, return to the trail junction and follow the sign to Grizzly Peak. This path crosses the lake's usually dry outlet and heads steadily uphill at such an even grade that the huge elevation gain seems less difficult than might be expected. Bear-

Old-growth Douglas firs line the Pamelia Lake Trail.

grass blooms put on a spectacular display approximately every third summer along the route. After climbing 2.1 miles from the lake, the trail switchbacks at a cliff edge with the climb's first viewpoint.

Here's a secret: this first viewpoint is in many ways a better goal than the actual summit of Grizzly Peak, a difficult 0.7-mile climb beyond. The bird's-eye view of Mount Jefferson is identical from here, and this cliff edge offers a far better look down at Pamelia Lake. What's more, the path is snow-free to this point by mid-June, when drifts still clog the route ahead. On the other hand, only the actual summit has a view south across the wilderness to the Three Sisters.

Pamelia Lake from Grizzly Peak.

Mount Jefferson from Grizzly Peak.

The trail follows tumbling, mossy Pamelia Creek.

Getting There

From exit 253 of Interstate 5 in Salem, drive 62 miles east on North Santiam Highway 22. Between mileposts 62 and 63 (beyond Detroit 11 miles), turn left on Pamelia Road 2246 for 3.7 miles to the trailhead parking lot at road's end. A Northwest Forest Pass is required to park here. The pass costs $5 per day or $30 per season.

WILDFLOWERS OF CENTRAL OREGON

The colorful alpine meadows of the Central Oregon Cascades share many of Mount Hood's wildflowers *(see p75)*, but here you'll find many other kinds of gardens as well, from sagebrush steppe in the east to rainforest marsh in the west.

ASTER *(Aster sp.)*. This purple daisy-like flower blooms late in summer, from July to September.

MARSH MARIGOLD *(Caltha biflora)*. This early bloomer likes high marshes full of snowmelt.

GENTIAN *(Gentiana calycosa)*. In high, damp meadows, gentians open only in strong, direct sunlight.

STONECROP *(Sedum oreganum)*. This plant survives on bare, rocky slopes by storing water in fat leaves.

PHLOX *(Phlox diffusa)*. Like a colorful cushion, phlox hugs arid rock outcrops with a mat of blooms.

CONEFLOWER *(Rudbeckia occidentalis)*. Like an odd, petalless daisy, coneflower grows waist-high.

PRAIRIE STAR *(Lithophragma parviflorum)* blooms in May amid sagebrush and pine near Bend.

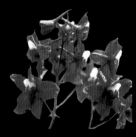

LARKSPUR *(Delphinium menziesii)*. Stalks of larkspur stand up to two feet tall in high meadows.

PINK MONKEYFLOWER *(Mimulus lewisii)*. Clumps of these showy flowers line alpine brooks *(at left)*.

GRASS OF PARNASSUS *(Parnassia fimbriata)*. Look for this saxifrage on grassy streambanks.

Warm Springs Indian Reservation

Five tribes share the vast, arid Warm Springs Indian Reservation. Learn about their culture, artifacts, and songs at the **Museum at Warm Springs.** This first-rate interpretive center on Highway 26 in the city of Warm Springs is open from 10am to 5pm daily. Adults are $6, children age 5-12 are $3.

The Museum at Warm Springs uses native designs.

The tribes also run the sunny **Kah-Ne-Tah Resort**, 11 miles north of Highway 26 from Warm Springs. The resort features a large swimming pool fed by warm springs, a hotel, rentable tepees, a golf course, salmon bakes on summer Saturdays, and the adjacent **Indian Head Casino**. Call 1-800-554-4SUN.

GETTING THERE: From Bend drive Highway 97 north 32 miles to Madras. Then veer left on Highway 26 toward Mount Hood and Portland for 11 miles to Warm Springs.

Deschutes River

Each year thousands of rubber rafts and whitewater dories drift the rimrock-lined Deschutes River. Two stretches of the river are particularly popular: the two-day, 45-mile drift from the Highway 26 bridge near Madras to Maupin, and the two- or three-day, 51-mile segment from Maupin to the Columbia River. Both sections include several thrilling and dangerous rapids and countless lesser riffles. The lower portion has a mandatory portage at Sherar Falls.

An abandoned railroad grade on the Deschutes River's east bank is open to hikers and bicyclists in several places, including this 7.4-mile segment from Highway 26 north to Trout Creek.

Boaters must bring a Deschutes River pass, available at local sporting goods stores. Fishing is banned from boats or floating devices. Jet boats and motors are banned on the portion of the river bordering the Warm Springs Indian Reservation and are restricted elsewhere. Camping is not allowed on islands, and campfires are banned except in enclosed pans in winter.

Kayaker on the river.

GETTING THERE: From Madras take Highway 26 toward Portland 11 miles to the Deschutes River bridge.

Cove Palisades

Where the Billy Chinook reservoir backs up three rivers into a dramatic cliff-edged desert canyonland, this popular park packs a sunny peninsula

The Tam-a-lau Trail climbs 1.3 miles from Cove Palisades' campground to The Peninsula, a basalt plateau overlooking the reservoir's canyon.

with 272 campsites, three ramps for launching powerboats, and a marina. The park even rents log cabins and houseboats that sleep ten *(see p191)*.

GETTING THERE: Turn off Highway 97 at a sign for The Cove State Park (either 15 miles north of Redmond or in the town of Madras) and follow similar signs, zigzagging west.

4 Sisters

A charming Western-theme town packed with upscale shops and art galleries, Sisters slows traffic on Highway 20 to a crawl. Crowds are perhaps big-

A footbridge over Whychus Creek connects the picnic and camping areas of Sisters Park, a cool grassy oasis amid giant ponderosa pines on the east edge of town.

gest for the outdoor show of nearly 1000 quilts on a Saturday in early July. Quilts are on display year-round in local shops. A smaller event in late September, the Sisters in Sisters Celebration, features reunions of sisters.

GETTING THERE: Drive Highway 20 west of Bend 21 miles.

The 1912 Hotel Sisters, now called Bronco Billy's Ranch Grill & Saloon, specializes in nachos and burgers.

HIKE 39 Canyon Creek Meadows

Moderate (to lower meadow)
4.5-mile loop　　　400 feet elevation gain
Open mid-July through October
Use: hikers, horses
Map: Mt. Jefferson (Geo-Graphics)

Difficult (to viewpoint)
7.5-mile loop　　　1400 feet elevation gain
Open August through October

One of the easiest routes to the High Cascades' wildflower meadows, this loop is ideal for children and amblers. More energetic hikers can continue up to a viewpoint beneath Three Fingered Jack's summit pinnacles. Although a forest fire swept through this area in 2003, leaving black snags along the first mile of the trail, the groves surrounding Canyon Creek Meadows are as beautiful as ever.

From the Jack Lake campground parking area, start hiking on the trail to the right, skirting Jack Lake's shore. This path climbs 0.3 mile to a well-marked fork at the Wilderness boundary: the start of the loop.

Three Fingered Jack, a long-extinct volcano, has been eroded by ice to a crag. A small glacier remains.

To limit the number of people you meet, the Forest Service asks that you hike the loop clockwise. So bear left at this junction, climb gradually amid snags, pass two ponds atop a small ridge, and descend through unburnt woods to the lower meadow.

Here the view of Three Fingered Jack's snow-clad crags emerges and the wildflower displays begin in earnest. Do not trample these delicate alpine gardens. Stay on the main trail and choose a picnic spot amid trees. Backpackers must camp at least 100 feet from trails or water.

If you still have plenty of energy, continue 0.7 mile up the trail to the rim of the rock-strewn upper meadow, a glacial outwash plain. From here the 0.8-mile route to the 6500-foot-elevation viewpoint becomes less distinct.

Climb south up a steep, rocky moraine to a notch overlooking a stunning, green cirque lake at the foot of Three Fingered Jack's glacier. Next the path follows the somewhat precarious crest of the moraine, scrambling steeply up to a windy saddle, where the view stretches

join the trail from Wasco Lake. But before turning right to return to the car, follow the sound of falling water to a footbridge below the first of Canyon Creek Falls' two lovely, 12-foot cascades.

Peak season for the masses of blue lupine and red paintbrush is the end of July—a trade-off, because mosquitoes are still a nuisance and snowdrifts usually still block the trail to the upper meadow until August.

The lower meadow is a wildflower field with rushing streams, while the upper meadow is a rocky plain.

from Mount Jefferson to the Three Sisters. Sharp eyes can often spot climbers on the spires of Three Fingered Jack.

To return via the loop, hike back to the bottom of the lower meadow and turn left. This path follows Canyon Creek past a fascinating beaver workshop, where dozens of large pines have been ringed and felled. Rings six feet above the ground prove the beavers are active even when winter snowdrifts remain.

Half a mile beyond the beaver trees,

Getting There

Drive Highway 20 east of Santiam Pass 8 miles. At a "Wilderness Trailheads" sign near milepost 88 (1 mile east of Suttle Lake or 12 miles west of Sisters), turn north on paved Jack Lake Road 12 for 4.4 miles. Then turn left on one-lane Road 1230 for 1.6 miles, and finally turn left onto Road 1234, climbing 5 miles to the trailhead at the primitive Jack Lake campground. A $5-per-car Northwest Forest Pass is required.

5 Head of the Metolius

Rustic but upscale, the Camp Sherman store stocks brie as well as beans.

The Metolius River emerges at the rate of fifty thousand gallons a minute from gigantic springs at the base of Black Butte. Stroll a paved 0.2-mile path to this mystic source. Then drive 2 miles downstream to the forest village of Camp Sherman to admire the resulting river, and its fish, from a Metolius River bridge.

GETTING THERE: Drive Highway 20 east of Sisters 9 miles (or west of Santiam Pass 10 miles). Near milepost 91, turn north at a "Metolius River" sign for 2.5 miles, then fork right, following a "Campgrounds" pointer, for 1.5 miles to the parking turnoff.

The Metolius River emerges fully grown at a spring.

 ## HIKE 40 Metolius River

Moderate
5.4 miles round trip   100 feet elevation gain
Open except in winter storms
Use: hikers   Map: Metolius River (Imus)

The Metolius, most magical of all Oregon rivers, emerges fully grown from the base of Black Butte. Sample the river's wizardry with a hike along the riverbank from a park-like fish hatchery to a gushing spring.

Start by inspecting the rustic build-

At the Wizard Falls hatchery, you can buy fish food from automats for 25 cents to feed the fish.

ings and open-air concrete ponds of the Wizard Falls state fish hatchery. Although the hatchery has no formal tours, friendly staff members always seem to be on hand to answer questions and show, for example, the indoor tank of two-headed fish. Fish food can be purchased from dispensing machines for 25 cents.

Then walk back to the bridge across the Metolius River. The name "Wizard Falls" originally referred to a small side springs, but because the hatchery drained the springs, the moniker now clings to a rapids above the bridge, where the river slides over a long ledge.

The most interesting trail from this bridge heads upstream along the right-hand bank. This path crosses a few side seeps that muddy unwary hikers' tennis shoes, so consider wearing boots.

Just beyond Wizard Falls the river splits around a series of long islands, bushy with monkeyflower, lupine, and hellebore. Birds delight in these islands. Look for goslings paddling about, bright yellow tanagers hopping in streamside shrubs, and the peculiar robin-sized water ouzels that "fly" underwater.

At the 2.4-mile mark, spectacular springs enter the river from the far

Black Butte's volcano erupted directly over the Metolius River. Today the river seeps into the ground at Black Butte Ranch, percolates underground beneath the butte, and reemerges on the far side as if nothing had happened.

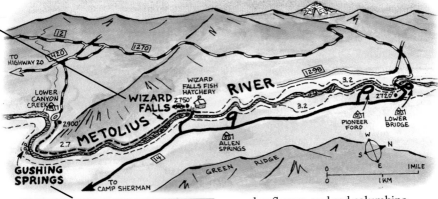

Gushing springs pour out of the riverbank like hydrants.

monkeyflower, and red columbine.

If you continue another 0.3 mile the trail ends at a small primitive campground where Canyon Creek joins the Metolius River—a good picnic stop before turning back.

bank, gushing like a dozen opened fire hydrants. The river winds through a steep canyon here with old-growth ponderosa pine and lots of May-June wildflowers: purple larkspur, yellow

Getting There

Drive Highway 20 east of Sisters 9 miles (or west of Santiam Pass 10 miles). Just west of Black Butte, near milepost 91, turn north at a sign for the Metolius River. After 2.5 miles fork to the right at a "Campgrounds" pointer, follow paved Road 14 for another 7.6 miles, and then turn left on the Wizard Falls entrance road for 0.3 mile to a river bridge at the fish hatchery.

Black Butte

Difficult
3.8 miles round trip   1600 feet elevation gain
Open July through October
Use: hikers
Map: Metolius River (Imus)

Bobcats are nocturnal, so people rarely see them in Oregon.

Plunked in the midst of the Central Oregon plateau, Black Butte looks like a misplaced mountain. This symmetrical, 3000-foot pile of cinders is one of the tallest such volcanoes in the state. A steep but view-packed trail climbs to the panoramic summit.

The butte's unusual placement east of the High Cascades makes it ideal as a fire lookout site. In 1910 one of Oregon's

The 1995 tower on Black Butte is staffed each summer.

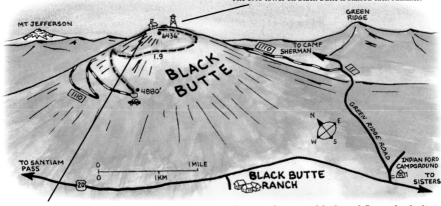

The fire lookout staff live in a log cabin near the tower.

earliest fire detection structures was built here: a simple "squirrel's nest" platform wedged between two adjacent treetops. That original lookout is gone, but Black Butte has collected a variety of other lookout structures since then: an intact cupola-style building from 1923, the ruins of a collapsed 1934 tower, and a modern 62-foot tower from 1995. In 1980 a one-room log cabin was constructed in

Sisters, disassembled, and flown by helicopter to Black Butte's summit as living quarters for the fire lookout staff.

From the trailhead at road's end, the path climbs steadily through a forest of orange-barked old-growth ponderosa

Balsamroot blooms along the trail in July.

The 1923 cupola-style fire lookout on Black Butte has a front-row view of Three Fingered Jack.

pine. The golf courses of Black Butte Ranch appear as miniature meadows in the forest far below.

After 1.1 mile, the trail crosses a treeless slope that's white in June with the blooms of serviceberry bushes. Expect other wildflowers too: big yellow balsamroot, purple larkspur, and red paintbrush.

Next the path climbs sharply — a hot, dusty stretch that makes this hike tough for small children. The trail gains the butte's broad, eastern ridge amidst wind-stunted whitebark pines and follows the ridge up to the top.

Do not attempt to climb or enter the lookout structures. The log cabin is the residence of the modern lookout tower's staff; respect their privacy. And bring your own drinking water, as the staff has none to spare. They diligently collect snow each spring and allow it to melt, filling a concrete cistern.

Getting There

Drive Highway 22 west of Sisters 5.5 miles (or east of Black Butte Ranch 2.5 miles) to Indian Ford Campground, near milepost 95. Turn north onto paved Green Ridge Road 11. After 3.8 miles, turn left onto gravel Road 1110 for 5.1 miles to a parking area at the road's end. A \$5-per-car Northwest Forest Pass is required.

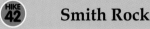

HIKE 42 — Smith Rock

Moderate
4-mile loop   800 feet elevation gain
Open all year
Use: hikers
Map: Redmond (USGS)

Smith Rock juts from the Central Oregon lava plains like an orange-sailed ship in the desert. Oregon's most popular rock-climbing area, this state park challenges mountaineers with 3 miles of rhyolite cliffs and Monkey Face, a 350-foot-tall natural sculpture.

Hikers can experience Smith Rock's scenic drama too. For an easy trip, walk along the aptly named Crooked River as it curls past the base of Monkey Face. For a steep shortcut back, climb steps to cliff-edge views of the High Cascades.

△ The Crooked River loops through the park.
Smith Rock resembles an orange-sailed ship. ▷

The area is best in spring, when high desert wildflowers bloom, or in winter when other trails are blocked by snow. Just avoid July and August when the park bakes in 100-degree heat.

Park near the restrooms and walk to an overlook at the far right end of the picnic area. Follow a gated dirt road down through an aromatic stand of tall sagebrush, cross the river bridge to a trail junction, and turn left along the riverbank. You'll soon round a bend and come to three side trails signed for The Dihedrals and Asterisk Pass; these climb up stairs and end at cliffs where climbers dangle, jangling their

With more than 1000 named routes, Smith Rock is Oregon's top rock climbing site.

Just beyond a house-sized boulder, turn right at a junction and switchback up to a ridge, where views extend to peaks from the Three Sisters to Mount Hood.

If you're not afraid of heights, you can take a side trail down to the right to a precipice opposite Monkey Face's cave-mouth. Otherwise continue straight on the loop trail, contouring 200 yards to the edge of

Monkey Face, a 350-foot tower overhanging on all sides, was unclimbed until 1960.

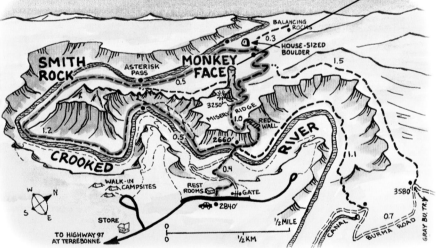

gear. Continue downriver on the main trail, watching the plentiful bird life. Black-and-white magpies swoop from gnarled junipers. Pigeons coo in rock cracks. The eagles that hunt these birds soar from aeries high on the cliffs. At the 2-mile mark the trail rounds the tip of a peninsula and soon offers the first view ahead to Monkey Face. Look for climbers resting in the mouth cave.

Ignore a fork to the right for Angel Flight Buttress, just below Asterisk Pass, and continue along the river half a mile.

Misery Ridge. Here several steep stair-cases have taken the misery out of the switchbacking descent to the Crooked River footbridge.

Getting There

Drive Highway 97 to Terrebonne, 6 miles north of Redmond or 20 miles south of Madras. Following "Smith Rock State Park" signs, turn east for 3.3 zigzagging miles to the parking area. An automat accepts bills or change for the $3 parking fee.

6 McKenzie Pass

Snow closes Highway 242 from about mid-November to June. Vehicles over 23 feet in length are banned.

Perhaps no other drive in Oregon is as scenic as the winding old McKenzie Pass Highway, crossing alpine lava fields with the craggy spires of Mount Washington and North Sister towering silently on either hand.

Closed by snow eight months of the

Mount Washington rises above snow-dusted lava fields from the Dee Wright Memorial Observatory.

year, the 37-mile route includes a dozen hairpin switchbacks. Stop at the summit of the pass to see the **Dee Wright Memorial Observatory**, a rock lookout hut with peepholes identifying nearby mountain peaks. Here, too, is a paved half-mile nature loop through the lava. The loop visits a portion of an 1877 wagon road.

For a picnic, a swim, or a longer hike,

A half-mile path leads to a rustic shelter at Hand Lake, beside a meadow and a lava flow. The trail starts at a highway pullout 4.5 miles east of McKenzie Pass.

head for **Scott Lake**. To find it, drive 5.6 miles west of the McKenzie Pass summit. Between mileposts 71 and 72, turn north on a gravel road for 1.5 miles to its end at a lakeside walk-in campground.

GETTING THERE: From Interstate 5 exit 194a in Eugene, drive McKenzie River Highway 126 east 55 miles. Beyond McKenzie Bridge 4 miles, turn right onto Highway 242 to McKenzie Pass. If you're coming from Bend, drive Highway 20 west 21 miles to the far edge of Sisters and fork left onto Highway 242 to McKenzie Pass.

Alpenglow from the Three Sisters reflects in Scott Lake at McKenzie Pass. A primitive, walk-in campground by the lake is a good base for short hiking or canoeing explorations.

Between 20 and 60 feet of snow fall on the Central Oregon Cascades each winter. Plowed roads lead to recreation centers at Mount Bachelor, Santiam Pass, and Willamette Pass. Sno-Park permits, required for cars, cost about $4 per day or $16 per season at outdoor stores.

April icicles frame Broken Top in the Three Sisters Wilderness.

MOUNT BACHELOR

A half-hour drive west of Bend or Sunriver, this 9065-foot volcano *(left)* boasts powder snow and a world-class ski resort with 11 lifts (tickets about $49, info at *www.mtbachelor.com*). Sno-Parks along the road to Mount Bachelor serve as bases for nordic ski or snowshoe tours on free, ungroomed trails to eight rustic shelters with woodstoves.

Nordic skier

SANTIAM PASS

Though lower and wetter than Mount Bachelor, Santiam Pass has views of Mount Washington and Three Fingered Jack *(at right)*. Hoodoo Ski Bowl offers half a dozen lifts (tickets about $36, info at *www.hoodoo.com*). Nearby, Benson Sno-Park has nordic ski/snowshoe trails to three shelters.

Snow-bent trees.

WILLAMETTE PASS

The closest snow center to Eugene, Willamette Pass *(left)* has an ambitious little ski area with a six-seat express lift (tickets about $36, info at *www.willamettepass.com*). A mile west, the Gold Lake Sno-Park is a base for nordic ski and snowshoe tours to six backwoods shelters.

The Gold Lake Sno-Park's nordic center

North Sister from the Arrowhead Lakes after a September storm.

HIKE 43　Obsidian Trail

Difficult
12-mile loop　　1800 feet elevation gain
Open mid-July through October
Use: hikers, horses
Map: Three Sisters (Geo-Graphics)

The Obsidian Trail leads to Sunshine, one of the most beautiful alpine areas in Oregon. Brooks meander through the wildflower meadows nestled here between Middle Sister and Little Brother. Snowmelt tarns shimmer from plateaus strewn with black obsidian glass.

To limit crowds, the Forest Service requires that Obsidian Trail users pick up a special permit in advance at the McKenzie Ranger Station on Highway 126 just east of McKenzie Bridge. Call at 541-822-3381 for information. Note that permits are issued to a limited number of groups for each day, so plan ahead if you want

Red-naped sapsucker.

a weekend reservation. Also note that Wilderness rangers strictly enforce a total ban on campfires, and that tents are prohibited within 100 feet of trails or water.

The trail begins at a message board at the far end of the parking loop and immediately forks. Head right, following a "White Branch Creek" pointer. The first mile of the path is dusty, climbing through a hot forest of lodgepole pine and beargrass. After passing a side trail to Spring Lake, climb steadily through cooler woods of lichen-draped mountain hemlock and red huckleberry.

At the 3.4-mile mark, traverse up the face of a fresh, blocky lava flow to a viewpoint of Cascade snow-peaks from Mount Jefferson to Middle Sister. Beyond the lava, the path crosses White Branch Creek and reaches a junction in a meadow of blue lupine wildflowers.

The loop begins here. Follow the "Linton Meadows" pointer to the right. This route climbs a mile to a plateau of flashing obsidian chips. This black volcanic glass forms when silica-rich rhyolite lava oozes to the surface without contacting water. If the lava meets water it explodes upon eruption, forming frothy pumice instead.

The trail follows a brook in a meadow decorated with western pasque flower—the early, anemone-like bloom

The Pacific Crest Trail traverses a field of lupine north of Collier Cone.

The Arrowhead Lakes' alpine plateau has close-up views of North Sister (left) and Middle Sister (right).

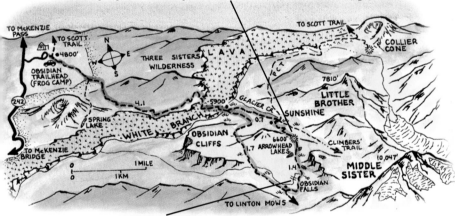

that develops a dishmop seed head known as "old man of the mountain."

At the Pacific Crest Trail junction, turn left and climb past 20-foot Obsidian Falls to a spring atop a glorious alpine plateau dotted with ponds.

Obsidian Falls.

Pass a stunning view of North Sister and switchback down to Sunshine, a meadow beside Glacier Creek.

Sunshine Shelter was demolished in the 1960s, but the trail junction here is still a crossroads for wilderness traffic. Turn left to continue the loop, following Glacier Creek steeply down to White Branch's meadow and the return route to the car.

Getting There

To find the trailhead, drive McKenzie Highway 242, the scenic old road between Sisters and McKenzie Bridge. West of McKenzie Pass 6.2 miles (between mileposts 70 and 71), turn off at a sign for the Obsidian Trailhead and drive 0.4 mile to a maze of small parking spots. A Northwest Forest Pass is required to park here. The pass costs $5 per day or $30 per season.

HIKE 44 Tam McArthur Rim

Difficult
5 miles round trip   1200 feet elevation gain
Open mid-July to mid-October
Use: hikers, horses
Map: Mt. Jefferson (Geo-Graphics)

Surrounded by 500-foot cliffs, the viewpoint on the edge of Tam McArthur Rim has a birds-eye view of the Three Sisters. Even in August patches of snow remain among the struggling trees and wildflowers of the rim's tablelands.

From the trailhead at Three Creek Lake, the path climbs steeply 0.2 mile, levels off for a bit, and then climbs hard again up to the rim's plateau. Notice how porcupines have gnawed patches of bark off some of the pines. These mostly nocturnal, spiny rodents can also subsist on lupine, though it causes selenium poisoning in other mammals.

The trail climbs gradually for half a mile across the rim's tilted tableland before views begin to unfold. To the north, look for (left to right) Belknap Crater, Mount Washington, Three Fingered Jack, Mount Jefferson, Mount Hood, and the tip of Mount Adams.

The wildflowers of this sandy plateau grow in scattered clumps to preserve moisture and to fight the winds. The bright purple trumpets are penstemon. The clumps of yellow balls are sulfur

Broken Top beckons from the viewpoint atop Tam McArthur Rim's 500-foot cliff.

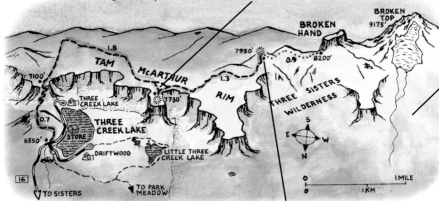

The Three Sisters line up along the skyline from a cinder knoll near the end of Tam McArthur Rim.

plant. And the off-white, fuzzy flowers are dirty socks—source of a suspicious odor wafting across the hot sand.

Finally, at an unmarked fork, take a small right-hand path 200 yards along the rim to the cliff-edge viewpoint. Three Creek Lake and its cousin, Little Three Creek Lake, are over 1000 feet below. To the east, sunlight glints off metal roofs in Bend and Sisters. To the south is snowy Mount Bachelor, striped with ski slopes.

If you have energy left after reaching this viewpoint, invest it in a 1.3-mile continuation of the hike. Return to the main trail and turn right toward Broken

From this nameless tarn below McArthur Rim, Broken Hand is a small snowless knob to the left of Broken Top.

Top. After a mile of sandy, alpine country, climb a snowfield and turn left up what appears to be a small red cinder cone—but which is in fact a ridge end. Stop at the ridgecrest amid a scattering of drop-shaped lava bombs, and admire the view here stretching south to Mount Thielsen. It's possible to continue even farther toward Broken Top, but the trail becomes faint and dangerous as it traverses Broken Hand's cliffs.

Getting There

Drive to downtown Sisters and turn south on Elm Street at a sign for Three Creek Lake. Follow Elm Street and its successor, Road 16, for 15.7 miles. After 1.7 miles of gravel, notice the trailhead sign on the left, opposite the entrance road to Driftwood Campground. Park at a lot 100 feet down the campground road and walk back to the trail. A Northwest Forest Pass is required to park here. The pass costs $5 per day or $30 per season.

HIKE 45 — Green Lakes

Difficult
8.4 miles round trip   1100 feet elevation gain
Open mid-July through October
Use: hikers, horses
Map: Three Sisters (Geo-Graphics)

This classic route to the famous alpine basin of the Green Lakes leads past a string of waterfalls and through a strangely idyllic canyon walled by an enormous lava flow. Although the trail is dusty from extremely heavy use, you can avoid the worst traffic by skipping August and September weekends.

Campfires are banned throughout the entire basin and tents are allowed only at posted, designated sites. Dogs must be on leash.

The trail starts at the far end of the parking loop, where a Wilderness Info trailer is parked from July through September. After 200 yards the trail crosses swift, glassy Fall Creek on a footbridge. Half a mile beyond is the first waterfall, a 25-foot-wide curtain of water. But don't spend all your time here. Just 100 yards upstream is another major cataract. In fact, the creek puts on a trailside performance for the next 1.5 miles, tumbling through chutes, juggling over boulders,

△ South Sister from the largest of the Green Lakes.
Broken Top from a spring on the optional lake loop. ▷

Pink monkeyflower crowds the banks of alpine creeks.

and falling headlong into pools.

After a trail splits off toward Moraine Lake on the left, cross Fall Creek again on a footbridge in a meadow with glimpses ahead to South Sister and Broken Top. Blue lupine, yellow composites, and

Green Lakes Basin thousands of years ago by damming Fall Creek.

Finally you'll reach a 4-way trail junction just before the lakes. To prowl the area on an optional 2.9-mile loop, continue straight, skirting the right-hand shore of the largest lake. After crossing

An alternate, less steep route to the Green Lakes skirts Broken Top from a trailhead on a very rough dirt road.

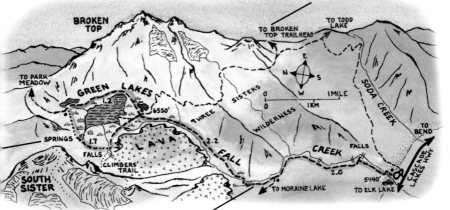

The Fall Creek Trail passes a succession of cascades.

pink monkeyflower bloom here in August. Then the trail climbs through the woods for a mile before returning to Fall Creek in an eerie meadow flanked by a massive lava flow on the left. This wall of blocky obsidian created the

a footbridge over the third lake's outlet creek, leave the trail and head cross-country to the left around the largest lake. Stay on the cinder plain because the lakeshore meadows are swampy here. The route passes an enormous spring and a milky outwash creek from Lewis Glacier. To complete the loop, cross Fall Creek on narrow, tippy logs and go straight.

Getting There

Take the Cascade Lakes Highway 26.4 miles west of Bend (4.4 miles past the Mount Bachelor Ski Area) and turn right at a sign for the Green Lakes Trailhead. A Northwest Forest Pass is required to park here. The pass costs $5 per day or $30 per season.

HIKE 46   South Sister

Difficult (to Moraine Lake)
7.3-mile loop   2000 feet elevation gain
Open August to mid-October
Use: hikers, horses
Map: Three Sisters (Geo-Graphics)

Very Difficult (to summit of South Sister)
11 miles round trip   4900 feet elevation gain

Oregon's third tallest peak has a path to its top. Admittedly, the trail up South Sister is exceedingly steep, long, and rugged, but no technical climbing skills are required and the rewards are great. From the summit—a broad, snowy crater with a small lake—you can see half the state. If this sounds too demanding, here's a secret: the loop to Moraine Lake, half-way up the moun-

A blue, a butterfly of alpine meadows.

tain, is just as picturesque. What's more, the weather's better here. The summit often generates its own wisp of clouds, a scenic feature when viewed from below, but a nuisance at the top. Hikers with dogs must keep them on leash here from July through September.

From the Devils Lake Trailhead,

start out on the South Sister Climbers Trail. This path crosses a footbridge over glassy Tyee Creek before crossing the highway. Then the trail promptly launches steeply uphill through a dense mountain hemlock forest.

After 1.5 grueling, viewless miles, the path emerges from the forest at the edge of a vast, sandy plateau. South Sister and Broken Top loom ahead. Signs at a 4-way trail junction indicate Moraine Lake is to the right, but to see the recommended viewpoint first, continue straight on the climbers' trail.

This portion of the hike is a lark—strolling up the open tableland, admiring views of a dozen mountains and lakes. Wind-gnarled trees pose in occasional clusters. Scraggly, red-leaved dogbane plants dot the sand. At the upper end of Moraine Lake's valley the trail swerves left around a rock outcrop. Just above it is a great lunch spot, a viewpoint amid boulders that serve as tables.

If you're turning back here, be sure to visit Moraine Lake. Simply return 1.1 mile to a fork in the trail and veer left down a sandy ridge to the lake. This ridge is the actual *moraine*—a pile of sand and rocks left by a glacier. The Lewis Glacier carved the lake's U-shaped valley in the Ice Age, and the debris it

If there's a cloud on South Sister when you reach Moraine Lake, the summit may have a snowstorm instead of a view.

Teardrop Pool, the state's highest lake, forms in South Sister's summit crater each summer.

The Lewis Glacier now ends at an unnamed lakelet, green with the glacial silt of pulverized rock.

pushed here now cups the lake.

If you're backpacking, note that tents near Moraine Lake are allowed only at sites designated by a post. Campfires are banned. The quickest way back to your car from Moraine Lake is to return on the climbers' trail, but if you don't mind an extra 1.2 miles, consider a gentler, prettier loop via Wickiup Plain (see map).

If you're climbing South Sister, pause at the lunch stop viewpoint to size up the weather. If you can't see the summit, don't go on. What looks like a fluffy white cloud ahead can prove to be a dangerous blizzard at the top. Above the lunch stop viewpoint, the trail steepens drastically, climbing 1.1 mile to a resting point in a sandy saddle—the current terminal moraine of Lewis Glacier, overlooking a small green cirque lake. A climbers' trail from Green Lakes joins here on the right. The route to the summit heads up the ridge to the left.

After another 0.7 mile you'll crest the lip of South Sister's broad crater. Follow the rim right 0.4 mile to the summit, a

The recommended loop to Moraine Lake includes views of Broken Top.

rocky crest with a benchmark. Bend, Sisters, and Redmond are clearly visible. To the north, the green Chambers Lakes dot the barren, glacial landscape below Middle Sister.

Getting There

Drive 28.5 miles west of Bend on the Cascade Lakes Highway. Beyond the Mount Bachelor Ski Area 6.5 miles, turn left at a Devils Lake Trailhead sign and park at the end of the campground loop. A $5-per-car Northwest Pass is required.

7   Bend

Founded in 1905, Bend boomed in 1911 when the railroad arrived and sawmills sprang up to log Central Oregon's ponderosa pine forests. After a sleepy half century, Bend boomed again, this time as the recreation capital of a sunny region where skiing, mountain biking, and white-water boating are so popular that thousands turn out for a Pole, Pedal, Paddle race each May.

Banners decorate downtown.

The 1936 Pine Tavern restaurant has a 250-year-old ponderosa pine growing through its roof.

One of Oregon's fastest growing cities, Bend now has traffic jams, strip malls, and a freeway. But downtown retains its small-town charm. Start at the pine-shaded lawns of **Drake Park**, where Mirror Pond reflects Cascade peaks. Beside the park is the 1936 **Pine Tavern** (967 NW Brooks Street), a historic restaurant with a riverside garden.

Then stroll by the upscale shops and galleries of **Wall and Bond Streets**, the

Ducks paddle in the Deschutes River at Drake Park.

next two streets up from the river. For breakfast or brunch, try the **Alpenglow Cafe** (1040 NW Bond), where the food is so fresh they offer a $1000 reward if you find a can opener in the kitchen. Next door is the **Deschutes Brewery & Public House**, a pub featuring Black Butte Porter and Mirror Pond Pale Ale. Ask for directions to the actual brewery, a mile away at 901 SW Simpson Street (free tours from noon to 4pm on Saturdays).

Bend brewpub sign.

Finally drive a mile south and look for three tall silver smokestacks marking the **Old Mill District**, where the red wooden buildings of a former riverside sawmill have been renovated as eclectic shops.

GETTING THERE: Take Revere Avenue exit 137 of Highway 97 and follow Hill Street (which becomes Wall Street) to downtown.

8   High Desert Museum

Open 9am-5pm daily except major holidays. Adults $12, $11 for seniors, and $7 for children age 5-11.

Walkways amid ponderosa pines lead to outdoor exhibits of river otters, porcupines, owls, and eagles at this first-rate interpretive center. Other displays feature Native American culture, a working sawmill, desert lore, and Oregon Trail pioneers.

Wild porcupines have been known to climb into the outdoor pen to fraternize with the museum's animals.

GETTING THERE: Drive 3.5 miles south of Bend on Highway 97.

Plan to spend half a day touring the museum.

9 Lava Butte

Open 9am-6pm from May 1 to October 19. $5-per-car Northwest Forest Pass required.

Lava Butte's fire lookout.

The Lava Lands Visitor Center has interesting displays, friendly rangers, and paved paths through lava, but the top draw here is the spiraling road up Lava Butte, a cinder cone with a crater, a lookout, and a fabulous view of Central Oregon.

GETTING THERE: Drive 8 miles south of Bend on Highway 97 to the Lava Lands Visitor Center turnoff near milepost 150.

Hike a quarter-mile loop trail around Lava Butte's crater rim to soak in the view of the High Cascades.

10 Lava River Cave

Open May 1 to October 31. Adults $2.50, teenagers $2. Children under 12 free. Gas lantern rental $1.50.

Oregon's longest lava tube extends a mile under Highway 97. Bring flashlights and warm clothes. The cave is a chilly 42° F year-round. Three-foot-tall ice stalagmites remain in the first chamber until June. After 0.4 mile the sandy-floored route passes Two Tube Tunnel, where the cave briefly splits into tiers.

GETTING THERE: Drive 11 miles south of Bend on Highway 97. A mile past the Lava Lands Visitor Center (and just before milepost 151), turn left at a sign for Lava River Cave. The area is gated in winter to protect bats.

The cave entrance is a cliff-rimmed pit in a ponderosa pine forest with scampering Townsends chipmunks.

LAVA TUBES

Central Oregon's lava fields are riddled with sinuous caves, some of them up to a mile long. These "lava tubes" form when molten basalt lava pours from a volcano. After a crust hardens on the surface of the runny lava flow, liquid rock continues flowing underneath, draining tube-shaped caverns.

Look for lines on the cave walls, the

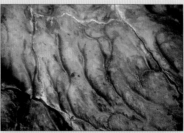

Shiny folds on cave walls and "lavacicles" on the ceiling form when superheated gas remelts the rock.

"high-water marks" left by ebbing lava flows. Also look for lavacicles — inch-long stone drips left when superheated gases roar through the cave near the end of the eruption, remelting the walls.

Most lava tubes are closed from November to May to protect hibernating bats. If the bats wake up in winter they use up the energy they need to survive.

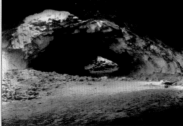

Lava tubes are discovered only if a roof collapse has exposed an entrance.

Lava Cast Forest

Open May through November.

A basalt lava flow from the Newberry volcano swept through a stand of trees 6000 years ago. The runny lava washed up against the trunks and cooled before they could burn. Today a paved, 1-mile loop path visits the circular rock wells.

GETTING THERE: Drive Highway 97 south of Bend 13 miles to milepost 153. Opposite the Sunriver exit, turn left on Road 9720 and follow this washboard gravel road 9 miles uphill to a turnaround at road's end. A Northwest Forest Pass ($5 per car) is required.

Most of the circular molds in the Lava Cast Forest are from standing trees, but this one was from a fallen log.

 ## Newberry Caldera

Closed by snow November through June. Northwest Forest Pass required ($5 per car per day or $30 per season), available at entry fee booth.

The giant Newberry volcano has sputtered, collapsed, and leaked lava for half a million years, leaving a vast outdoor museum of geologic oddities, now pro-

Paulina Peak, above Paulina Lake, is on the caldera rim of a gigantic, collapsed volcano, as at Crater Lake.

tected as the Newberry National Volcanic Monument. Two of the volcanic sights are conveniently near Highway 97, Lava Butte and Lava River Cave (see p187), but to see the source of the fireworks you'll need to drive a paved side road up into the caldera itself, a 6-mile-wide mountain crater with lakes and lava flows.

Start at the Paulina Creek Falls picnic area, where the caldera's outlet creek spills over a pair of 60-foot waterfalls. Ahead half mile on the left is Paulina Lake Lodge, an old-timey resort with a rustic general store, a

Paulina Lake Lodge's restaurant.

tiny marina that rents boats, an unpretentious restaurant, and a collection of rentable cabins (see p193). A very

A picnic area beside Paulina Creek Falls has trails to viewpoints below the falls and atop the far shore's cliff.

beautiful 8.6-mile trail circles Paulina Lake; hikers should park at Little Crater Campground on the far shore.

Next drive the main paved road just past a fee booth and turn right for 3 miles to the summit of Paulina Peak, where you can see across the collapsed volcano's 6-mile-wide caldera to the peaks of the High Cascades.

Then return to the main road and drive another 1.8 miles east to a large parking area on the right for the Obsidian Trail. This path climbs a staircase and loops 0.8 mile through the frothy black glass of the 1300-year-old Big Obsidian Flow.

The 8.6-mile trail around Paulina Lake passes a submarine warm springs, a lava flow of obsidian glass, and a cinder cone.

In winter, Paulina Peak's sweeping view of Central Oregon is accessible only by ski or snowmobile.

GETTING THERE: Drive Highway 97 south of Bend 22 miles (or north of La Pine 7 miles). At a "Newberry Caldera" sign between mileposts 161 and 162, turn east on a paved road for 12.2 miles to Paulina Creek Falls.

The five campgrounds around Paulina Lake and its twin, East Lake, are crowded only for the opening of the fishing season in early July, when snowdrifts and mosquitoes are problems.

An 0.8-mile path explores the Big Obsidian Flow, a square mile of black glass that erupted 1300 years ago.

HIKE 47 Salt Creek Falls

Easy
3.4-mile loop   400 feet elevation gain
Open May through November
Use: hikers, bicycles
Map: Diamond Peak Wilderness (Imus)

Waterfalls! This stroll starts at the state's second tallest waterfall and loops along a canyon rim to lacy Diamond Creek Falls, hidden in a mossy grotto.

From the parking turnaround, first walk 100 feet past a kiosk to an overlook of 286-foot Salt Creek Falls. The falls have cut a dramatic canyon in the edge of a High Cascades basalt lava flow.

To start the actual hike, however, follow a concrete pathway upstream, cross Salt Creek on a footbridge, and look for a small sign directing hikers 200 feet through the woods to a well-marked trail junction. Turn right and climb 0.2 mile to a different viewpoint of Salt Creek's canyon. Here the trail crosses rock worn smooth by Ice Age glaciers. Notice the honeycomb-shaped fracture pattern characteristic of basalt.

In another 200 yards a short side trail to the left leads to Too Much Bear Lake, a brushy-shored pond. Continue on the

Salt Creek Falls is the state's second tallest cascade.

In winter, nordic skiers and snowshoers follow the snowed-under loop trail to icy Diamond Creek Falls.

For a longer hike, leave the loop at Diamond Creek and hike up Fall Creek to a view of Mount Yoran from Vivian Lake. Above: Mount Yoran from Divide Lake.

Getting There

From Oakridge exit 186 of Interstate 5 just south of Eugene, take Willamette Highway 58 east 66 miles to a sign for Salt Creek Falls (5 miles west of Willamette Pass or 1 mile east of the highway tunnel) and follow the paved entrance road to a turnaround with an information kiosk, restrooms, and picnic tables. A Northwest Forest Pass is required to park here. The pass costs $5 per day or $30 per season.

on the right.

Take this steep, 0.2-mile side trail down to a footbridge in a misty grotto below the fan-shaped, 100-foot cascade. Look for scarlet salmonberry blossoms, yellow monkeyflowers, and pink bleeding hearts among the ferns.

Then return to the main trail and switchback up past another viewpoint to a trail junction. Turn left to complete the loop to your car, crossing a gravel road twice in 1.2 miles.

main trail 1.2 miles, passing viewpoints, rhododendrons (blooming in June), and two small clearcuts before reaching the signed turnoff for Diamond Creek Falls

WHERE TO STAY

Campgrounds (map p161)

		Campsites	Water	Showers	Flush Toilet	Fee
2	**ALLEN SPRINGS.** On the Metolius River amid ponderosa pines, this is the closest camp to the Wizard Falls fish hatchery (see p170). Open April to mid-October. Drive paved Road 14 north of Camp Sherman 5 miles.	17	●			$$
6	**BIG LAKE.** Powerboaters and RVers dominate this very scenic camp near the Pacific Crest Trail. At Santiam Pass turn south past the Hoodoo ski area 2 miles. **Mount Washington from Big Lake.** ▷	38	●			$$
4	**CAMP SHERMAN.** On the Metolius River, this fly-fishing haven is beside the charming forest hamlet of Camp Sherman (see p170). Open April to mid-October.	15	●			$$
1	**COVE PALISADES.** In a spectacular desert canyon beside a sinuous, three-armed reservoir (see p167), this large state park camp has three deluxe cabins that rent for $55-65 and a marina with three rental houseboats ($125 for 11 people, $85 for 7). Reservations: 800-452-5687.	272	●	●	●	$$
23	**CRESCENT LAKE.** Beside a rustic resort, this camp amid lodgepole pines borders a high mountain lake with powerboats. Open May to late October. Reservations: 877-444-6777. Drive Highway 58 east of Willamette Pass 7 miles to Crescent Junction and take Road 60 for 2.2 miles.	47	●			$
12	**DEVILS LAKE.** Carry your gear a few yards to spectacular, quiet sites on this high mountain lake at the South Sister trailhead (see pp184-85).	9				$
10	**DRIFTWOOD.** Below scenic Tam McArthur Rim (see p180), this camp borders Three Creek Lake (no powerboats). Open July to mid-September.	15				$
13	**ELK LAKE.** Beside a rustic mountain resort with a store, restaurant, boat rentals, and windsurfing, this lakeside camp is open June to September. From Bend, drive the Cascade Lakes Highway west 32 miles.	22	●			$

WHERE TO STAY

Campgrounds *(map p161)*

	Campsites	Water	Showers	Flush Toilet	Fee
21 **FALL RIVER.** Like the Metolius, this river emerges from a spring among pines. The camp has flyfishing and a 3-mile trail. Open mid-April to October. Drive south of Bend 16 miles on Highway 97. At Vandevert Road, turn right 12 miles on what becomes Cascade Lakes Highway 42.	10				$
25 **GOLD LAKE.** A mile west of Willamette Pass on Highway 58, turn north on Road 500 to this quiet lakeside camp, open late May to mid-September.	21	●			$$
20 **HOT SPRINGS.** Perhaps the quietest camp in the Newberry Caldera *(see p189)*, this camp beside East Lake has no hot springs, but rather warm water welling up at the lakeshore. Open July through September.	50	●			$
22 **LA PINE.** On the Deschutes River, this large state recreation area has Oregon's largest ponderosa pine, a log cabin meeting hall, three yurts ($27-30), and ten rental cabins ($38-70). Reservations: 800-452-5687. Take Highway 97 south of Bend 23 miles. ▷	145	●	●	●	$$
15 **LAVA LAKE.** This lakeside camp with views of South Sister is beside a rustic resort with showers and a store. Open April to October. From Bend, drive the Cascade Lakes Highway west 39 miles.	43	●			$
19 **LITTLE CRATER.** In Newberry Caldera *(see p189)*, this camp has paths along Paulina Lake, to lava, and around a crater. Open May to October.	50	●			$$
16 **LITTLE LAVA LAKE.** At the headwaters of the Deschutes River, this camp has sites on both the river and a mountain lake, a mile from Lava Lake *(see above)*. Open April to late September.	12	●			$
17 **McKAY CROSSING.** In ponderosa pines, this quiet camp along Paulina Creek has a 15-foot waterfall. Open April to September. Drive Highway 97 south of Bend 22 miles, turn left toward Newberry Caldera 3 miles, and veer left on dirt Road 2120 for 3 miles.	10				$
27 **NORTH WALDO.** By an 8-mile, crystal clear lake that's great for sailboats or canoes, this camp is open mid-June to early October, but has mosquitoes in July. Drive Highway 58 west of Willamette Pass 3 miles and turn north on paved Waldo Lake Road 11 miles.	58	●		●	$$
18 **PAULINA LAKE.** Near a rustic resort on a large mountain lake *(see p189)*, this camp in Newberry Caldera is open May to late October.	69	●		●	$$
5 **RIVERSIDE.** Carry your gear a few yards to campsites among pines on the Metolius River just 1 mile below its headwater springs *(see p170)*. Open May through September.	16	●			$
9 **SCOTT LAKE.** Canoe or hike from this scenic walk-in lakeside camp at McKenzie Pass *(see p176)*. Open July to early October. Mosquitoes are a problem in July. Northwest Forest Pass required ($5 per car).	20				free
26 **SHADOW BAY.** At the south end of lovely, large Waldo Lake (see North Waldo, above), this camp is open July through mid-September.	92	●		●	$$
8 **SISTERS.** Amazingly convenient and nice, this city park has campsites on pine-shaded lawns along Whychus Creek. Beside Highway 20 at the east edge of the town of Sisters. Open April to mid-October.	60	●		●	$
3 **SMILING RIVER.** A mile north of Camp Sherman *(see p170)*, this is the roomiest of a string of five campgrounds among ponderosa pines on the east bank of the enchanting Metolius River. Open May to mid-October. **Metolius River.** ▷	38	●			$$

WHERE TO STAY

Campgrounds (map p161)

	Campsites	Water	Showers	Flush Toilet	Fee
14 **SOUTH.** On Hosmer Lake (the quiet, motor-free neighbor to busy Elk Lake) this camp is a base for canoeing and fly-fishing, with a view of Mount Bachelor. Open May to October. From Bend, drive the Cascade Lakes Highway west 35 miles, turn left 2 miles on Road 4625.	23				$
7 **SOUTH SHORE.** The largest of three campgrounds on Suttle Lake (fishing, waterskiing), just off Highway 20, east of Santiam Pass 7 miles. Open April to late September. Reservations: 877-444-6777.	39	●			$$
24 **TRAPPER CREEK.** By Odell Lake's Shelter Cove Resort (store, laundry, boat rentals), this camp is open June through October. From Highway 58 at Willamette Pass, turn south on Road 5810 for 2 miles.	32	●			$$
11 **TUMALO.** This convenient state park on the Deschutes River has seven yurts that rent for $29 apiece. Reservations: 800-452-5687. From Bend, drive Highway 20 toward Sisters 5 miles and turn left a mile.	87	●	●	●	$$

Deschutes River at Tumalo Park. ▷

B&Bs and Quaint Hotels (map p161)

	Rooms	Private bath	Cont. breakfast	Full breakfast	Rate range
4 **ASPEN MEADOW LODGE.** This themed bed & breakfast lodge is on 8 acres of aspen and ponderosa pine beside Whychus Creek, 1.5 miles north of Sisters at 68733 Junipine Lane, Sisters, OR 97759. The 1970 lodge has an outdoor hot tub, a lava rock fireplace, and a log swing. Pets OK. Info: 866-549-4312 or www.sisterslodging.com.	5	●		●	$59-119
1 **BLACK BUTTE RANCH.** Rent a lodge room, condo, or private home in this sprawling mountain resort and you gain entry to outdoor pools, tennis courts, golf courses, and bike paths. West of Sisters 8 miles on Highway 20. Info: 800-452-7455 or www.blackbutteranch.com.	300	●			$100-950
3 **BLUE SPRUCE.** Four blocks from downtown Sisters at 444 S. Spruce Street, Sisters, OR 97759, this modern bed & breakfast inn has a wraparound porch, gaslight fireplaces, bicycles, and themed rooms (fishing, hunting, logging). Info: 888-328-9644 or www.blue-spruce.biz.	4	●		●	$160
2 **CONKLIN'S GUEST HOUSE.** Once a schoolhouse, this 1910 Craftsman farmhouse is a bed & breakfast inn with a Cascade view and heated pool. A quarter mile north of Sisters at 69013 Camp Polk Road, Sisters, OR 97759. Info: 800-549-4262 or www.conklinsguesthouse.com.	5	●		●	$70-150
5 **LARA HOUSE.** In downtown Bend overlooking Mirror Pond, this 1910 Craftsman home is a bed & breakfast inn with a hot tub. At 640 NW Congress St., Bend, OR 97701. Info: 800-766-4064 or www.larahouse.com.	6	●		●	$90-175
7 **MILL INN.** Between downtown Bend and the trendy Old Mill shopping district, this restored 1917 home is a bed & breakfast inn at 642 NW Colorado Ave., Bend, OR 97701. Info: 877-748-1200 or www.millinn.com.	10	5		●	$30-100
9 **PAULINA LAKE LODGE.** This old-time resort in Newberry Caldera (see pp186-89) has 13 rental log cabins (sleep 2-10) with kitchens. Snowed in Dec-April, the resort stays open for guests who ski or snowmobile 2.5 miles from a Road 21 sno-park. Info: 541-536-2240 or www.paulinalakelodge.com.	13	●			$75-230
6 **THE SATHER HOUSE.** Afternoon tea is served by the fireside in winter at this elegant 1911 Victorian home, now a bed & breakfast inn. Three blocks from downtown Bend at 7 NW Tumalo Avenue, Bend, OR 97701. Info: 888-388-1065 or www.satherhouse.com.	4	●		●	$95-140
8 **SUNRIVER.** Rent a lodge room, condo, or private home in this sprawling Deschutes River resort and you gain entry to outdoor pools, tennis courts, golf courses, and bike paths. South of Bend 13 miles off Highway 97. Info: 800-801-8765 or www.sunriver-resort.com.	400	●			$139-850

SOUTHERN OREGON

Crater Lake National Park stars in a region rich with rivers, theater, and history.

The rugged region where the Klamath and Cascade mountain ranges intersect has long been one of the wildest corners of the continent.

Indian tribes isolated in these hills spoke half a dozen different languages. The first wagon train to pass through Southern Oregon blazed the Applegate Trail in 1846. Settlers who survived that trek told of a nightmarish voyage through canyons of death.

When the discovery of gold lured thousands of miners here in the 1850s, supplies were so short that salt traded even with gold dust by weight. The railroad line built through Southern Oregon in 1887 was the final link of a system of railroads tracing the perimeter of the United States. Even today locals claim the wilds here are the last retreat of Bigfoot, the mythical ape-man of the backwoods.

But Southern Oregon is starting to show up on traveler's maps. Half a million people a year marvel at the intense blue of Crater Lake, an astonishingly deep mountain pool in a collapsed volcano. Thousands of theater lovers flock to the small town of Ashland, the setting for one of the world's largest Shakespearean festivals. Others come to fish or float on sunny whitewater rivers.

One of area's greatest charms is that so much of the landscape still has an "undiscovered" feel. Just beyond the tourist loop at Crater Lake and the shopping malls of Medford lie mile upon mile of forests, mountains, and trails known only to adventurous souls – if not to the legendary Bigfoot.

◁ **Wizard Island is a cinder cone in Crater Lake.**   △ **The gold rush boomtown of Jacksonville dates to 1851.**

Exploring
SOUTHERN OREGON

L ike beads on a necklace, a string of Southern
Oregon cities from Ashland to Roseburg are
linked by Interstate 5. The freeway also separates
the snow-capped Cascade Range on the east from
a jumble of ridges to the west, known variously
as the Siskiyou or Klamath Mountains. Start your
exploration of the area by driving along the scenic
North Umpqua or Rogue Rivers to the high country
at Crater Lake National Park.

North Umpqua River

A dozen major waterfalls *(p198)*
and a natural hot springs *(p200)*
line this scenic river between
Roseburg and its headwaters at
Diamond Lake *(p202)*.

Crater Lake

Most visitors to this National Park
merely drive along the rim to
viewpoints. Stop at historic Crater
Lake Lodge *(p206)*, where a trail
leads to a view atop Garfield
Peak *(p207)*. The only access to
the lake itself is a 1.1-mile path
down to Cleetwood Cove *(p210)*,
where you can catch a boat tour
around Wizard Island. Snow
closes the 33-mile Rim Drive from
November to July, but you can
still drive up to the Rim Village —
or circle the lake on skis.

Rogue River

Famed for its whitewater, this
mischievous river actually has
many moods. It begins at massive
springs near Crater Lake *(p204)*,
churns underground through
a lava tube *(p215)*, lazes past
the Medford area's Table Rocks
(p216), and finally roars through
a wilderness canyon *(pp222-25)*.
Hikers trace this wild western
segment on a 40-mile trail *(at left)*.
while others brave the rapids by
raft or kayak.

Ashland

This small but culturally awake
college town *(see pp218-19)* tried
its luck as a spa resort in 1914,
laying out a landscaped creekside
park with bubbly lithium
springs. A Shakespearean stage
opened beside the park in 1935,
blossoming into a world-class
theater festival with modern and
classic plays on three stages from
February to November. Upscale
galleries, brewpubs, and bed &
breakfast inns now fill the city.

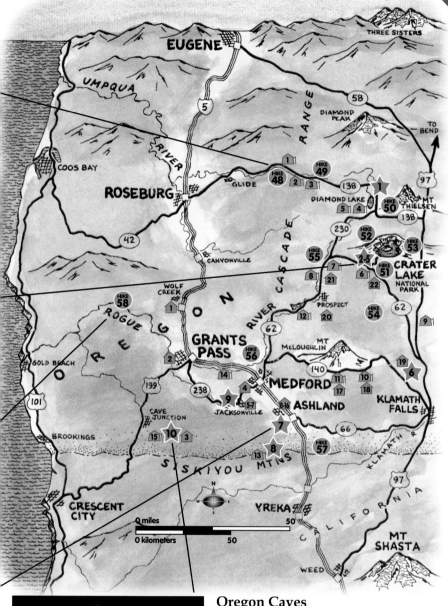

THREE SISTERS

EUGENE

UMPQUA RIVER

58

DIAMOND PEAK

TO BEND

COOS BAY

5

GLIDE

138

97

1

HIKE 48

2

3

HIKE 49

ROSEBURG

DIAMOND LAKE

5

4

HIKE 50

MT THIELSEN

138

42

230

HIKE 52

HIKE 53

CANYONVILLE

HIKE 55

2-5

HIKE 51

CRATER LAKE NATIONAL PARK

8

7

WOLF CREEK

21

6

22

HIKE 58

1

PROSPECT

62

HIKE 54

9

12

20

GRANTS PASS

HIKE 56

MT McLOUGHLIN

19

6

GOLD BEACH

2

14

140

11

10

199

238

4

MEDFORD

17

18

KLAMATH FALLS

101

9

57

8-16

ASHLAND

CAVE JUNCTION

JACKSONVILLE

7

BROOKINGS

15

10

3

13

8

HIKE 57

66

97

CRESCENT CITY

SISKIYOU MTNS

CALIFORNIA

N
W E
S

YREKA

0 miles   50
0 kilometers   50

MT SHASTA

WEED

Oregon Caves

At this National Monument, guided tours lead through narrow passageways and up rock staircases to halls of marble stalactites. Outside are an interpretive center, a historic lodge, and a loop trail to Big Fir, a Douglas fir tree 13 feet in diameter.

KEY

5 Star attraction

HIKE 12 Featured hike

2 Campground

6 B&B or quaint hotel

? Information:

Medford area
800-469-6307
www.visitmedford.org

Southern Oregon
www.sova.org

HIKE 48 North Umpqua Waterfalls

Easy (5 short trails)
6 miles total   940 feet elevation gain
Open except in winter storms
Use: hikers

Driving along the North Umpqua River is always scenic, but the trip's more fun if you stop to walk to water-

Salmon and steelhead leap 8 feet up Deadline Falls.

falls on the way. Here are five of the best. Because the trails are so short, it's possible to hike them all in a day.

The first of these cataracts, Deadline Falls, drops only 8 feet, but it's a good place to watch salmon leaping upstream. From the Tioga Trailhead, the route follows the first 0.2 mile of the 79-mile North Umpqua Trail. Beware of lush 3-leaved poison oak around the viewpoint.

The path to the second waterfall, Susan Creek Falls, starts across Highway 138 from a picnic area and climbs 0.7 mile to a 70-foot punchbowl plume emerging from a slot. A rougher path continues 0.3 mile to the Indian Mounds, an overgrown vision quest site.

The shady trail to the third waterfall, Fall Creek Falls, squeezes though a crack in a house-sized boulder on its way 0.9

The path to Susan Creek Falls is accessible even to wheelchairs.

The spectacular Fall Creek Trail squeezes through a split boulder, visits a pool at a lower 50-foot cascade, and then climbs to the top of a smaller falls.

Toketee Falls pours out of columnar basalt cliffs to smash into a wave-tossed pool.

The North Umpqua River, famed for its whitewater rafting and steelhead fishing, also has a 79-mile trail, open to bicyclists and horses, that climbs to the river's source in the Mount Thielsen Wilderness.

mile up to a plunging double cascade. The trail first visits a misty pool at the base of Fall Creek Falls' lower, 50-foot cascade, and then switchbacks up to a gravel road crossing the top of a smaller upper falls.

Toketee means "pretty" in the Northwest Indians' old trade jargon. The 0.4-mile trail to 90-foot Toketee Falls leads past a churning gorge to a railed viewpoint deck.

Western red cedar trees often grow near waterfalls.

The fifth and final cascade is 272-foot Watson Falls, tallest in Southern Oregon. An 0.8-mile path loops across a zigzagging footbridge over bouldery Watson Creek. Just beyond is a T-shaped trail junction. To the left a 100-yard path climbs to the misty base of Watson Falls' amazingly tall horsetail plume.

Getting There

From Interstate 5 in Roseburg, take exit 124 and follow "Diamond Lake" signs east on Highway 138.

▶ **Deadline Falls.** Drive Highway 138 for 22 miles. A mile past the Idleyld Park store, turn right at a "Swiftwater Park" sign, cross the river bridge, and park at the Tioga Trailhead on the left.

▶ **Susan Creek Falls**: Drive another 6.3 miles east on Highway 138 to the Susan Creek Picnic Area on the right, beyond milepost 28.

▶ **Fall Creek Falls.** Drive another 3.9 miles east on Highway 138 to a trailhead sign on the left between mileposts 32 and 33.

▶ **Toketee Falls**. Drive another 26.4 miles east on Highway 138. Between mileposts 58 and 59, turn left onto Toketee-Rigdon Road 34. Then keep left at all junctions for 0.4 mile.

▶ **Watson Falls.** Drive another 2.3 miles east on Highway 138. Between mileposts 60 and 61, turn right on Fish Creek Road 37 for 200 yards.

HIKE 49 Umpqua Hot Springs

Easy
0.6 miles round trip　100 feet elevation gain
Open except in winter storms
Use: hikers, horses, bicycles
Map: Potter Mountain (USGS)

An unmarked path leads to a rustic shelter with a spa-sized, 105° F hot springs pool overlooking the North Umpqua River. An equally easy trail on the far shore that leads to a pair of astonishing *cold* springs.

Start by crossing the North Umpqua River on a 150-foot bridge. After 100 yards, take a steep side trail up to the right for 0.2 mile to the hot springs. Just before the shelter, ignore a small trail

ally built up a 100-foot dome-shaped rock knoll above the river's bank.

After soaking a while and hiking back to the parking lot, why not take another short hike to see the cold springs? This trail starts beside the parking lot's outhouse, climbs to the road, follows it 100

Swimsuits are rare at Umpqua Hot Springs' shelter.

Mysterious Columnar Falls has no apparent source.

A footbridge at the trailhead is part of the 79-mile North Umpqua River Trail.

feet, and then descends into the woods. After 0.3 mile you'll pass Surprise Falls, which roars out of the ground just below the trail, and Columnar Falls, where springs spill over a cliff and vanish.

down to the right that leads to riverside campsites. On summer weekends, expect to wait an hour for a turn in the hot springs.

All the springs in this area resulted when lava flows from the High Cascades buried thousands of stream channels, leaving snowmelt to percolate underground to find an outlet. Here an active fault heats the water. The hot water carries dissolved minerals that have gradu-

Getting There

Drive 58.6 miles east of Roseburg (or 20 miles west of Diamond Lake) on Highway 138. Between mileposts 58 and 59, turn north onto Toketee-Rigdon Road 34. After 0.2 mile keep left alongside Toketee Lake's dam. Continue 2 miles, fork right onto (possibly unmarked) gravel Thorn Prairie Road 3401 for precisely another 2 miles, and look for a huge parking lot on the left. A Northwest Forest Pass is required to park here. The pass costs $5 per day or $30 per season.

A paved 11.5-mile bike path circles Diamond Lake. ▷

⭐ Diamond Lake

This popular mountain lake is surrounded by mountain views, over 400 campsites, five boat ramps, a resort lodge, and a paved 11.5-mile loop trail.

The 3,015-acre lake has an average depth of only 20 feet, so it becomes swimmably warm in August. It's also heavily stocked to provide catchable trout—although the emphasis on fishing has introduced alien species that have ravaged the lake's ecosystem. Note that boats are limited to 10 miles per hour and that mosquitoes are thick in June and early July, when fishing is best.

Diamond Lake Lodge makes a good starting point for a lakeshore tour. The compound includes not only a restaurant and store, but also a marina shop where you can rent boats and bicycles. If you're hiking, simply walk to the sandy picnic beach in front of the lodge, follow the lakeshore to the right, and climb to

Diamond Lake Lodge.

the paved bike path. After 1.7 miles, the trail briefly joins a road to cross Lake Creek, the lake's outlet, a good turnaround spot.

Perhaps the most beautiful short hike at Diamond Lake follows Silent Creek to the largest spring feeding the lake. To find this unpaved trail from the Diamond Lake Lodge, drive 2.7 miles south on Road 6592, turn right at a "South Shore Picnic Area" pointer, follow Road 4795 for 1.5 miles, and park on the left immediately after the Silent Creek bridge. This path heads upstream through an oasis in the pine forests.

GETTING THERE: From Roseburg, follow "Diamond Lake" signs east on Highway 38 for 70 miles to a sign for the Diamond Lake Recreation Area and turn right on paved Road 6592 to a "Lodge" pointer.

A view of Mount Bailey and Diamond Lake spreads below Mount Thielsen's summit. Climbing skills are required for the final 80 feet to Thielsen's top.

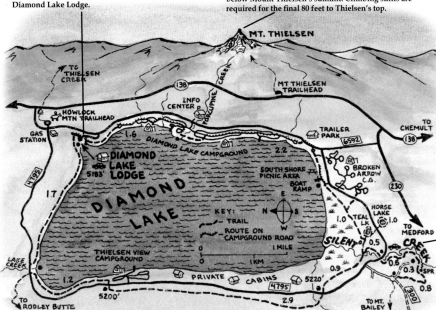

HIKE 50 Mount Thielsen

Very Difficult
10 miles round trip   3800 feet elevation gain
Open end of July through October
Use: hikers
Map: Mount Thielsen Wilderness (USFS)

Towering above Diamond Lake, Mount Thielsen's stony spire commands views from Mount Shasta to the Three Sisters. A popular path climbs to the Pacific Crest Trail on Mount Thielsen's flank. Hardy hikers can follow a scramble trail to a dizzying ledge at the base of the summit spire, and many dare to scale the final pitch as well. The

The "Lightning Rod of the Cascades," Thielsen's summit has fulgurites, rock recrystalized by lightning.

name Thielsen (pronounced *TEEL-sun*) honors a Danish-American pioneer railroad engineer.

The trail climbs a dry, sparsely forested ridge, so bring plenty of water. After 3.8 miles the path officially ends at the Pacific Crest Trail, but a climbers' trail continues straight up the ridgecrest. Above timberline this braided, rocky path gives out amidst slippery scree

Mount Thielsen towers above the forests at its base.

and broken rock. Only sure-footed hikers should venture upward. The correct route veers slightly to the right, spiraling around to a dizzying ledge at the eastern base of the summit spire.

This ledge, practically overhanging Thielsen Creek

Mount Thielsen's summit register.

2000 feet below, is an excellent place to declare victory and turn back. The final 80 feet are nearly vertical and require the adept use of hands and feet to chimney up cracks in the rock. Hikers attempting this do so at their own risk.

Silent Creek is the glassy inlet of Diamond Lake.

Getting There

From Medford, take Highway 62 east and follow "Diamond Lake" signs a total of 81 miles. At that point do not take the "Diamond Lake Recreation Area" turnoff. Instead continue 300 yards to a "Roseburg" pointer and turn left onto Highway 138. In 1.4 miles you'll find the Mount Thielsen Trailhead parking area on the right. If you're coming from Roseburg, take Highway 138 east for 81.6 miles. Ignore a "Diamond Lake Recreation Area" turnoff and continue 3 miles to the trailhead sign on the left. A $5-per-car Northwest Forest Pass is required.

Exploring
CRATER LAKE

Crater lake fills the caldera of Mount Mazama, a volcano that collapsed in a cataclysimic eruption in 5700 BC. The explosion blew 14 cubic miles of rock into the sky. The deepest lake in North America, Crater Lake has no outlet but maintains its level by evaporation and seepage. The lake's purity and 1958-foot depth account for its stunning blue color.

Golden-mantled ground squirrel.

Townsend's chipmunk.

Klamath tribal legends claim the lake is the haunt of an evil spirit named Llao. Native Americans refused to speak of the lake, so it was not discovered early by white explorers. National Park status came in 1902.

A 2.4-mile path from the Crater Rim Viewpoint pullout on Highway 230 follows the Rogue River to its source at Boundary Springs. Pets are banned on all park trails.

Wizard Island, here seen in April, was named for its resemblance to a sorcerer's hat. The island is one of two cinder cones that erupted in the caldera left by Mount Mazama's massive explosion. The lake has covered the other cone.

The park receives up to sixty feet of snow each winter. Only the south access road from Highway 62 to the Rim Village is plowed. Mazama Village, open from early June to mid-October, has a campground, grocery store, gas station, and motel.

A few National Park rules: Pets are permitted on leash only, and are not allowed on trails. Horses are limited to the Pacific Crest Trail, and grazing is banned. If you're backpacking, pick up the required, free backcountry camping permit at park headquarters.

GETTING THERE: From Medford, follow "Crater Lake" signs on Highway 62 for 73 miles and turn left to the park's entrance booth. Expect to pay $10 per car here for a day pass or $25 for an annual pass. Then continue seven miles to the Rim Village.

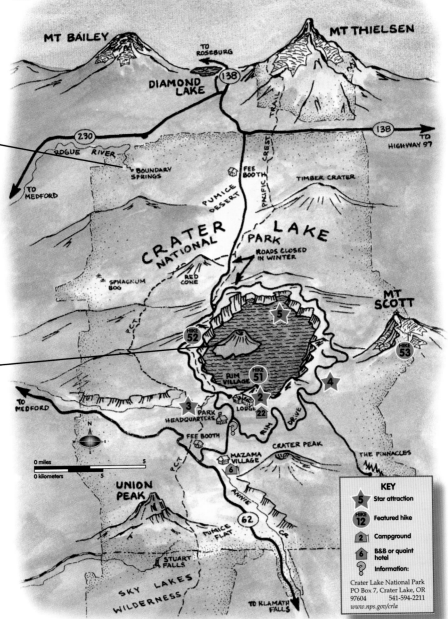

KEY

5 — Star attraction

HIKE 12 — Featured hike

2 — Campground

6 — B&B or quaint hotel

? — Information:

Crater Lake National Park
PO Box 7, Crater Lake, OR
97604   541-594-2211
www.nps.gov/crla

2 Crater Lake Lodge

Open late May to mid-October. Info:
541-830-8700 or www.craterlakelodges.com.

Crater Lake's grand old lodge was not always grand. Built between 1909 and 1915 for just $50,000, it originally opened with tarpaper on its outside walls and flimsy beaverboard between rooms. After years of neglect, it was slated for demolition in the 1980s, but a public outcry

Garfield Peak rises behind Crater Lake Lodge.

pushed the Park Service to spend $35 million renovating it instead.

The rebuilt lodge still has a rustic ambiance, with finely crafted stone walls and woodwork. All 71 of the guest rooms now have private baths. Reservations are essential in the elegant dining room, but you can order the same menu, without reservations, from the comfortable chairs of the Great Hall.

For less spendy fare, follow a scenic walk along the lake's rim to a gift shop and cafe at the other end of the Rim Village. Along the way you'll pass a Visitor

Cedar bark decorates the walls of the lodge's Great Hall.

Center where friendly rangers answer questions about the park.

GETTING THERE: From the Crater Lake turnoff on Highway 62, drive 7 miles north to the Rim Village and keep right for 0.3 mile to a parking turnaround.

3 Park Headquarters

Open daily 9am to 5pm (winter 10am to 4pm).

Open year-round, the Steel Information Center at park headquarters has helpful rangers, a 16-minute movie, and a selection of books and gifts. Two short walks begin here. A 0.6-mile path

The Information Center was built as a dormitory in 1936.

loops past the historic park headquarters buildings along Munson Creek. Across the road, a 0.4-mile trail leads to the 0.4-mile Castle Crest wildflower loop.

GETTING THERE: From the Crater Lake turnoff on Highway 62, drive 4 miles north.

Waiters offer to serve drinks and snacks to visitors in the rawhide rocking chairs on the lodge's scenic stone terrace.

Stepping stones on the Castle Crest loop path cross Munson Creek amid alpine wildflowers.

From Garfield Peak, the glowing blue of Crater Lake gapes below like a 4-cubic-mile pool from a high-dive tower.

HIKE 51 Garfield Peak

Moderate
3 miles round trip   970 feet elevation gain
Open mid-July through October
Use: hikers
Map: Crater Lake W and E (USGS)

One of the prettiest trails in Crater Lake National Park follows the lake's craggy rim from the historic lodge to the wildflowers and views of Garfield Peak. As on all park trails, pets and flower-picking are banned.

From the back porch of Crater Lake Lodge, head to the right on a paved pathway. Pavement soon yields to a broad trail through meadows of blue lupine, orange paintbrush, yellow groundsel, purple daisy-shaped fleabane, and pearly everlasting. The trail switchbacks up past cliffs of *breccia* — welded volcanic

Getting There

Drive to the far end of the Rim Village and park at Crater Lake Lodge.

WHITEBARK PINES

The bent, struggling trees you see at timberline on Cascade peaks are often whitebark pines. These five-needle pines grow only above 7000 feet. Their amazingly supple limbs allow them to bend, rather than break, in winter gales. The pine's seeds are a favorite food of the Clark's nutcracker *(see p162)*. By flying from peak to peak with the seeds, this bird helps the whitebark pines spread.

Whitebark pine branches can be tied in knots.

rubble from Mt. Mazama's early mountain-building eruptions.

Snow patches linger across the trail until August at the top, where the panorama stretches from the Three Sisters to Mount Shasta.

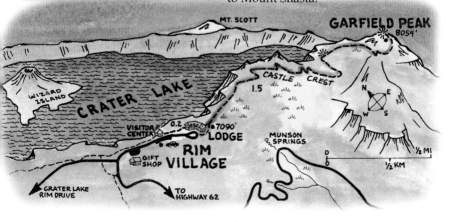

HIKE 52 The Watchman

Moderate
1.6 miles round trip   420 feet elevation gain
Open mid-July through October
Use: hikers
Map: Crater Lake West (USGS)

A popular but steepish trail on Crater Lake's rim climbs to The Watchman, where a lookout tower commands an eagle's-eye view across the amazingly blue lake to Wizard Island.

From the parking area, follow a paved sidewalk along the highway 100 yards to the actual trailhead. Look here for the fuzzy seedheads of western pasque flower and the blue trumpets of penstemon.

The broad hiking trail—actually a portion of the original 1917 rim road—traverses a snowfield that lingers until August. Turn left at a junction just beyond the snow and climb 0.4 mile to the summit tower, staffed each summer with friendly rangers who spot fires and answer hikers' questions.

Getting There

From Crater Lake's Rim Village, take the Rim Drive clockwise 4 miles to the trailhead, at a large viewpoint parking lot with a rail fence. If you're coming from Diamond Lake, turn right when you reach the Rim Drive junction and continue 2.2 miles to the parking lot.

The Watchman's lookout tower dates to 1931. The peak won its name in 1886 when surveyors set up here to track the location of a boat. The boat crew was testing the lake's depth with almost 2000 feet of piano wire—and still ran out.

Rim Drive

4

The spectacular 33-mile loop road around Crater Lake's rim passes dozens of viewpoint pullouts and several picnic areas. It's also the only access for the trails to Mount Scott *(see p210)*, Sun Notch *(see below)*, and Cleetwood Cove's boat tours *(p210)*. Plan at least half a day to complete the circuit.

Two bulldozers begin clearing the Rim Drive of snowdrifts in April, but the loop seldom opens before mid-July. Fresh snow closes it again after October.

GETTING THERE: Start either at Rim Village or at a junction near park headquarters.

Sunset lights up Cloudcap from the viewpoint at Sun Notch, one of many overlooks along Crater Lake's Rim Drive.

PHANTOM SHIP

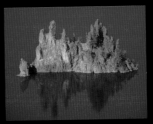

A small craggy island at the foot of Dutton Cliff *(below)*, Phantom Ship is the 400,000-year-old core of ancient Mount Mazama. This volcanic plug was so hard that it survived the explosion that created Crater Lake. To see the island's many moods *(at right)*, hike a 0.2 mile path from the Rim Drive to an overlook at Sun Notch.

5 Boat Tours

$23.50 for adults, $14 for children age 3-11. Boats leave Cleetwood Cove every 60 minutes between 10am and 4pm from early July to early September.

The switchbacking 1.1-mile trail from Rim Drive down to Cleetwood Cove's tour boat dock is the most popular path in Crater Lake National Park—and the only allowed route to the lake itself.

From the boat dock, ranger-guided tours sail to Wizard Island, where you can stop for a picnic and catch the next boat, if you like. Then the tour boats loop around the lake's smaller island, Phantom Ship. Pack a warm coat and possibly an umbrella, because the 60-seat boats have no roofs and tours last two hours.

Start at the ticket office in a trailer at the Cleetwood Cove Trailhead on Rim Drive. The office opens at 8:15am. On busy summer weekends, it's not a bad idea to arrive by 9am. To make sure hikers don't miss their boat, sales for each tour stop 40 minutes before it leaves. Pets are not permitted.

The only access to Crater Lake's popular boat tours is the switchbacking 1.1-mile Cleetwood Cove Trail.

GETTING THERE: From Crater Lake's Rim Village, take Rim Drive clockwise 10.6 miles to the trailhead. If you're coming from the park's north entrance off Highway 138, turn left along Rim Drive for 4.6 miles.

CRATER LAKE IN WINTER

Skiing around Crater Lake's snowed-under Rim Drive is a rugged 33-mile trek, best undertaken in March or April.

For an easier tour, join a ranger-led, 90-minute showshoe walk around Rim Village at 1pm any Saturday or Sunday from Thanksgiving to the end of March. The tours are free—even snowshoes are provided—but sign up first at park headquarters.

Skiing around Crater Lake is a three-day trek.

HIKE 53 Mount Scott

Difficult
5 miles round trip　1030 feet elevation gain
Open mid-July through October
Use: hikers
Map: Crater Lake East (USGS)

Mt. Scott's lookout tower is the only place where hikers can fit the whole sweep of Crater Lake into an average camera viewfinder. And although this is a major mountain—tenth tallest in Oregon's Cascades—the trail is so well-graded that even families with children sometimes tackle it.

The trail begins as an ancient road track

Getting There

From a junction near park headquarters, take Rim Drive 11 miles east to a parking pullout and trail sign on the right. If you're coming from Diamond Lake, turn left on Rim Drive for 13 miles to the trailhead.

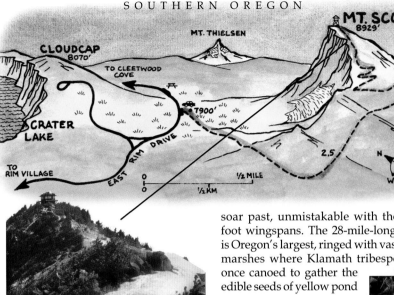

Expect to cross a few snow patches on the Mount Scott Trail until August.

amid whitebark pines. The trail's second mile switchbacks up a slope of pumice pebbles. Views open up to the south to Klamath Lake's flats and the white cone of Mount McLoughlin. The Crater Lake panorama from the summit is breathtaking, but so is the view north to Mount Thielsen and the distant Three Sisters.

The tower's view frames Crater Lake.

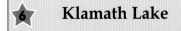

⑥ Klamath Lake

Half a million birds descend on Upper Klamath Lake's national wildlife refuge during the great migrations of April and October. Hundreds of bald eagles hunt ducks while strings of white pelicans

soar past, unmistakable with their 8-foot wingspans. The 28-mile-long lake is Oregon's largest, ringed with vast tule marshes where Klamath tribespeople once canoed to gather the edible seeds of yellow pond lilies.

The best way to see the lake is still by canoe, on 9.5 miles of marked water trails meandering through the marshes. If you have your own boat, use the free Malone Springs launch. Or start at the rustic Rocky Point Resort (see p229), where you can rent a canoe or kayak for $30 per half day or $40 per day.

Trail sign.

For maps and information, contact the refuge at 530-667-2231 or *www.klamathnwr.org.*

GETTING THERE: Drive east of Medford 6 miles on Highway 62 and turn right on Highway 140 toward Klamath Falls for 43.5 miles. (If you're coming from Klamath Falls, head west on Highway 140 for 25 miles.) Between mileposts 43 and 44, turn north on Westside Road for 3 miles to Rocky Point, or an additional 4 miles to Malone Springs.

Canoe trails explore Upper Klamath Lake's marshes.

HIKE 54 Seven Lakes Basin

Difficult
11.4-mile loop   900 feet elevation gain
Open early June through October
Use: hikers, horses
Map: Sky Lakes Wilderness (USFS)

The tourists who visit Crater Lake National Park rarely discover the Sky Lakes Wilderness, a lake-dotted mountain landscape immediately to the south. Sample the region with a hike to the Seven Lakes Basin—and perhaps an optional loop to a view at the summit of craggy Devils Peak.

Snow usually melts from the trail here by early July, but mosquitoes are thick from mid-July to mid-August, so it's best to visit later.

Black bear cub.

Also note several regulations: Backpackers must tent at least 100 feet from lakeshores and are encouraged to use the four signed camp areas. Equestrians are required to use the eight designated horse camps. Horses are not allowed within 200 feet of lakeshores (except on trails or at designated watering spots) and grazing is usually banned.

From the Sevenmile Trailhead, hop across a creek on rocks to find the start of the trail. Heavy horse use has left the path dusty in the dry lodgepole pine woods. After 1.8 miles, turn left on the Pacific Crest Trail in a cooler forest of mountain hemlock and Shasta red fir. The distant river roar audible in the canyon to the right is the Middle Fork Rogue, gushing from Ranger Spring.

Lake Alta is half a mile long, but surprisingly narrow.

Devils Peak rises above Cliff Lake, a good swimming lake.

At the 4.5-mile mark, fork to the right on the Seven Lakes Trail—the start of a delightful little loop tour. In another 0.3 mile, side trails branch off to the right to designated camp areas by Grass Lake. Take time for a detour to the right along Grass Lake's shore, where you'll see mountain views, fuzzy pink spirea blooms, blue dragonflies, and zillions of thumbnail-sized Cascade toads.

Then return to the Seven Lakes Trail and continue the loop tour 1 mile to a junction, passing huckleberry patches, wildflower meadows, and sandy-bottomed Middle Lake

Lakeshore sign.

along the way. At the junction, turn right 100 yards to find a short spur trail on the left to Cliff Lake. With a dramatic view of Devils Peak, a rockslide full of curious pikas, and a 30-foot diving cliff popular with daredevil swimmers, Cliff Lake is a popular destination. Heavy use has left much of its lakeshore closed for revegetation, but there's an approved camping area on a low ridge close by.

Day hikers will probably have to turn back here, completing the little loop tour by following signs back to the Pacific Crest Trail. Backpackers, however, can continue on a spectacular, larger loop to

△ From the summit of Devils Peak, the pools of the Seven Lakes Basin resemble pips on green dice.

◁ Devils Peak dominates the view from the reedy shore of Grass Lake.

the top of Devils Peak. From Cliff Lake, continue west on the Seven Lakes Trail 1.7 miles to a forested pass, turn left for 1.3 view-packed miles to a junction in another pass, turn left on the Pacific Crest Trail along a slope for 0.3 mile, and take a steep unmarked side trail to the left 0.2 mile to Devils Peak's summit. The view here encompasses most of the Sky Lakes Wilderness from Crater Lake to Mount McLoughlin. On the way down, fork left to find a different route to the PCT. Then go left on this well-graded trail to complete the loop.

Getting There

Start by driving to Fort Klamath, a hamlet near milepost 90 of Highway 62, east of Crater Lake 16 miles and 38 miles north of Klamath Falls. At an abandoned gas station in the middle of town, turn west on Nicholson Road. Follow this paved road absolutely straight 3.9 miles. Heeding "Sevenmile Trailhead" signs, fork left on gravel Road 3300 for 0.4 mile, and then fork to the right on Road 3334 for 5.6 miles to road's end. A Northwest Forest Pass is required to park here. The pass costs $5 per day or $30 per season.

WILDFLOWERS OF SOUTHERN OREGON

Although the Crater Lake area has many of the same alpine wildflowers as the Central Oregon Cascades (see p166) and Mount Hood (p75), the Siskiyou/Klamath range is a different world altogether, with a host of showy newcomers and botanical oddities.

BIGELOW SNEEZEWEED (*Helenium bigelovii*). These bulbous blooms grow near timberline.

OOKOW (*Dichelostemma congestum*) blooms in dry, grassy meadows from April to June.

FRITILLARY (*Fritillaria glauca*). This odd, nodding brown lily likes subalpine meadows.

ELEGANT BRODIAEA (*Brodiaea elegans*) blooms in dry grasslands in early summer.

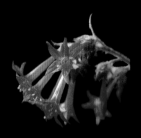

SCARLET GILIA or SKYROCKET (*Ipomopsis aggregata*) blooms on dry, open slopes all summer.

FAREWELL TO SPRING (*Clarkia amoena*). This Clarkia blooms in dry grasslands as summer arrives.

POND LILY (*Nuphar polysepala*). Indians gathered this water plant's seeds for flour or popcorn.

WILD ONION (*Allium falcifolium*). This pungent bloom hugs the ground in dry, rocky areas.

MONKSHOOD (*Aconitum columbianum*) blooms on head-high stalks in damp subalpine meadows.

INDIAN CARTWHEEL (*Silene hookeri*). Also called stringflower, this bloom likes dry rocky ground.

JACOBS LADDER (*Polemonium occidentale*), often pale blue, likes damp spots in mid-elevation woods.

HIKE 55 Natural Bridge

Easy
2.4-mile loop   300 feet elevation gain
Open mid-March through November
Use: hikers
Map: Union Creek (USGS)

The upper Rogue River briefly vanishes underground in the popular Union Creek resort area. The secret behind the river's stunt is an ancient lava tube, left by lava flows from Crater Lake's volcano several thousand years ago. The river now funnels through the tube like water through a hose.

From the Natural Bridge parking area, follow a paved path across the river on a long footbridge. Pavement ends in 0.2 mile at a railed viewpoint. Below, the frothing river appears to be sucked into solid rock. Water pressure in the 200-foot lava tube

Blacktail deer.

is so great that spray sputters out from cracks in the cave roof.

Although you could turn back here, a lovely, quiet portion of the Upper Rogue River Trail continues upstream. A mile beyond Natural Bridge turn right across the river on a footbridge over a churning chasm. At a T-junction with the Rogue Gorge Trail, turn right for 1.1 mile to your car.

A footbridge spans the Rogue a mile above Natural Bridge.

Getting There

Drive Crater Lake Highway 62 east from Medford 55 miles (or west of Union Creek 1.1 mile), and turn off the highway at a "Natural Bridge Campground" sign near milepost 55. Then keep left for 0.7 mile to the Natural Bridge parking area. A Northwest Forest Pass is required to park here. The pass costs $5 per day or $30 per season.

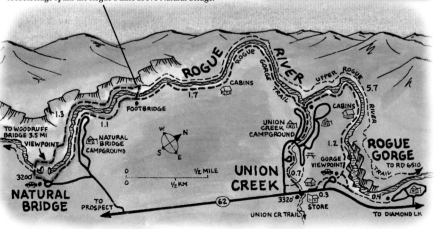

HIKE 56   Table Rocks

Moderate (Upper Table Rock)
2.8 miles round trip   720 feet elevation gain
Open all year
Use: hikers
Map: Sams Valley (USGS)

Moderate (Lower Table Rock)
5.4 miles round trip   780 feet elevation gain

These two U-shaped mesas near Medford are havens for hikers and endangered wildflowers. Visit in spring to catch the best flower displays and to avoid summer's merciless heat. Dogs, horses, fires, and flower picking are banned on both Table Rocks trails. Keep an eye out for triple-leafletted poison oak.

Each mesa has its own trail, but the

Getting There

To find the Upper Table Rock trailhead from Interstate 5 take Central Point exit 33 (just north of Medford), drive east on Biddle Road 1 mile, turn left on Table Rock Road for 5.2 miles to a curve, and turn right on Modoc Road for 1.5 miles to the trailhead parking lot on the left, just opposite an electric substation.

To find the Lower Table Rock trailhead instead, drive Table Rock Road north of Medford to milepost 10 and turn left on Wheeler Road 0.8 mile.

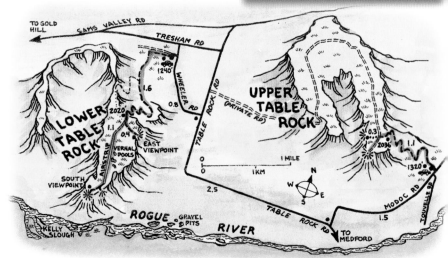

Lower Table Rock, overlooking the Rogue River near Medford, served as an Indian fortress in an 1853 war.

path to Upper Table Rock is shorter and slightly easier. This trail climbs through a scrub grassland ablaze with spring wildflowers. After 1.1 mile you emerge onto the table's amazingly flat, grassy summit. To find the best viewpoints, explore straight ahead or to the left.

The trail to Lower Table Rock, though longer and rockier, climbs through shadier woods to a viewpoint atop a taller cliff. Most of Lower Table Rock was dedicated as a nature preserve in 1979 by The Nature Conservancy, the non-profit organization that built the trail. After 1.6 miles, at the mesa's top, the path becomes an old road and then an ancient grassy airstrip. Hike a mile to the airstrip's far end for the best views.

Popular with rock climbers as well as hikers, Pilot Rock is a remnant of a 30-million-year-old lava flow that fractured into hexagonal columns.

HIKE 57 Pilot Rock

Moderate
1.2 miles round trip   810 feet elevation gain
Open late May through November
Use: hikers
Map: Siskiyou Pass (USGS)

Pioneers once looked to Pilot Rock to find the easiest pass across the Siskiyous from California to Oregon. Today Interstate 5 may miss this mountaintop Gibraltar by a few miles, but the landmark's sweeping viewpoints and dramatic columnar basalt cliffs are just a short hike away in the Cascade-Siskiyou National Monument.

Great-horned owl.

From the parking area, walk across the road to find the Pacific Crest Trail. This level path passes small incense cedars, Jeffrey pines, and blue elderberry bushes. After 300 yards, fork to the right on a wide, unmarked path toward Pilot Rock.

Mount Shasta from the base of Pilot Rock.

It's safest to declare victory at the base of the cliffs, where the view opens up across Shasta Valley to Mount Shasta. If you're willing to risk an unstable scramble route, veer left up a dusty scree slope at the cliff's base. Then go straight up a very steep gully, using hands and feet to climb past a tricky spot to the summit.

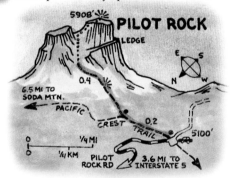

Getting There

Drive Interstate 5 to Mount Ashland exit 6 and follow a "Mount Ashland" pointer onto old Highway 99, paralleling the freeway south. After 0.7 mile go straight under the freeway, following the old highway another 1.2 miles. Beyond the Siskiyou summit 0.4 mile turn left onto Pilot Rock Road 40-2E-33. After 1 mile on this bumpy one-lane gravel road, ignore a Pacific Crest Trail crossing. After another 1 mile, keep right past an old rock quarry. When the road crests at the 2.8-mile mark, pull into an unmarked parking area on the right.

7 Ashland

This little university town has a Shakespearean theme, charming visitors with elegant parks, quaint shops, galleries, and world-class theater performances.

Start at the triangular **Plaza**, where a drinking fountain spouts **Lithia Water.** Piped from nearby springs as part of a 1914 spa scheme, this bubbly, bitter water contains lithium, sodium, calcium, iron, "and other healthful minerals."

A row of interesting, upscale shops faces the Plaza, but be sure to walk around to the back of this historic city block to see the open-air cafes and brewpub balconies lining Ashland Creek. An outdoor crafts fair sets up on the creekside promenade on summer weekends.

Then stroll upstream through **Lithia Park**, in a woodsy canyon with duck-filled lakes, playgrounds, flowerbeds, and the bouldery cascades of Ashland Creek. The park extends a mile upstream.

Next return to the Plaza and head south through **downtown** on East Main Street for window shopping. Favorite haunts of locals include Bloomsbury Books (290 E. Main) with its funky upstairs cafe, Pangea's Grill & Wraps, and the Northwest Nature Shop,

Downtown is dominated by the 7-story Lithia Hotel from 1925, restored as the posh Ashland Springs Hotel.

Ashland Creek powered the 1852 sawmill that led to the city's founding. Now the creek is the centerpiece of Lithia Park, with trails, playgrounds, and duck ponds.

A fountain in the triangular Plaza dispenses bitter Lithia water, piped from a naturally carbonated soda spring.

a block south of Main at 154 Oak Street.

GETTING THERE: From Interstate 5, take Ashland exit 14 or 19 and follow signs 2.5 miles to downtown.

SHAKESPEAREAN FESTIVAL

Ashland college professor Angus Bowmer converted an abandoned lecture hall into a replica of Shakespeare's open-air Globe theater in 1935, launching a tradition of performing plays beside Lithia Park.

Today Ashland's Shakespearean Festival has blossomed into a world-class theater event, performing a

Ashland's open-air Elizabethan Stage is modeled on the Globe, Shakespeare's London theater.

dozen plays each year, including world premieres by modern playwrights. The 600-seat Bowmer Theatre and the 300-seat New Theatre host plays from late February to early November. The 1200-seat, open-air Elizabethan Stage (*above*) operates on summer evenings and cancels in case of rain.

Banners and Tudor architecture grace Ashland streets.

Tickets run $22-72. Sell-outs are common, so make reservations well in advance at 541-482-4331.

Check *www.osfashland.org* for the current play list, or drop by the box office at 15 South Pioneer Street, one block south of the Plaza. A tip if you can't get reservations: When the box office opens at 9:30am, unclaimed tickets for that day's plays are offered for sale.

Catering to the theater crowds, Ashland has more bed & breakfast inns than any other Oregon city (*see pp228-229*).

8 Mount Ashland

Highest peak in the Siskiyous, 7531-foot Mount Ashland is a popular center for summer hiking and winter skiing, just ten miles from Interstate 5.

To see the peak's wildflowers, hike a fairly level 3.4-mile segment of the Pacific Crest Trail through alpine meadows from Road 20 to a picnic shelter at Grouse Gap. The trail is hikable from mid-June to mid-November.

The Mount Ashland Ski & Snowboard Resort, with four   chairlifts

Patches of snow remain on Mount Ashland in June, as seen from the ski area's lodge.

and 23 runs, is open from the end of November to the start of April, if there's enough snow. Tickets run about $39 for adults and $31 for children age 7 to 17.

GETTING THERE: Drive Interstate 5 south of Ashland 10 miles and take Mount Ashland exit 6. Following "Mt. Ashland Ski Area" pointers, parallel the freeway for 0.7 mile and turn right on Mount Ashland Road 20. After 7.2 paved miles (400 yards beyond milepost 7) park at a pullout on the right for the Pacific Crest Trail—or continue 2.1 miles to the ski area.

The Pacific Crest Trail skirts Mount Ashland through alpine wildflower meadows.

9 Jacksonville

This well-preserved gold mining boomtown from the 1800s is more than just a living museum; it's an active cultural center with art galleries, a first-rate summer music festival, and miles of hiking trails through recently-acquired parklands.

Miners on their way to California's more famous Gold Rush discovered gold here in Rich Gulch in 1852. The

tent-and-plank town that sprang up was briefly Oregon's largest. After the easy gold was panned out, giant hydraulic hoses washed away acres of land in search of gold dust. Some locals later planted fruit orchards.

When the new railroad line through Southern Oregon bypassed Jacksonville in favor of Medford in 1886, however, the city slipped into a kind of suspended animation, lacking the money to build or even to tear down buildings. The entire city was declared a historic landmark

Banker Cornelius Beekman built this house in 1873. It's open as a museum in summer.

The 1860 McCully House is an upscale restaurant and inn.

in the 1960s, and restoration began.

For a historic walking tour, start at an 1891 railroad depot converted to a visitor center on Oregon and C Streets. Follow a trail across California Street to the **Britt Music Festival** gardens, where pioneer photographer Peter Britt's home once stood. On summer evenings, an outdoor stage here hosts the festival's classical and popular music concerts.

From the Britt garden a path up Jackson Creek is the start of a 2-mile loop hike through the **Jacksonville Woodlands**, visiting a knoll-top panorama

△ The oldest church in Southern Oregon, this 1854 building served both Methodists and Episcopalians.

◁ The 1881 Presbyterian Church has elegant Victorian Gothic lines.

Beneath an oak at the summit of the Jacksonville Woodlands trail system, a bench overlooks the historic town.

and the historic Rich Gulch mining area.

For a shorter tour of the city, return to California Street and head east into town. For the area's best coffee, detour half a block up Oregon Street to the **Good Bean Coffee Company**. For reasonably priced food and local brew, don't miss the restored 1856 **Bella Union Saloon** on California Street between Oregon and Third Streets.

Then follow the dotted route shown on the map to visit the clapboard 1860 McCully House, the Victorian Gothic 1881 Presbyterian Church, the 1883 county courthouse (now serving as the fascinating **Jacksonville Museum**), and rival Protestant and Catholic churches from the 1850s.

GETTING THERE: From Interstate 5, take Medford exit 30 and follow signs 7 miles to Jacksonville on Highway 238. At a "Britt Parking" sign opposite the Jacksonville Museum, turn right on C Street for four blocks to its end at a visitor center and parking lot.

◁ Jacksonville's cemetery, dating to the 1850s, has separate plots for Catholics, Jews, Germans, Masons, and Oddfellows. Pick up a cemetery tour brochure at the visitor center.

The 1856 Bella Union Saloon (at left) joins a row of porched shops along California Street in the historic downtown.

HIKE 58 Rogue River

Moderate (to Whisky Creek)
7 miles round trip   300 feet elevation gain
Open all year
Use: hikers
Map: Wild Rogue Wilderness (USFS)

Difficult (entire trail, with shuttle)
40 miles one way   3800 feet elevation gain

At times the irascible Rogue River idles along in lazy green pools, but elsewhere it's misty mayhem, plunging over Rainie Falls or boiling through Mule Creek Canyon's Coffeepot. Trekkers who trace the entire 40-mile Rogue River Trail can either tent or stay in rustic lodges. If you're just out for a day hike, sample the eastern section of the famous trail with a 3.5-mile jaunt to Whisky Creek.

Although the trail is open all year, avoid August's blazing heat and winter's cold rains. Backpackers should bring stoves because campfires are allowed within 400 feet of the river only if they're kept in firepans. Wear good boots because the trail is rough in spots, and wear long pants because of occasional poison oak along the trail. To discourage nosy black bears, hang food

Flora Dell Falls plunges 20 feet into a swimmable pool.

The Rogue River Trail crests a cliff at Inspiration Point.

at least 10 feet high in a tree at night.

From the trailhead at Grave Creek the path climbs 0.2 mile to an overlook of Grave Creek Rapids, a rock-walled chute. After 1.8 miles a short fork to the left leads to the shore beside Rainie Falls. Continue on the main trail 1.6 miles, pass a cluster of campsites at a beach, and then cross Whisky Creek on a bridge. Here a spur to the right leads up to a historic log cabin with mining

The 1903 Rogue River Ranch has been restored as a ranching museum.

traverses rocky slopes high above the river. Attractions down the trail include Horseshoe Bend's dramatic river loop, Western author Zane Grey's (private) log cabin at Winkle Bar, and the restored 1903 Rogue River Ranch museum at Marial. It's possible to drive to Marial on a narrow, winding gravel road, but the drive to the next trailhead

The free Whisky Creek Cabin museum is an 1880 gold miner's house.

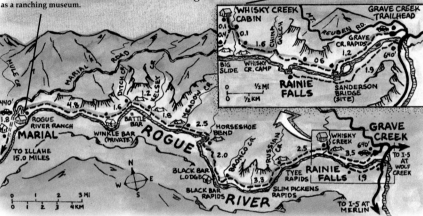

memorabilia.

Trekkers continuing downstream will find the Rogue River Trail mostly

Getting There

To find the eastern trailhead at the Grave Creek bridge, take Interstate 5 north of Grants Pass 18 miles (or south of Roseburg 48 miles) to Wolf Creek exit 76, drive half a mile to the Wolf Creek Tavern, turn off into town two blocks, go under a railroad overpass, turn left, and follow this paved road 15 miles. Just before the Grave Creek bridge, turn right to a boat ramp and trail parking area. A Northwest Forest Pass is required to park at all trailheads. The pass costs $5 per day or $30 per season.

To shuttle a car to the western trailhead at Illahe, drive south from Grave Creek 8 miles to Galice, turn right on paved Bear Camp Road 23 for 31 miles, turn right along the Rogue River on Road 33 for 2 miles to a bridge, and fork to the right toward Illahe on a paved, one-lane road 3.5 miles to a spur on the right.

at Illahe follows paved roads, so most long-range hikers shuttle cars there.

If you're hiking past Marial, keep left on a dirt road 1.8 miles to find the final, 15-mile section of the Rogue River Trail. This path climbs 0.7 mile to a spectacular clifftop at Inspiration Point. In another 1.4 miles the trail crosses Blossom Bar Creek, with campsites and a swimmable creek pool near Blossom Bar Rapids.

In another mile a fork to the left leads to Paradise Lodge. Another 2.9 miles

Hikers pass a gnarled tree near Inspiration Point.

downstream is Brushy Bar, a forested plain with a large campground. In the next 2.8 miles the trail skirts the scenic cliffs of Solitude Bar and reaches Clay Hill Lodge. Then it's 6 miles to the Illahe trailhead, passing lovely 20-foot Flora Dell Falls along the way.

Cougars are rarely seen, and have killed no one in Oregon's history.

Commercial lodges along the route charge about $120 per person per night, including meals. Study the map and then reserve well in advance at your choice of Black Bar Lodge (541-479-6507), Marial Lodge (541-474-2057), Paradise Lodge (541-247-6968), or Clay Hill Lodge (503-859-3772). Note that Black Bar Lodge is across the river, so you must arrange a time for pickup by boat. Jet boat connections to Paradise Bar and Clay Hill Lodge can be arranged from Gold Beach or Foster Bar by calling Rogue River Mail Boats (800-458-3511) or Jerry's Rogue Jets (800-451-3645).

RAFTING THE ROGUE

The 40-mile stretch of Rogue River between Grave Creek and Illahe is Oregon's most famous and popular three-day whitewater trip.

Whitewater boaters have hardly left the launch before they hit the spray of Grave Creek Rapids. Half an hour later the increasing roar of 15-foot-tall Rainie Falls warns boaters to portage. On the second day (or third, for slower drifters), boats accelerate toward Mule Creek Canyon, a chasm so narrow and turbulent that boats can span the walls sideways or spin for minutes in the Coffeepot's maelstrom. A mile beyond is Blossom Bar's treacherous boulder field.

The Coffeepot spins boats in Mule Creek Canyon.

Whitewater raft.

Expect to pay $500-1000 per person for a commercially guided Rogue River trip with overnight stays at private lodges. If you'd rather go on your own, you'll need a permit during the restricted season from May 15 to October 15. For information, contact the BLM's Smullin Visitor Center at Rand (541-479-3735). The permits are hard to get, because only 120 are issued for each day, chosen by lottery.

△ Blossom Bar's boulder field resembles a giant pinball machine for whitewater boaters.
A whitewater raft drifts through Mule Creek Canyon's chasm. ▷

10 Oregon Caves

Poet Joaquin Miller's praise of the "great Marble Halls of Oregon" helped win National Monument status for Oregon Caves in 1909. Visitors today can join a guided tour for $7.50 ($5 for children under 17), exploring narrow passageways and stairs to rooms of cave formations.

Vanilla leaf carpets the forest floor outside the caves.

A forest trail loops to a giant Douglas fir.

The caves' marble began as a tropical island reef in the Pacific Ocean. When the land rose and the caves drained, dripping water gradually deposited calcite inside.

Early entrepreneurs damaged the cave by encouraging visitors to break off stalactites as samples and sign their names on the walls. The National Park Service now urges visitors not to touch anything in the cave. Lighting is dim to discourage the algae that grows near artificial lights.

From the parking area, walk up the road 0.2 mile to the gift shop and cave entrance on the left. Cave tours leave every 15 minutes from 9am to 6:30pm in summer, and on the hour from 10am to 4pm in spring and fall. There are no tours between December 1 and mid-March. You don't need a flashlight, but because it averages 41° F in the cave year-round, you'll want warm clothes.

The 75-minute tour climbs 0.3 mile through the cave to an upper exit. From there the quickest return route is a 0.3-mile trail to the right. For a free hike above ground try the 3.4-mile Big Tree Loop to one of Oregon's largest Douglas firs. Pets are banned on all park trails.

GETTING THERE: Take Highway 199 south from Grants Pass 29 to Cave Junction and follow "Oregon Caves" pointers east on Highway 46 for 20 miles to a turnaround.

The Chateau, a 1934 lodge, is faced with shaggy incense cedar bark.

The half-mile cave tour includes 500 stairsteps. Children must be at least 42 inches tall and be able to climb a set of test stairs to be allowed to join a tour.

Elijah Davidson discovered the Oregon Caves in 1874 when his dog chased a bear into the entrance.

WHERE TO STAY

Campgrounds *(map p197)*

	Campsites	Water	Showers	Flush Toilet	Fee
10 **ASPEN POINT.** Swim or waterski at this camp at Lake of the Woods, open late May through September. Drive Highway 140 east of Medford 50 miles or west of Klamath Falls 30 miles. Reservations: 877-444-6777. **Mount McLoughlin from Lake of the Woods.** ▷	61	●		●	$$
9 **COLLIER STATE PARK.** An outdoor museum of logging and log cabins adjoins this riverside camp on Highway 97, north of Klamath Falls 30 miles or south of Bend 108 miles. Open April through October.	68	●	●	●	$$
4 **DIAMOND LAKE.** Strung along almost two miles of shore at a large mountain lake *(see p202)*, this popular camp can be noisy and smoky. Open mid-May to the end of October. Reservations: 877-444-6777.	240	●	●	●	$$
11 **DOE POINT.** On Fish Lake (fishing, resort, boat rentals) a mile from the Pacific Crest Trail, this camp is open mid-May to late September. Drive Highway 140 east of Medford 35 miles or west of Klamath Falls 40 miles.	30	●		●	$$
3 **EAGLE ROCK.** A rock pillar towers above this North Umpqua River campground, open late May to late September. Drive Highway 138 east of Roseburg toward Diamond Lake 51 miles.	25	●			$
15 **GRAYBACK.** This camp on a woodsy creek has a footbridge to a nature trail. From Cave Junction drive 12 miles east toward Oregon Caves. Open mid-May to mid-September. Reservations: 541-592-3311.	39	●		●	$
2 **HORSESHOE BEND.** In a North Umpqua River loop 48 miles east of Roseburg on Highway 138, this camp is open late May through September.	24	●		●	$$
6 **MAZAMA.** Just inside the south entrance of Crater Lake National Park *(see map p205)*, this is the closest camp to the famous lake. Adjacent are a nature trail, store, and laundry. Open June to early October.	200	●	●	●	$$
13 **MOUNT ASHLAND.** Carry your tent a few feet to campsites with views across alpine meadows to Mount Shasta. Open June through October. Drive half a mile past the Mount Ashland ski area *(see p219)*.	6				free
8 **NATURAL BRIDGE.** Along the upper Rogue River, this wooded camp is on the loop trail to the river's natural bridge *(see p215)*. Open May through October.	17				$

WHERE TO STAY

Campgrounds (map p197)

		Campsites	Water	Showers	Flush Toilet	Fee
12	**STEWART STATE PARK.** On Lost Creek Reservoir (swimming, waterskiing, 19-mile hiker/biker loop trail), this park is open March through October. From Medford, drive Highway 62 east 34 miles.	201	●	●	●	$$
1	**SUSAN CREEK.** This camp along the North Umpqua River has a trail that leads to Susan Creek Falls (see p198). Open May to early October.	31	●	●	●	$$
7	**UNION CREEK.** In an old-growth forest where Union Creek meets the upper Rogue River, this camp has miles of beautiful riverbank trails (see map, p215). Winter closure dates vary depending on snow.	78	●			$
14	**VALLEY OF THE ROGUE.** Noisy but conveniently situated between Interstate 5 and the Rogue River, this state park halfway between Medford and Grants Pass has 6 yurts ($29). Reservations: 800-452-5687.	167	●	●	●	$$
5	**THIELSEN VIEW.** This is by far the quietest and prettiest camp at popular Diamond Lake, amid pines on the less-visited west shore (see map, p202). Open mid-May to mid-October.	60	●			$

Thielsen View Campground's view. ▷

B&Bs and Quaint Hotels (map p197)

		Rooms	Private bath	Cont. breakfast	Full breakfast	Rate range
8	**BAYBERRY INN.** Walk four blocks to theaters from this 1925 Craftsman-style home decorated with a country English theme at 438 N. Main Street, Ashland, OR 97520. Info: 800-795-1252 or www.bayberryinn.com.	8	●		●	$100-225
9	**COLONEL SILSBY'S.** This bed & breakfast in an 1896 Victorian home is a block from downtown Ashland at 111 Third Street. Three rooms have Jacuzzis and fireplaces. Info: 800-927-3070 or www.silsbysinn.com.	6	●		●	$75-169
10	**COOLIDGE HOUSE.** Afternoon tea is served at this bed & breakfast in an 1875 Italianate home (see photo p219) two blocks from Ashland theaters at 137 N. Main Street. Info: 800-655-5522 or www.coolidgehouse.com.	6	●		●	$95-195
11	**COWSLIP'S BELLE.** Two blocks from Ashland theaters, this 1913 bungalow and carriage house is a bed & breakfast inn at 159 N. Main Street, Ashland, OR 97520. Info: 800-888-6819 or www.cowslip.com.	5	●		●	$130-210
22	**CRATER LAKE LODGE.** Lavishly renovated, this grand old National Park lodge on Crater Lake's scenic rim (see p206) is open from late May to mid-October. Info: 541-830-8700 or www.craterlakelodges.com.	71	●			$129-248
17	**FISH LAKE RESORT.** This 1940s fishing resort near the Cascade crest has boat rentals, a tiny store, a cafe, and 11 cabins with water and electricity. Open all year despite snow. Pets are $15 extra. Drive Highway 140 to milepost 30, east of Medford 35 miles or west of Klamath Falls 38 miles. Info: 541-949-8500 or www.fishlakeresort.net.	11	7			$60-200
12	**IRIS INN.** This 1905 Victorian home with antiques and gardens has been a bed & breakfast inn since 1982. It's four blocks from Ashland theaters at 59 Manzanita Street, Ashland, OR 97520. Info: 800-460-7650 or www.irisinnbb.com.	5	●		●	$80-155
2	**IVY HOUSE.** Expect a traditional English breakfast at this inn, in a quiet historic district of Grants Pass, in a 1908 brick arts-and-crafts-style home at 139 SW "I" Street, Grants Pass, OR 97526. Info: 541-474-7363.	5	1		●	$55-80
5	**JACKSONVILLE INN.** This 1861 brick inn in the middle of historic Jacksonville has eight rooms, four honeymoon cottages with Jacuzzis, and a multi-star restaurant. Complimentary wine-tasting upon arrival. Located at 175 E. California St., Jacksonville, OR 97530. Info: 800-321-9344 or www.jacksonvilleinn.com.	12	●		●	$145-395

The Iris Inn in Ashland. ▷

WHERE TO STAY

B&Bs and Quaint Hotels (map p197)

	Rooms	Private bath	Cont. breakfast	Full breakfast	Rate range
18 LAKE OF THE WOODS RESORT. This old-timey mountain lodge has 26 rustic cabins, most with kitchenettes. Drive Highway 140 east of Medford 50 miles or west of Klamath Falls 30 miles. Info: 866-201-4194 or *www.lakeofthewoodsresort.com*.	26	●			$69-269
13 McCALL HOUSE. This 1883 Italianate manor (with original stained glass) and an adjacent carriage house serve as a bed & breakfast inn a block from downtown Ashland at 153 Oak Street. Closed in January. Info: 800-808-9749 or *www.mccallhouse.com*.	10	●		●	$100-225
6 McCULLY HOUSE. The oldest Oregon home serving as an inn, this 1860 Gothic revival mansion (*see p220*) is a bed & breakfast and restaurant, surrounded by rose gardens at 240 E. California Street, Jacksonville, OR 97530. Info: 800-367-1942 or *www.mccullycountryhouseinn.com*.	3	●			$135
15 OAK HILL. Near Southern Oregon University 2 miles from downtown Ashland (2190 Siskiyou Blvd), this inn offers a front porch swing and breakfast on a garden deck. Info: 888-482-1554 or *www.oakhillbb.com*.	6	●		●	$89-169
3 OREGON CAVES LODGE. The Chateau, the grand 1934 lodge of Oregon Caves National Monument (*see p226*), includes a restaurant, gift shop, and classic 1930s soda fountain. Two-bedroom suites run $125-135. Open May 1 to October 1. Info: 541-592-3400 or *www.southwestoregon.com*.	23	●	●		$80-125
7 ORTH HOUSE. Also known as the Teddy Bear Inn, this 1880 Italianate villa in historic Jacksonville is decorated with Victorian antiques and teddy bears. Located at 105 W. Main Street, Jacksonville, OR 97530. Info: 800-700-7301 or *www.orthbnb.com*.	3	●		●	$110-170

The Orth House Bed & Breakfast. ▷

	Rooms	Private bath	Cont. breakfast	Full breakfast	Rate range
20 PROSPECT HISTORICAL HOTEL. Teddy Roosevelt stayed in this 1889 stagecoach inn en route to Crater Lake. Decorated with period antiques, it still makes a nice stop in the hamlet of Prospect, 45 miles east of Medford on Highway 62. Info: 800-944-6490 or *www.prospecthotel.com*.	10	●		●	$85-150

19 ROCKY POINT RESORT. This rustic, low-key resort on Upper Klamath Lake (*see p211*) has a dock, tiny store, restaurant, and lodge, open April to November. Four cabins that sleep 2-6 people run $110-150. Pets are $2 extra. Info: 541-356-2287 or *rockypointoregon.com*.

◁ Rocky Point's restaurant overlooks the lake.

	Rooms	Private bath	Cont. breakfast	Full breakfast	Rate range
ROCKY POINT RESORT	5	●			$75
4 UNDER THE GREENWOOD TREE. This 1862 farmhouse amid orchards between Medford and historic Jacksonville serves as a quiet bed & breakfast inn, at 3045 Bellinger Lane, Medford, OR 97501. Info: 541-776-0000 or *www.greenwoodtree.com*.	5	●		●	$120-140
21 UNION CREEK RESORT. A waystation on the road to Crater Lake since the 1920s (*see map, p215*), this hamlet includes a lodge, a rustic store, a cafe, and 23 cabins. Cabins that sleep 2-6 run $70-225. Open all year, despite heavy winter snow. Info: 866-560-3565 or *www.unioncreekoregon.com*.	9				$48-58
14 WINCHESTER COUNTRY INN. This 1983 bed & breakfast with Victorian styling is a block from downtown Ashland at 35 S. Second Street. Info: 800-972-4991 or *www.winchesterinn.com*.	19	●		●	$129-239
1 WOLF CREEK INN. Oregon State Parks restored this 1883 stagecoach tavern, now open as an inn and restaurant in Wolf Creek, 18 miles north of Grants Pass at Interstate 5 exit 76. Info: 541-866-2474 or *www.rogueweb.com/wolfcreekinn*.	9	●		●	$70-107

Wolf Creek Inn. ▷

	Rooms	Private bath	Cont. breakfast	Full breakfast	Rate range
16 WOODS HOUSE. This 1908 bed & breakfast inn is 5 blocks from Ashland's theaters at 333 N. Main Street. Info: 800-435-8260 or *www.woodshouse.com*.	6	●		●	$125-140

NORTHEAST OREGON

Echoes of the Old West linger here, from gold rush ghost towns to the Wallowa's alps.

When Oregon Trail pioneers drove their covered wagons into Northeast Oregon in the 1840s, many were outraged. Ahead lay hundreds of miles of sagebrush and mountains — hardly the green Eden they had hoped to find in Oregon.

In the 1850s the US Army actually forbade pioneers from settling in the eastern half of the state, deeming it an untamable land suitable only for Indians.

That policy changed in 1862, when gold strikes in the Blue Mountains sent tens of thousands of men storming into Northeast Oregon. For a time, the boomtowns of Auburn and Canyon City became the largest cities in the state.

When the gold rush faded, some miners decided the landscape here was more attractive than they had first thought. Beyond the sagebrush slopes were well-watered valleys of grass for cattle and well-timbered mountains with sparkling alpine lakes and snowpeaks.

To make room for ranchers and settlers the Army rounded up or drove out the native tribes in the 1870s, including the Nez Perce under Chief Joseph. Completion of a transcontinental railroad across Northeast Oregon in the 1880s brought a flush of prosperity.

But then time seemed to stand still — and this too is part of the region's charm. Today the population of some Eastern Oregon counties is actually lower than it was a century ago. A stroll through the ghost town of Granite or a hike through the Wallowa Mountains is a walk back to a time when the American West was wild and young.

◁ Pine Lakes in the southern Wallowa Mountains.   △ Gold rush mural on a building in downtown Canyon City.

Exploring
NORTHEAST OREGON

Do not judge this vast landscape by the sagebrush along Interstate 84! Instead explore a backroad along the John Day River past painted hills and basalt gorges to a green valley of ranches. Or drive a paved loop road around the craggy Wallowa Mountains, with a side trip to the mile-deep chasm of Hells Canyon. Or prowl about the impressive Elkhorn Range to find the ghost towns and railroads of gold rush days.

John Day Fossil Beds
This National Monument showcases colorful badlands with fossils ranging from tortoises to camels. The monument includes three separate areas 50 miles apart *(see pp234-35)*.

Strawberry Mountain

With snowy peaks and mountain lakes, the Strawberry Mountain Wilderness *(see p236)* seems like a chunk of the Canadian Rockies dropped in the midst of Eastern Oregon's ranchlands. One of the prettiest drives in Oregon traces the John Day River through Picture Gorge to the historic towns of John Day and Canyon City *(see p238)* at the foot of Strawberry Mountain.

Baker City
Over 100 restored buildings line the streets of Baker City's turn-of-the-century downtown *(see p240)*, including the turreted Geiser Grand Hotel, built in 1889 as the grandest hostelry between Portland and Salt Lake City.

KEY

5   Star attraction

HIKE 12   Featured hike

2   Campground

6   B&B or quaint hotel

?   Information:

Eastern Oregon Visitors Association
PO Box 1087
Baker City, OR 97814
800-332-1843
www.eova.com

Wallowa Mountains Visitor Center
88401 Highway 82
Enterprise, OR 97828
541-426-4978
www.fs.fed.us/r6/w-w

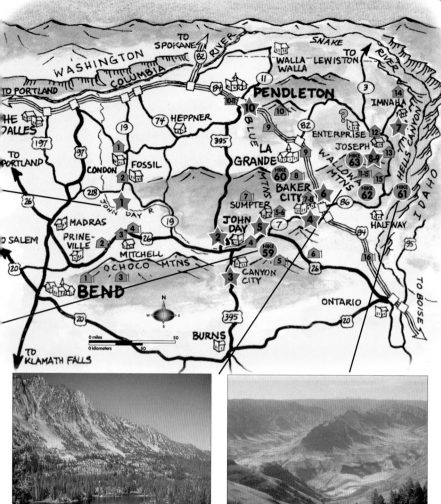

Wallowa Mountains

The Wallowas have been called America's Little Switzerland because of their alp-like peaks and mountain lakes (above, Douglas Lake). Trails into the Eagle Cap Wilderness explore the range (pp246-47, 252-54), while Wallowa Lake (p251) and Joseph (p250) offer dramatic views.

Hells Canyon

The deepest river gorge in the United States, Hells Canyon is bigger than the Grand Canyon, but less famous because it is less accessible. One paved road visits a dam at the canyon's lower end (see p245), and a long gravel road climbs to the Hat Point lookout on the canyon rim (see p248).

John Day Fossil Beds

More than 50 miles of highway separate the three parts of the John Day Fossil Beds National Monument, but each area has a different story to tell.

Start your tour at the **Clarno Unit**. A 0.3-mile trail from the picnic area parallels the highway to a message board. From there, head uphill to the

Fossilized leaf in a trailside boulder.

right on the **Trail of the Fossils**, a 0.2-mile loop lined with boulders that fell from the rimrock far above. The boulders are riddled with leaf and branch fossils from an ancient subtropical forest.

A different short trail from the message board climbs uphill to the left for 0.2 mile to **Clarno Arch**, a ten-foot span carved into the rimrock cliff by water.

To find the next area of the National Monument, drive 19 miles east to Fossil and turn right on Highway 19 for 59 miles. Between mileposts 118 and 119, turn left to the **Blue Basin** parking lot.

From here the **Island in Time Trail** ambles 0.6 mile up a green creekbed into an eerie badlands canyon of fluted green volcanic ash *(see photo, p232)*. Exhibits by

Footprints last for years in the soft soil of the Painted Cove Trail, so it's important to stay on the trail.

the trail display replicas of tortoise and saber-tooth-cat-like fossils discovered in the eroding ash.

Next drive south on Highway 19 another 3.2 miles to see the displays at the **National Monument's visitor center**, in a historic farmhouse at Sheep Rock.

Then drive another 2.2 miles to the layered lava canyon of **Picture Gorge**, and turn right on Highway 26 for 38 miles. Beyond Mitchell 4 miles (between mileposts 62 and 63), turn right on Burnt Ranch Road at a sign for the Painted Hills. After 6 miles, turn

The rounded, colorfully striped Painted Hills began as ash that erupted from the ancestral Cascades volcanoes 33 million years ago and settled in a vast lake. The resulting yellow clay was colored by traces of iron and manganese.

The Clarno Unit's rimrock cliff is riddled with fossils that were trapped in a mud flow 44 million years go.

beside the school's football field is full of **leaf fossils**, and is open to amateur collectors for free.

GETTING THERE: To find the Clarno Unit from Portland, drive Interstate 84 east beyond The Dalles 16 miles to Biggs exit 104, turn south on Highway 97 for 59 miles to Shaniko, and then turn left for 26 miles on Highway 218 through Antelope and Clarno. Beyond the John Day River bridge 3.3 miles, park in a picnic area on the left. To drive here from Bend, take Highway 97 north 61 miles to Willowdale, fork right to Antelope 12 miles, and keep right on Highway 218 another 16 miles to the picnic area on the left.

The county courthouse in the town of Fossil.

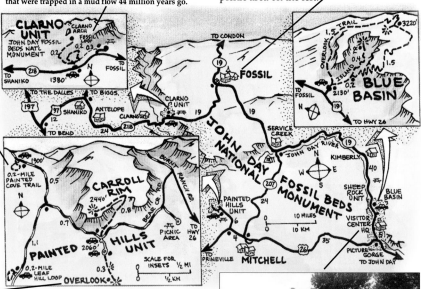

left on Bear Creek Road for 1.2 miles, mostly on gravel, and then turn left 0.2 mile to the **Painted Hills Overlook** parking area.

From here, stroll out the 0.3-mile path to a photogenic viewpoint. Then drive another 1.2 miles to the **Painted Cove Trail**, a 0.2-mile loop with a boardwalk that crosses the colorful claystone.

Note that visitors are not permitted to dig for fossils in the National Monument. But here's a tip: When you drive through the city of Fossil, stop by the town's high school. The shaley hillside

Behind the National Monument's visitor center you'll find a rustic fossil laboratory and a view of Sheep Rock.

HIKE 59 Strawberry Lake

Moderate (around the lake)
4-mile loop   550 feet elevation gain
Open July to mid-November
Use: hikers, horses
Map: Strawberry Mtn Wilderness (USFS)

With alpine lakes, snowy crags, and waterfalls, the Strawberry Mountain Wilderness seems like a chunk of the Canadian Rockies dropped onto the sagebrush plains of Eastern Oregon. For a picture-postcard view of this surprising range, hike 1.3 miles to Strawberry Lake. The trail begins at Strawberry Campground by a message board at the far end of the parking area.

Two-tailed swallowtail butterfly.

Getting There

Drive Highway 26 to Prairie City (13 miles east of John Day). Turn south in the middle of Prairie City, following a pointer for Depot Park and Strawberry Lake. After 0.4 mile you'll reach a stop sign at a T-shaped junction. Turn left for two blocks, and then turn right at a "Strawberry Campground" arrow onto Bridge Street, which becomes County Road 60 and eventually Forest Road 6001. Continue a total of 10.7 miles (the last 7.6 on gravel) to road's end at Strawberry Campground. A campsite here costs about $6, but hikers park free.

Keep right at all junctions to the edge of Strawberry Lake at the 1.3-mile mark. Although the main trail turns left here, you'll get better views if you turn right on a smaller path around the quieter,

Rabbit Ears is the remnant of an ancient volcanic plug on the ridge above Little Strawberry Lake.

Strawberry Falls cascades 60 feet onto mossy boulders. Strawberry Lake. ▷

west side of the lake.

This path crosses the lake's underground outlet. Strawberry Lake formed when giant landslides dammed the valley. The lake now drains down a whirlpool, leaving the outlet "creek" gurgling beneath the landslide's rocks.

For a short hike, simply loop counterclockwise around the lake and head back to your car. For a longer trip, hike to the far end of Strawberry Lake, turn uphill on a steep, unmarked side path 50 yards and then turn right on a larger trail that climbs to Strawberry Falls. From the top of the falls, trails lead left to Little Strawberry Lake and right to the summit of Strawberry Mountain itself.

Inside the Kam Wah Chung Museum are an altar, apothecary, and opium den used by pioneer Chinese.

⭐2 John Day

In downtown John Day, stop for a look at the **John Day Historic Church,** with

its white wooden steeple and Carpenter Gothic frills. On the west edge of town, the **City Park** has the county's only public swimming pool (an inexpensive treat on a hot summer day) and the fascinating Kam Wah Chung Museum.

The **Kam Wah Chung Museum** was built by Chinese gold miners in the late 1860s as a combination pharmacy, cultural center, temple, opium den, and fortress. Now the oldest building in John Day, this two-story stone structure is filled with artifacts

The John Day Historic Church.

The Kam Wah Chung Museum preserves the gold-rush-era store of a pioneer Chinese doctor.

from the culture of pioneer Chinese immigrants. It's open from May through October, Monday through Saturday 9am-12noon and 1pm-5pm, and Sunday from 1pm-5pm. Admission runs $1.50 to $3.

GETTING THERE: Drive Highway 26 east of Prineville 122 miles to John Day.

⭐3 Canyon City

Gold was discovered along Canyon Creek on June 8, 1862, and soon a boomtown of 10,000 sprang up. Today the town is still the county seat, but its population has declined to about 700.

Walk a few blocks around Canyon City's downtown to see the old stone buildings, the city park's **historic**

The 1865 cabin of poet Joaquin Miller.

murals, and the **Grant County Historical Museum,** where you'll find the 1865 plank cabin of **Joaquin Miller,** the "Poet of the Sierras" who practiced law and wrote poems here 1863-69. The museum is open 9:30am-4:30pm Monday through Saturday (Sundays 1pm-5pm) from June 1 to Sept 30.

GETTING THERE: Drive Highway 395 south of John Day 2 miles.

WILDFLOWERS OF NORTHEAST OREGON

From the Ochocos to the Wallowas, the mountains of Northeast Oregon are cut off from the Cascade Range, surrounded by semi-arid rangelands. As a result, the flora has grown in isolation. Wildflowers here more closely resemble those of the Rocky Mountains.

PENSTEMON *(Penstemon sp.)*. Look for these red, purple, or blue trumpets in high, rocky areas.

BLANKETFLOWER *(Gaillardia aristata)*, alias brown-eyed Susan, blooms in grassy foothills all summer.

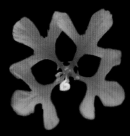

HONEYSUCKLE *(Lonicera ciliosa)*. This fragrant, viny shrub blooms in canyons early in summer.

BROAD-LEAVED FIREWEED *(Epilobium latifolium)*, just inches tall, likes sandy alpine creekbanks.

MOUNTAIN BLUEBELL *(Mertensia sp.)*. A favorite browse for elk, these plants fill subalpine meadows.

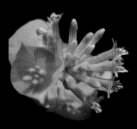

CLARKIA *(Clarkia pulchella)*. Named for Lewis and Clark, this bloom covers canyonsides in June.

GENTIAN *(Gentiana calycosa)*. These thumb-sized blooms near alpine lakes open only in full sun.

FAWN LILY *(Erythronium grandi-florum)* blooms within days after snow melts from high meadows.

YELLOW BELL *(Fritillaria pudica)*. Just 6 inches tall, this lily blooms in sagebrush grasslands in spring.

ELEPHANTS HEAD *(Pedicularis groenlandica)*. You'll see pink elephants like this in alpine bogs.

ASTER *(Aster sp.)*. These purple daisy-like flowers grow at all elevations and bloom until fall.

4   Baker City

Over 100 restored buildings line the streets of Baker City's turn-of-the-19th-century downtown. Pick up a free brochure describing a 1-mile walking tour at **Betty's Books** (1813 Main Street). For a quick cuppa, cross the street to the Front Street Cafe & Coffee Company, with an impressive menu of coffee drinks and breakfast specials.

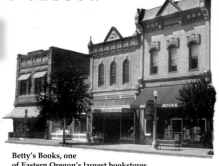

Betty's Books, one of Eastern Oregon's largest bookstores, occupies an 1888 building on Main Street.

It's hard to miss the imposing **Geiser Grand Hotel** at 1996 Main Street. Restored in 1998 at a cost of $7 million, this elaborate, turreted 1889 building is worth a visit even if you don't book a room. Consider taking a table beneath the stained glass ceiling of the Palm Court, where liveried waiters serve steaks, pasta, or chicken.

Several benign ghosts are said to haunt the 1889 Geiser Grand Hotel.

Then cross the street to the US Bank (2000 Main) to see its astonishing **gold display**, a glass case filled with gold pebbles, gold dust, and a monstrous five-pound, fist-sized gold nugget. Walk on to **Barley Brown's Brew Pub**, 2190 Main Street. Dare to order the gigantic Death Burger, or go with chicken nachos and a pint of the Jubilee Golden Ale.

Identical 1880s buildings on Main Street house the Adler Museum and the Baer House Bed & Breakfast next door.

Another block down Main Street is the **Adler House Museum**, a restored 1889 home at 2305 Main, packed with original antiques. It's open May 1 to October 1, Thursday through Saturday 1pm-4pm and Sunday 11am-2pm. Adults are $5; children under 7 are free.

GETTING THERE: Take Interstate 84 exit 304, go west a mile, and turn left on Main Street.

5   Sumpter

Founded by gold miners in 1862, Sumpter boomed to 3500 after the railroad line from Baker City reached here in 1896, but dwindled after a 1917 fire burned nearly every building and even the planked Main Street.

A stained glass ceiling lights an elegant yet affordable restaurant in the Geiser Grand Hotel's Palm Court.

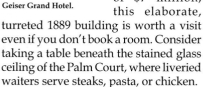

The Sumpter Dredge is a 1200-ton gold mining ship that dug its own lake as it went.

sion steam train on 5 miles of restored track from the Sumpter Dredge west to McEwen Station. Trains leave McEwen Station at 10am, 12:30pm, and 3pm on weekends and holidays from Memorial Day weekend through September. The return train leaves Sumpter at 11:30am, 2pm, and 4:30pm. Expect to pay $9 per adult for the round trip. For details call 800-523-1235.

GETTING THERE: From downtown Baker City, drive south on Main Street (which becomes Highway 7) for 23 miles to the Sumpter Valley Railway's McEwen Station, or continue onward 5 miles to the dredge in Sumpter itself.

Start your visit at the **Sumpter Dredge**, a 1200-ton, 60-foot-tall gold mill floating in a lake of its own making. The odd ship dug up $4.5 million in gold 1935-1954, but left miles of farmland churned to a moonscape of rock tailings. Now restored as a state heritage site, the dredge is open 9am-4pm daily from May 15 to September 15 and 9am-3pm Thursday to Monday from September 16 to October 31.

Nicknamed the "Stump Dodger" because it helped log the area's ponderosa pine forests in the 1890s, the narrow-gauge **Sumpter Valley Railroad** has reopened as an excur-

Nicknamed the "Stump Dodger," the 1890s Sumpter Valley Railroad now serves as an excursion steam train.

GHOST TOWNS

Whitney lost its population when the railroad line here closed.

Sumpter bills itself as the "Liveliest Ghost Town in Oregon," with a population that varies from about 140 in summer to 80 in winter.

To see a town with a higher ghost-to-human ratio, drive the main paved Road 73 west of Sumpter 17 miles to **Granite**.

Granite's city hall has a bell tower because it was first used as a school.

This 1862 gold boomtown shrank to a population of one in the 1960s, and although it has rebounded to about 25, the weathered old city hall, Wells Fargo office, and dance hall remain abandoned.

The ghost town of **Whitney**, on the other hand, is completely deserted. To find it, drive back to Sumpter and take Highway 7 toward John Day 9 miles. A logging center, Whitney faded when the Sumpter Valley Railroad closed its line in 1947.

HIKE 60 Anthony Lake

Easy (around Anthony Lake)
1-mile loop   No elevation gain
Open July through October
Use: hikers
Map: Anthony Lake (USGS)

Difficult (around Gunsight Mountain)
8.2-mile loop   1330 feet elevation gain

A glacier scoured out Anthony Lake's granite basin from the crest of the Elkhorn Range during the Ice Age. Today subalpine firs and wildflower meadows ring the lake. To explore the area on foot, start at a lakeshore picnic gazebo, walk down to the lake, and turn left along the shoreline trail. After strolling clockwise 0.3 mile around the lake you'll reach a boat ramp and face a decision. Two trails set off from the far right-hand side of the boat ramp's road turnaround — the Black Lake Trail on the left and the Hoffer Lake Trail on the right.

Gentians by the lake.

For an easy, 1-mile loop hike, take the right-hand trail and keep right around

Some of the Elkhorn Range's white granite was polished to a shiny finish by glaciers thousands of years ago.

Anthony Lake to return to your car. To make the loop more interesting, detour 0.6 mile up to the lovely Hoffer Lakes.

The most spectacular loop hike in the area, however, is an 8.2-mile trip around Gunsight Mountain. Start as before from the picnic gazebo, but after walking 0.3 mile to the boat ramp, veer left toward Black Lake for 0.5 mile and then keep straight on the Elkhorn Crest Trail.

This well-graded path climbs 950 feet in 2.1 miles to a breathtaking view at Angell Pass. Continue downhill 0.6 mile to a junction in Dutch Flat Saddle, a good

In summer you can hike or canoe around Anthony Lake for views of Gunsight Mountain.

In winter Anthony Lake is a snow sports center with a nearby chairlift for skiers and snowboarders.

The Hoffer Lakes are backed by a granite slab that rears up to form Lees Peak.

A side trail climbs between granite boulders to The Lakes Lookout.

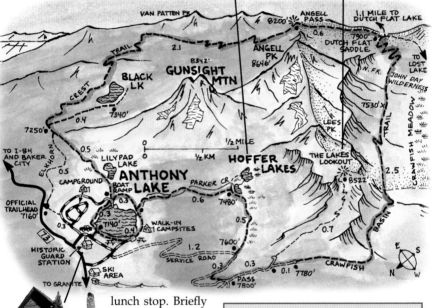

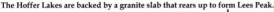

Anthony Lake's historic 1930s guard station.

lunch stop. Briefly detour 100 feet left for a view of Dutch Flat Lake, a mile below.

Then return to the saddle and take the Crawfish Basin Trail downhill. This path skirts above Crawfish Meadow before ending at a dirt road. Go straight along this road 0.4 mile to a pass with a 4-way junction. Look to the right at this pass to find an unmarked trail angling downhill. Take this path to cut off the service road's first switchback. At the road's second switchback, turn right on the Hoffer Lakes Trail for the prettiest route back to your car.

Getting There

Drive Interstate 84 north of Baker City 19 miles (or south of La Grande 24 miles) to North Powder exit 285 and follow "Anthony Lakes" signs 21 paved miles west on what becomes Road 73. If you're hauling a horse trailer or backpacking equipment, plan to park in the well-marked Elkhorn Crest Trailhead lot on the left, where there's a self-pay station for the required parking pass. If you're just out for a day hike, however, drive onward 0.3 mile and turn left at an Anthony Lake Campground sign. After 100 yards fork to the right toward a picnic area, and in another 100 yards park on the left at a lakeshore picnic gazebo. Here no parking fee is required, but dogs are allowed only on a leash.

6 Oregon Trail Interpretive Center

Open 9am-6pm daily from April to October and 9am-4pm from November to March.
Adults $5, seniors $3.50, kids under 16 free.

The Conestoga wagons of the Oregon Trail crossed Flagstaff Hill to a dramatic view of the rugged Blue Mountains ahead. Today a world-class interpretive center perches atop the panoramic hill, with walk-through dioramas, a covered wagon camp, a gold mine replica, and trails to the original wagon ruts.

Start by touring the walk-through exhibits in the interpretive center building. After you come back out of the front door, take stairs down to the left to the paved trail network. First switchback downhill a few hundred yards to a replica of a hard-rock gold mine.

If you're up to a longer walk, follow "Panorama Point" signs a mile down to a cliff-edged viewpoint with a deck and a shaded bench. Then continue downhill 0.5 mile to an X-shaped trail junction near a shade shelter with a bench.

To the left is the return trail—a rough dirt path that climbs 0.9 mile to your car. But first go straight on a 0.3-mile loop path that passes a covered wagon on the actual route of the Oregon Trail.

GETTING THERE: From Interstate 84 exit 302, just north of Baker City, drive east 5 miles on Highway 86 to the Oregon Trail Interpretive Center entrance road on the left.

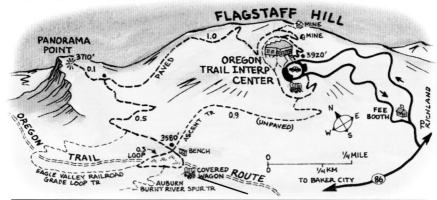

A covered wagon marks the route of the Oregon Trail, accessible from the museum by a 2.9-mile loop trail.

HIKE 61 Hells Canyon Dam

Easy
2.4 miles round trip   180 feet elevation gain
Open all year
Use: hikers
Map: Hells Canyon Nat'l Rec Area (USFS)

The Hells Canyon Dam's paved access road offers hikers an easy back door into this spectacular, mile-deep chasm.

Start by perusing the displays in the visitor center at road's end. Then go out the building's back door to the deck and take the stairs down to the boat launch.

Taking care to avoid triple-leaved poison oak alongside the path, follow a

HELLS CANYON BOAT TRIPS

Boat tours leave from a dock at road's end. Expect to pay $45 for a 3-hour jet boat tour with lunch (10am-1pm Pacific Time), $35 for a tour without lunch (leaves 1pm), and $127.50 for a 6-hour tour (leaves 9am). Longer trips in rubber rafts are also available. For reservations and information, call 800-422-3568 or check *www.hellscanyonadventures.com*.

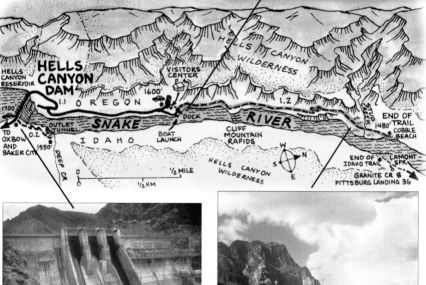

When the 330-foot-tall Hells Canyon Dam opened in 1956 it flooded 20 miles of the famous gorge and led to the demise of salmon runs for half of Idaho.

Getting There

Leave Interstate 84 at exit 302 just north of Baker City, drive Highway 86 east 65 miles to Oxbow, follow signs another 23 miles to Hells Canyon Dam, and continue 1.1 mile to a parking lot by the visitor information center at road's end.

For a sample of Hells Canyon's scenery, walk a 1.2-mile path from the end of the dam's road to Stud Creek.

walkway past a railed archeological site and continue downriver a mile to Stud Creek's gravelly outwash plain. Just beyond the creek crossing the path ends at a cobble beach. Return as you came.

HIKE 62   Eagle Creek

Difficult (to Eagle Creek Meadow)
8.8 miles round trip   1250 feet elevation gain
Open early July through October
Use: hikers, horses
Map: Wallowa Mountains (Imus Geographics)

Very Difficult (to Arrow Lake)
19.1-mile loop   4080 feet elevation gain

Most visitors to the alp-like Wallowa Mountains flock to the crowded northern trailheads near Wallowa Lake (see p251). But the much quieter Eagle Creek Trail on the southern side of the range is actually an easier route to the Wallowa's scenic high country. Even families with children can usually make it to Eagle Creek Meadow, an alpine glen surrounded by granite canyon walls. From there, trekkers can continue to half a dozen high lakes.

Note that the maximum group size in the Eagle Cap Wilderness is 12 people. Campsites must be at least 100 feet from any lakeshore, tethered horses must be at least 100 feet from water or campsites,

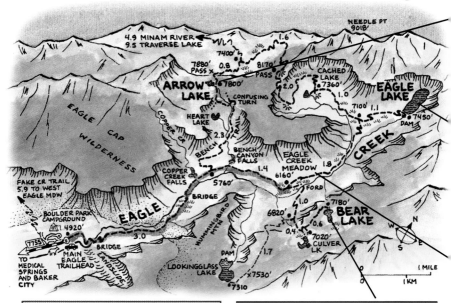

Getting There

From Baker City, take Interstate 84 north 6 miles to exit 298 and drive 19 miles on Highway 203 to Medical Springs, an old stagecoach stop. Here turn east on Eagle Creek Drive, following the first of many signs for Boulder Park. The road soon becomes gravel. After 1.6 miles, fork left onto one-lane Big Creek Road 67. After another 14.6 miles, turn left on Road 77 for 0.8 mile and then keep straight on Road 7755 for 3.7 miles to its end at the Main Eagle Trailhead, where a Northwest Forest Pass is required. It costs $5 per car per day or $30 per season.

An excellent 2-mile side trip climbs to Bear Lake.

and fires are strongly discouraged. Firewood may be gathered only from downed, dead trees.

From the trailhead beside the Boulder

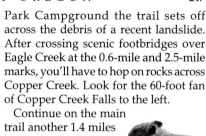

Park Campground the trail sets off across the debris of a recent landslide. After crossing scenic footbridges over Eagle Creek at the 0.6-mile and 2.5-mile marks, you'll have to hop on rocks across Copper Creek. Look for the 60-foot fan of Copper Creek Falls to the left.

Pikas live in alpine rockslides.

Continue on the main trail another 1.4 miles to the start of Eagle Creek Meadow. Where the trail enters the clearing you'll cross a well preserved example of glacial polish, granite bedrock smoothed to a shine by Ice Age glaciers.

If you're headed for Bear Lake, wade across Eagle Creek and take a trail 2 miles uphill. A substantial fir forest abuts Bear Lake on three sides, but the far end opens onto a large meadow with a colossal backdrop of cliffs. Another popular goal from Eagle Creek Meadow is Eagle Lake, in a stark granite basin at timberline. An ancient dam of hand-fitted rocks stores irrigation water in the lake.

Perhaps the grandest trip from Eagle Creek Meadow is a loop past Cached Lake and Arrow Lake through high alpine country, keeping left at all trail junctions. This 19.1-mile trek is for hikers only, as parts are too rough for horses.

A difficult but spectacular 19-mile loop visits Arrow Lake.

A small stone dam has converted Eagle Lake to a reservoir.

Eagle Creek Meadow makes a good day-hike goal. If you're backpacking, tent in the woods and not on the meadow plants.

7   Hat Point

Open early June to mid-November.

A meadow 3.7 miles down the Hat Point Trail from the lookout is a popular goal for hikers, but the return trip gains an arduous 2200 feet of elevation.

The long, gravel road to Hat Point leads to some of the best viewpoints on Hells Canyon's rim. On the way, the road passes Granny View Vista. Pull into the parking area here (not shown on map) and walk a 0.3-mile nature loop through the wildflower meadows for views of the vast Imnaha River canyon.

Hat Point's lookout tower.

Then drive another 6 miles to Hat Point. Park at a display board nearest the fire lookout tower, take a gravel 0.3-mile loop to the right through a picnic area to a viewpoint, and then climb up to the tower itself. Public stairs climb 60 feet to an observation deck. Only staff are allowed up to the 8-foot-square lookout cabin.

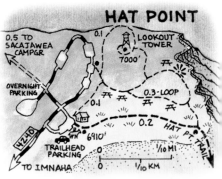

Stout-hearted hikers can take the Hat Point Trail from the parking area down into the Hells Canyon Wilderness toward the Snake River. Be warned, however, that the river is 5560 feet below Hells Canyon's rim. Every foot of elevation you lose will have to be gained back later — quite possibly under a hot afternoon sun.

Trail sign below Hat Point.

△ The Snake River caroms through the bottom of Hells Canyon, a vertical mile almost directly below Hat Point. The Imnaha River canyon and the distant, snowy Wallowa Mountains from Freezeout Saddle, near Hat Point. ▷

The store / tavern in Imnaha has an eclectic array of wares, but the nearest gasoline is 29 miles away in Joseph.

GETTING THERE: Top off your tank at the gas station in downtown Joseph. Then turn east beside the station at a "Hells Canyon Scenic Byway" sign for 29 paved miles to Imnaha. Drive straight through this village onto steep, narrow, gravel Hat Point Road 4240. The first 5 miles climb so relentlessly that you may need to pause in the shade to keep your car's engine from overheating. Beyond Imnaha 16.6 miles is Granny View Vista, and another 6 miles later you'll reach the parking areas below Hat Point's lookout tower. A Northwest Forest Pass ($5 per day or $30 per season) is required to park here.

Sign at the Hells Canyon Wilderness boundary.

8 Joseph

Backed by craggy Wallowa Mountain peaks, this Old West town has long been a jumpoff point for expeditions into the Eagle Cap Wilderness. But it's also become a center for Western art.

The monumental **bronze sculptures** lining Joseph's main street are the work of local foundries and artists — many of whom are also represented in local art galleries.

Monarch butterfly.

At the north edge of downtown, the large, private **Manuel Museum** will display Indian artifacts and bronze works until 2007, when it moves to Hot Lake, a restored 1906 hot springs resort 8 miles southeast of La Grande near exit 268 of Interstate 5.

The **Wallowa County Museum**, in a 1888 bank building at 110 South Main in the middle of downtown, includes a Nez Perce room with a tepee. The museum is open daily 10am-5pm from late May to mid-September. Admission is by donation.

GETTING THERE: Drive Interstate 84 to exit 261 in La Grande and follow Wallowa Lake signs on Highway 82 through Enterprise a total of 71 miles.

Bronze sculptures by local artists line the main street of Joseph, against a backdrop of the Wallowa Mountain peaks.

Most trails into the Wallowa Mountains' high country are long and difficult, but it's easy to ride the gondola up 8341-foot Mount Howard to sample the alpine environment on short loop paths. Views extend to Eagle Cap.

9 Wallowa Lake

Wedged against alpine peaks, this blue, 3-mile long lake fills the curving footprint of a vanished Ice Age glacier.

At the far end of the lake, **Wallowa Lake State Park** features a picnic area, marina, boat ramp, swimming beach, and popular 212-site campground. Near the park entrance, the rustic yet elegant **Wallowa Lake Lodge** offers rooms in the grand style of National Park lodges as well as affordable dining.

Beyond the park entrance 0.3 mile, the gondolas of the **Wallowa Lake Tramway** zoom visitors up 3700 feet of elevation in 15 minutes to views atop Mount Howard. The tramway is open 10am-5pm daily from May through September, and costs $19 per adult, $16 for kids age 13-17, and $12 for age 4-12.

GETTING THERE: Drive to Joseph and continue straight on Highway 82 for 6 miles.

Wallowa Lake fills the moraine left by an Ice Age glacier.

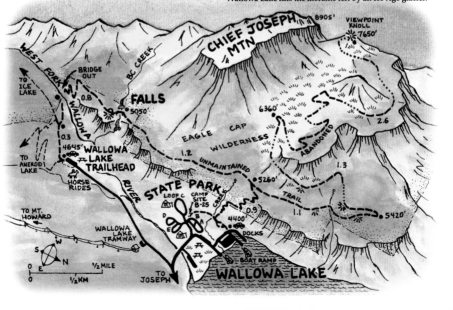

HIKE 63 — Eagle Cap

Difficult (to Mirror Lake)
14.8 miles round trip 2020 feet elevation gain
Open mid-July through October
Use: hikers, horses
Map: Wallowa Mountains (Imus Geographics)

Very Difficult (to Eagle Cap summit)
19.8 miles round trip 4000 feet elevation gain

Eight valleys radiate from 9572-foot Eagle Cap, the rock hub of the Wallowa Mountains. Although Eagle Cap is not quite the tallest peak in this range, its 360-degree view is unmatched, and a surprisingly well-graded trail climbs to the summit from the East Lostine River's

The trail along this meadow is nearly level for 2.3 miles to a stream crossing at the far end — a possible turnaround point.

If you're continuing, hop across the stream at a collapsed bridge. Beyond,

Mirror Lake from Eagle Cap.

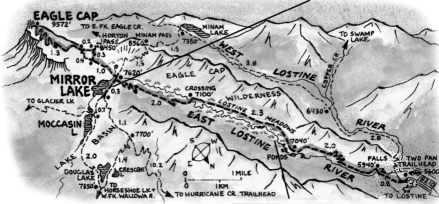

meadows. If your goal's the summit, plan on a two-day trip. If you're out for a day hike, settle for a view of the cliff-edged peak from the Lostine meadows or Mirror Lake.

Note that group size is limited to twelve on trails and six in camps. Tents must be at least 100 feet from lakeshores, grazing horses must be at least 200 feet from lakes, and campfires are banned within a quarter mile of Mirror Lake.

Start at the Two Pan Trailhead. When the trail forks after a few hundred yards, veer left on the East Fork Lostine River Trail. This path climbs steeply for 2.8 miles. Finally the path levels off beside several ponds at the start of a long, beautiful meadow.

Here at last is a grand view ahead to Eagle Cap. During the Ice Age, a glacier from Eagle Cap filled this high valley, sculpting it into a long U-shaped trough.

△ The East Lostine River meanders through meadows.
Eagle Cap reflects in a tarn near Mirror Lake. ▷

WILDLIFE OF EASTERN OREGON'S MOUNTAINS

On almost any drive through Eastern Oregon an alert watcher is likely to spot mule deer on hillsides or in fields, often by the dozen. The Blue Mountains alone are home to 150,000 deer. Although that range also has over 50,000 elk, they are more elusive. Likewise, black bears are common but rarely seen. Grizzly bears and wolves were hunted to extinction in Oregon long ago, although occasionally a wolf now ventures here from Idaho on its own. Hunting and diseases from domestic sheep wiped out Oregon's mountain goats and bighorn sheep in the early twentieth century, but both species have been reintroduced with success.

ELK. Bull elk can weigh 1000 pounds, collecting "harems" of up to 60 females and bugling to declare territory. Still, they're not seen a lot because they graze at night and bed in forest thickets by day.

BIGHORN SHEEP. Herds of a dozen or more graze cliffy slopes and alpine meadows at Strawberry Mountain, Hells Canyon, and Steens Mountain. Males butt heads at up to 20 miles per hour.

MOUNTAIN GOAT. Rare in the Wallowas but common in the Elkhorn Range west of Baker City, mountain goats sometimes descend from their cliff ledges to nibble an unwatched backpack for salt.

the trail climbs 2 miles to a rock cairn at a junction within sight of Mirror Lake.

Detour left to see the lake's reflection of Eagle Cap's snowy cliffs. Then return to the rock cairn and keep left at all trail junctions. After a mile the trail forks at a signless post. Horton Pass is to the right, but the left-hand path is a shorter, if snowier, route. The two trails rejoin on a ridgecrest and climb left 1.3 miles to Eagle Cap's windswept summit.

A green ammunition can holds the summit climbers' register. Below you, the Eagle Cap Wilderness spreads out like a colorful map, dotted with blue lakes and striped with green valleys.

The summit of 9572-foot Eagle Cap overlooks most of the wilderness, including blue-green Glacier Lake.

Getting There

Drive Interstate 84 to La Grande exit 261 and follow Wallowa Lake signs 55 miles on Highway 82 to Lostine. In the center of town, where the highway turns left, go straight on Lostine River Road, following a pointer for "Lostine River Campgrounds." This route is a two-lane paved road for the first 12.2 miles to the Lostine Guard Station. Then continue on a rougher, one-lane gravel road another 6.1 miles to road's end at the Two Pan Trailhead. A Northwest Forest Pass is required to park here. The pass costs $5 per day or $30 per season.

Pendleton

Stop in this well-preserved Old West city to take the **Pendleton Underground Tour**, exploring tunnels and opium dens built by Chinese railroad laborers in the 1880s. The 90-minute tour costs $10 for adults or $5 for children and begins at 37 SW Emigrant Street (reservations 800-226-6398).

The **Pendleton Woolen Mill**, founded 1909, still weaves Indian-inspired robes and shawls. At 1307 SE Court Place, the factory offers free tours Monday to Saturday at 9am, 11am, 1:30pm, and 3pm.

Downtown Pendleton.

The city puts on its spurs each year for the **Pendleton Round-Up,** a world-class rodeo during the second full week of September.

GETTING THERE: Take Interstate 84 exit 209.

CHIEF JOSEPH AND THE NEZ PERCE

Among the most peaceable of Northwest tribes, the Nez Perce caught salmon at the outlet of Wallowa Lake and bred prized Appaloosa ponies on the plains below.

Signs mark the tribe's 1877 route.

When the US Army ordered the 400-member Wallowa band to move to a small Idaho reservation in May 1877, Chief Joseph led his people across Hells Canyon, crossing the Snake River at flood stage. A shootout just short of the reservation, however, sent the tribe on a 4-month tactical retreat, ending with defeat just 30 miles short of political sanctuary in Canada. The tribe was exiled to distant reservations where Joseph died of what his doctor called "a broken heart."

In 1997 the federal government granted the tribe 10,000 acres of Wallowa County land as compensation for broken treaties. Since 1998 the tribe has held an annual summer friendship powwow along the lower Wallowa River.

A roadside monument just south of the town of Joseph overlooks Wallowa Lake. The monument contains the bones of Chief Joseph's father, moved here in 1925 without the tribe's permission.

Ordered by the Army to leave Oregon, Chief Joseph led his people across the Snake River at Dug Bar in 1877.

WHERE TO STAY

Campgrounds (map p233)

	Campsites	Water	Showers	Flush Toilet	Fee
8 ANTHONY LAKES. At a spectacular mountain lake (see pp242-43) with canoeing and hiking, this camp is open July through September.	37	●			$
15 BOULDER PARK. All you need is a Northwest Forest parking pass to stay at this camp beside the Main Eagle Trailhead (see pp246-47), high in the southern Wallowa Mountains. Open July through October.	8				free
1 CHIMNEY ROCK. Camp beside the Crooked River or climb 1.4 miles to a rimrock viewpoint from this canyon camp 16.6 miles south of Prineville on Main Street (which becomes Road 27).	20	●			$
9 EMIGRANT SPRINGS. In a Blue Mountains forest on the Old Oregon Trail route, this handy state park has freeway noise, so consider renting one of the seven log cabins ($20-$35; reservations 800-452-5687). Drive Interstate 84 east of Pendleton 25 miles to exit 234.	52	●	●	●	$$
16 FAREWELL BEND. Where the Oregon Trail left the Snake River, this state park has two log cabins ($38), four teepees ($29) and two covered wagons ($29) if you don't want to tent. Drive Interstate 84 between Baker City and Ontario to exit 353. Reservations: 800-452-5687.	131	●	●	●	$$
14 INDIAN CROSSING. Where the Imnaha River leaves the Eagle Cap Wilderness, this camp is open June through October. From Joseph, follow signs for the Hells Canyon Byway and Halfway for 40 miles and turn right on paved Road 3960 for 9 miles to its end.	14	●			$
4 MITCHELL. The city park lawn in this small town (population 180) is open for camping. It's popular with long-distance bicycle tourers.	5	●		●	free
2 OCHOCO DIVIDE. Amid ponderosas at the crest of the Ochoco Mountains, this Forest Service camp is open May through October. From Prineville, drive Highway 26 east for 30 miles to the Ochocos' summit at Ochoco Pass.	28	●			$
7 OLIVE LAKE. A 2.7-mile trail from a Forest Service camp circles this lake high in the forested Blue Mountains. Open June to mid-October. From Granite (see p241), drive west on Road 10 for 12.5 miles.	21				$
13 OLLOKOT. This forested camp beside the whitewater Imnaha River is open May through October. From Joseph, follow signs for the Hells Canyon Byway and Halfway 40 miles.	12	●			$
11 SHADY. Prepare for an Eagle Cap climb at this Lostine River camp half a mile before the Two Pan trailhead (see p252). Open June to October.	12				$
5 STRAWBERRY. At the Strawberry Lake trailhead (see p236), this quiet, woodsy camp beside a rushing creek is open June to mid-September.	11	●			$
10 UMATILLA FORKS. In a deep, forested canyon where river forks merge, this camp is open April through November. From Pendleton, drive Interstate 84 east 7 miles to exit 216, go north 2.1 miles, turn right on Mission Road 1.7 miles, turn left on Cayuse Road 11.2 miles, and turn right on Bingham Road 16 miles.	15	●			$
6 UNITY LAKE. On the grassy shore of a desert reservoir (motorboats OK), this state park is open April to late October and has two rentable teepees ($29). From John Day, drive Highway 26 east 50 miles and turn left 3 miles on Highway 245.	35	●	●	●	$$
12 WALLOWA LAKE. The busy state park at this popular mountain lake (see p251) has boat ramps, a swimming area, roving deer, trails, a cabin ($58-80), and two yurts ($29). Reservations recommended: 800-452-5687.	210	●	●	●	$$
3 WALTON LAKE. In the pine forests of the Ochoco Mountains, this quiet lakeside camp is open May through September. From Prineville drive Highway 26 east 17 miles, fork right at Ochoco Creek 8.3 miles, and veer left on paved Road 22 for 7 miles.	30	●			$

Wallowa Lake. ▷

WHERE TO STAY

B&Bs and Quaint Hotels *(map p233)*

	Rooms	Private bath	Cont. breakfast	Full breakfast	Rate range
10 A PLACE APART. This 1901 Colonial revival home is a bed & breakfast inn within walking distance of downtown Pendleton and a river promenade, at 711 SE Byers. Info: 888-441-8932 or *www.aplaceapartbnb.com*.	2			●	$65-95
8 BAER HOUSE. In downtown Baker City's historic district *(see p240)*, this 1882 Victorian bed & breakfast inn has 11-foot ceilings and country decor, at 2333 Main Street. Info: 800-709-7637 or *www.baerhouse.com*.	3	1		●	$85-95
2 BRIDGE CREEK FLORA INN. A three-story 1905 historic home serves as a bed & breakfast inn near Fossil's quaint downtown at 828 Main Street, Fossil, OR 97830. Info: 541-763-2355 or *www.fossilinn.com*.	9	2		●	$65-75
12 BRONZE ANTLER. Built in 1925 for a sawmill supervisor, this Craftsman bungalow is now a bed & breakfast inn at 309 S. Main in the charming downtown of Joseph *(see p250)*. Info: 866-520-9769 or *www.bronzeantler.com*.	3	●		●	$75-140
7 GEISER GRAND HOTEL. Restored to its original opulence *(see p240)*, this turreted 1889 Victorian hotel is a landmark in Baker City's historic downtown at 1996 Main Street. Info: 888-434-7374 or *www.geisergrand.com*.	30	●			$89-209
1 HOTEL CONDON. This renovated, artsy 1920 hotel in downtown Condon (population 790) has an inexpensive, upscale restaurant, at 202 S. Main, Condon, OR 97823. Info: 800-201-6706 or *www.hotelcondon.com*.	18	●	●		$55-105
14 IMNAHA RIVER INN. Surrounded by Hells Canyon scenery, this massive, modern log lodge is on a remote, paved road 5 miles north of Imnaha *(see p250)*. Info: 866-601-9214 or *www.imnahariverinn.com*.	7			●	$120
5 THE LODGE AT GRANITE. The ghost town of Granite has only 25 residents *(see p241)*, so your visit will be noticed if you stay in this modern log hotel. Info: 541-755-5200 or *www.visitbaker.com*.	9	●	●		$60
3 OREGON HOTEL. In downtown Mitchell (population 180), this 1860 hotel burned in 1937, but was rebuilt in 1938 and retains its authentic Old West ambiance, renovated with antiques. A single bunk in a hostel room runs just $10. Pets are $10 extra, but children stay free. Info: 541-462-3027. The Oregon Hotel in Mitchell. ▷	11	5			$29-59
11 PARKER HOUSE. A 1917 Italian Renaissance mansion with original Chinese silk wallpaper is an elegant bed & breakfast near downtown Pendleton at 311 N. Main Street. Info: 800-700-8581 or *www.parkerhousebnb.com*.	6	2		●	$85-145
15 PINE VALLEY LODGE. In the southern Wallowa Mountain hamlet of Halfway, artists have converted a 1900 rectory, 1920 home, and 1880 shack into an offbeat but upscale lodge and restaurant. Drive Highway 86 east of Baker City 52 miles. Info: 541-742-2027 or *www.pvlodge.com*.	7	4	●		$65-160
6 SCOOP N STEAMER. The lively ghost town of Sumpter *(see pp240-41)* includes this restaurant and four adjacent, modern log cabins (sleep 2-4) with kitchenettes. Info: 888-894-2236 or *www.scoop-n-steamer.com*.	4	●			$65-75
9 STANG MANOR INN. A 1923 timber baron's Colonial mansion serves as a bed & breakfast in this historic college town, at 1612 Walnut Street, La Grande, OR 97850. Info: 888-286-9463 or *www.stangmanor.com*.	4	●		●	$98-115
4 STRAWBERRY MOUNTAIN INN. Views from this 1906 inn include grazing cattle and snowy Strawberry Mountain. Drive Highway 26 east of John Day 13 miles to Prairie City and continue a quarter mile. Info: 800-545-6913 or *www.strawberrymountaininn.com*. ▷	5	3		●	$85-120
13 WALLOWA LAKE LODGE. This National-Park-style 1923 lodge at a mountain lake *(see p251)* includes an elegant, affordable restaurant and eight cabins ($95-210). Info: 541-432-9821 or *www.wallowalake.com*.	22	●			$75-160

SOUTHEAST OREGON

Oregon's sparsely populated high desert is a toybox of geologic marvels.

Sagebrush rules the high desert cattle country of Southeast Oregon, where vast fault-block mountains spawn rivers that die in alkaline playas—intermittent oases for waterfowl and wildlife. Annual precipitation averages only 10 to 15 inches a year, much of it as snowstorms in the harsh winters or as thundershowers in the hot summers. No other part of the United States, outside of Alaska, is so sparsely populated.

But this is also a land of breathtaking beauty. From Crack in the Ground to Borax Hot Springs, the geologic story has been painted across the high desert with the color of a Gauguin and the surreal whimsy of a Dali.

Although history records no major earthquakes here, the rocks do. Fresh fault scarps at Abert Rim, Hart Moun-tain, and Steens Mountain prove that blocks of earth have shifted 2000 to 5700 feet vertically, leaving plateaus and gaping valleys. The terrain here must have been mostly flat 10 million years ago, because Steens Mountain basalt lava flows of that age cover all these disjointed rims. The area's many hot springs also suggest ongoing crustal activity.

The Ice Age brought rain instead of ice to these high plains. A chain of vast, 50-mile long seas filled nearly every valley from Bend to Utah 200 feet deep. The Alvord Desert and other playas are the alkaline residue of the evaporated lakes. In spring and fall when water refills the playas and adjacent marshlands, millions of migrating birds stop for respite on their north-south trek across the continent.

◁ **Rock formations at Leslie Gulch** *(see p278).*   △ **Steens Mountain's summit in April** *(see pp268-71).*

Exploring
SOUTHEAST OREGON

Top off your gas tank before heading into Oregon's high desert, a vast landscape where signs of human habitation are routinely 50 miles apart, even on major highways. That said, don't miss the spectacular 146-mile drive from La Pine to Lakeview, with a side trip to Fort Rock's circular cliff. Even grander is a 265-mile drive around Steens Mountain, passing hot springs, mile-high cliffs, and wildlife marshes—but only one rustic gas station.

Fort Rock

Like a ship in the desert, Fort Rock was once a lake island. Geologic oddities nearby include Crack in the Ground (above), Hole in the Ground, and Derrick Cave (see pp262-63).

Hart Mountain

At the Hart Mountain National Refuge you really can spot antelope herds racing through the hills. A free campground includes an outdoor hot springs in a natural rock pool (see pp264-65). The cliffs of Poker Jim Ridge (at right) loom above the Warner Lakes, a chain of marshes and pools popular with canoeists and migrating birds.

Hot Springs

With half a dozen major thermal springs, Oregon's high desert is the right place to soak in the scenery. Choices range from a commercial indoor pool at Summer Lake (see p264) to scalding turquoise vents at Borax Hot Springs (at left and pp274-75). Other natural spas are at Hart Mountain (p265), beside the Alvord Desert (p273), and deep in the rock canyon of the Owyhee River (p277).

KEY

5 ★ Star attraction

HIKE 12 Featured hike

2 ⛺ Campground

6 🏠 B&B or quaint hotel

❓ Information:

Eastern Oregon Visitors Association
PO Box 1087
Baker City, OR 97814
800-332-1843
www.eova.com

Harney County Chamber of Commerce
76 East Washington
Burns, OR 97720
541-573-2636
www.harneycounty.com

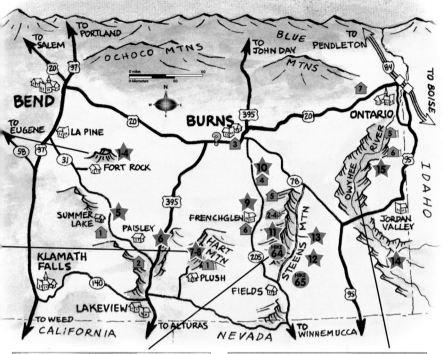

TO SALEM
TO PORTLAND
OCHOCO MTNS
BLUE MTNS
TO PENDLETON
TO JOHN DAY
BEND
TO EUGENE
LA PINE
BURNS
395
20
ONTARIO
TO BOISE
84
OWYHEE RIVER
IDAHO
95
FORT ROCK
SUMMER LAKE
PAISLEY
395
FRENCHGLEN
78
STEENS MTN
JORDAN VALLEY
KLAMATH FALLS
HART MTN
PLUSH
205
FIELDS
95
LAKEVIEW
TO WEED
CALIFORNIA
TO ALTURAS
NEVADA
TO WINNEMUCCA

Steens Mountain

Ice Age glaciers gouged colossal U-shaped valleys (*above, Kiger Gorge*) into 9733-foot Steens Mountain. Explore the peak on the highest road in Oregon (*see pp267-71*). Nearby, stop at the historic Frenchglen Hotel (*p266*) or take a birdwatching car tour through the Malheur Refuge (*p268*).

Owyhee River

This desert river winds through a cliff-walled canyon so remote that most of it can be seen only on long whitewater trips. For a few spectacular samples, however, drive down the pinnacle-lined canyon of Leslie Gulch (*see p278*) or venture into the depths of Three Forks (*see p276-77*).

⭐1 Fort Rock

An island in a sea of sagebrush, Fort Rock serves as a landmark for travelers heading southeast from Bend into the high desert. In a cave nearby, archeologists in 1938 unearthed a 9000-year-old cache of more than 70 sandals woven from sagebrush bark.

Start at the Fort Rock picnic area and climb 200 yards to a viewpoint beside a

Like a giant bathtub ring, a notch circling Fort Rock remains from the surf of a vanished Ice Age lake.

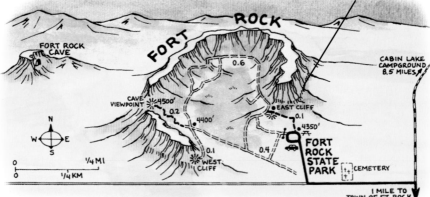

Fort Rock began as an explosion crater with sloping sides, but wave erosion reduced it to a ring of cliffs.

cliff. From here a 1-mile loop path circles the inside of Fort Rock's ring.

Before or after your visit, stop in the nearby hamlet of Fort Rock to see the **Homestead Village Museum** (open Friday through Sunday 10am-4pm in summer), a collection of homes and buildings salvaged from early 1900s dry-land farms.

GETTING THERE: From Bend, drive 29 miles south on Highway 97. Beyond La Pine, turn left at a "Silver Lake" pointer for 29.2 miles on Highway 31, and then turn left at a "Fort Rock" sign for 6.5 miles. Turn left again just beyond the Fort Rock store, following signs 1.7 paved miles to Fort Rock State Park.

⭐2 Hole in the Ground

This mile-wide pit certainly looks like a meteorite crater. But it's actually a *maar*, a volcanic explosion crater formed when a bubble of magma rises to the surface and bursts. Nearby Fort Rock is also a maar, but because it erupted in a lakebed it has been severely eroded.

GETTING THERE: From Bend, drive 29 miles south on Highway 97. Beyond La Pine, turn left toward Silver Lake for 22.4 miles on Highway 31. Then turn left on gravel Road 3125 and follow signs 5 miles.

Hole in the Ground is often mistaken for a meteorite crater, but is actually the pit left by a volcanic explosion.

3 Derrick Cave

★4 Crack in the Ground

To explore this quarter-mile-long lava tube fully you'll need a flashlight or lantern. You'll want a warm coat, too. In winter, dripping water from the ceiling forms three-foot-tall ice stalagmites. Look along the walls for stripes in the rock, the "high water marks" of the lava river that formed the cave.

GETTING THERE: Drive Highway 97 south of Bend 29 miles, turn left at a "Silver Lake" pointer on Highway 31 for 29.2 miles, turn left 6.5 miles to the village of Fort Rock and continue straight 5.8 miles toward Christmas Valley. At a corner, turn left on Road 5-12 for 9.1 paved, zigzagging miles to the Fort Rock Guard Station entrance, and continue straight on gravel 6.8 miles to a signed parking area.

This 70-foot-deep crack formed a few thousand years ago when the ground settled along a valley edge after a lava eruption. Walk a 0.2-mile path to the rock chasm, and hike through it for another 0.2 mile to a sandy gap. Beyond this the crack is blocked by boulders.

GETTING THERE: Take Highway 97 south of Bend 29 miles, turn left toward Silver Lake on Highway 31 for 29.2 miles, turn left 6.5 miles to the village of Fort Rock, and follow signs east another 27 miles to the town of Christmas Valley. At the far edge of town, turn left at a "Crack in the Ground" pointer onto a gravel road for 7.2 miles to a signed parking area.

Crack in the Ground is so narrow that boulders hang wedged overhead. Snow lingers in the bottom until May.

The first 200 yards of Derrick Cave are lit by natural skylights—two jagged holes in the lava ceiling.

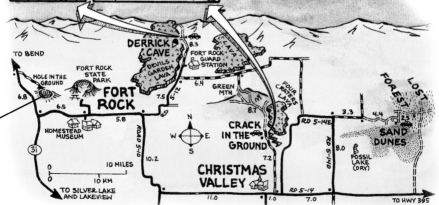

5 Summer Lake

The marshes of the Summer Lake Wildlife Area attract white pelicans, Canada geese, and sandhill cranes in summer, thousands of migratory birds in spring and fall, and bald eagles in winter. To see the birds, drive an 8.5-mile gravel road tour, following "Wildlife Viewing Loop" signs.

Summer Lake Hot Springs.

The refuge's campgrounds resemble gravel parking lots, but you can book a room across from the refuge headquarters at the Lodge at Summer Lake, which prides itself on a

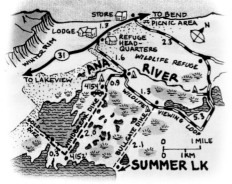

dinner menu of 2-pound steaks. For a fancier place to stay, drive 12 miles south on Highway 31 to the posh Summer Lake Inn (between mileposts 80 and 81). For a swim, drive 11 miles south to Summer Lake Hot Springs (near milepost 92), a rustic 1928 bathhouse with a 102°F pool, open 7am-9pm daily for a $3 fee.

GETTING THERE: Take Highway 97 south of Bend 29 miles and turn left through Silver Lake on Highway 31 for 70 miles. Turn left to the refuge headquarters near milepost 70.

Summer Lake's marshes attract thousands of birds.

6 Abert Lake

This vast alkali lake, overtowered by the colossal 2000-foot cliffs of Abert Rim, is the salty remnant of ancient Lake Chewaucan, which extended 40 miles to Summer Lake during the rainier climate of the Ice Age.

Abert Rim towers 2000 feet above alkali Abert Lake.

From the wildlife viewing pullout, drive or walk a rough dirt track down 300 yards to the lake's sandy shore, where sandpiper-like plovers and giant white pelicans sup on brine shrimp.

GETTING THERE: Drive 30 miles north of Lakeview on Highway 395. Between mileposts 85 and 84 (2 miles after the highway starts following Lake Abert's shore), park in a large gravel pullout marked "Wildlife Viewing Area."

7 Hart Mountain Refuge

Pronghorn antelope race across sagebrush highlands and pelicans sail in salty lakes at this national wildlife refuge. At pullouts along the road from Plush,

The Warner Lakes cluster below Poker Jim Ridge.

Popular with birds and canoeists, the alkaline Warner Lakes at Hart Mountain expand and merge after a wet winter.

short nature trails lead to bird blinds and viewpoints. The headquarter's visitor room, always open, has displays, brochures, and restrooms.

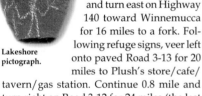

Lakeshore pictograph.

GETTING THERE: From Lakeview, drive 5 miles north on Highway 395 and turn east on Highway 140 toward Winnemucca for 16 miles to a fork. Following refuge signs, veer left onto paved Road 3-13 for 20 miles to Plush's store/cafe/tavern/gas station. Continue 0.8 mile and turn right on Road 3-12 for 24 miles (the last 10 miles on gravel) to refuge headquarters.

8 Hart Mountain Hot Springs

The only campground at Hart Mountain's wildlife refuge has free creekside sites and a free 102°F hot springs in a natural rock pool. Rules: No glass containers. No soap. Maximum stay 20 minutes if others are waiting.

GETTING THERE: From Hart Mountain Refuge's headquarters (*see above*), turn south on a gravel road and keep right for 4.5 miles.

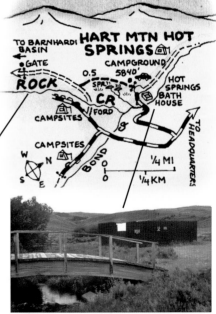

Hikers can explore up Rock Creek from the Hot Springs campground toward 8017-foot Warner Peak.

The wall around Hart Mountain's hot springs has been lowered to two feet to recapture the pool's natural look.

9 Frenchglen

This frontier hamlet at the foot of Steens Mountain consists of a few dozen buildings. The rustic **Frenchglen Hotel,** built in 1916, has been restored by the Oregon State Parks. The hostelry still has no public telephone or television. For meals, guests pack family-style around two large tables in the hotel's little lobby. Typical fare is herb-baked chicken with garlic roast potatoes and marionberry pie. Note that the hotel closes from November 1 to March 15 (see p279).

The 1916 Frenchglen hotel, restored by the Oregon State Parks, is a base for explorations of Steens Mountain.

GETTING THERE: From Burns, drive east on Highway 78 toward Crane for 1.7 miles and turn right on paved Highway 205 for 61 miles.

PETE FRENCH'S LEGACY

Peter French was sent to Oregon in 1872 by California ranching mogul James Glenn to buy cattle land. French ruthlessly amassed ranchland, including much of the present Malheur National Wildlife Refuge. In 1897 he was shot dead by a homesteader in broad daylight in front of witnesses. French had alienated so many locals that a jury acquitted his murderer.

Cows still rule in French's domain.

By 1901, Basque and Irish shepherds were grazing more than 140,000 sheep on Steens Mountain, obliterating once-lush grasslands. Domestic sheep were banned from public land on the mountain in 1972. Cattle were excluded from the mountain's fragile summit and canyons in 1982, and were banned from other wilderness upland areas in 2001. Ironically, cattle still graze the wildlife refuge, French's old domain.

The town of Frenchglen was named for its two original owners, French and Glenn. Pete French's impressive Round Barn, built to train horses for ranch work, is worth a visit although it is threatened by a rising lake. French's old headquarters, the P Ranch, was along the Donner und Blitzen River just east of Frenchglen. Visit it to see the horse barn and fields of the Old West cattle baron.

Pete French built this 100-foot-diameter Round Barn about 1880 to train horses for his vast cattle empire.

French's P Ranch, 1.5 miles east of Frenchglen on the Steens Mountain loop road, includes a horse barn.

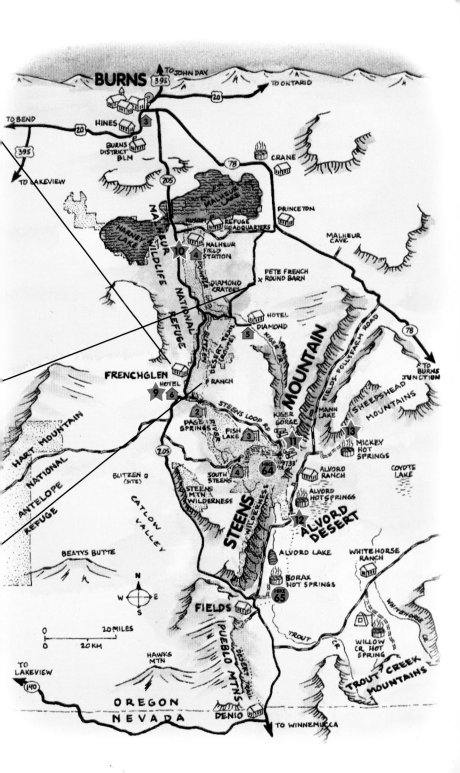

The Donner und Blitzen River (German for "thunder and lightning") was named by Army Colonel George Curry, who led a campaign against the Paiute Indians here in 1864 and forded the river in a thunderstorm.

10   Malheur Refuge

Most of Steens Mountain's winter snow melts into creeks that flow west to the marshlands of the Malheur National Wildlife Refuge. Huge flocks of migrating birds stop here from March through May: sandhill cranes, snow geese, egrets, swans, grebes, herons, pelicans, songbirds, and many kinds of ducks.

The great egret *(at left)* is slightly smaller and more common than the sandhill crane *(at right)*.

Bring binoculars or a spotting scope to watch birds from your car without disturbing them. Stop at the refuge headquarters to see a worthwhile, free museum (open dawn to dusk) with some 200 mounted specimens of birds. A nearby visitor center offers road tour maps, brochures, and tips on recent bird sightings.

GETTING THERE: From Burns, drive east 1.7 miles on Highway 78, turn right toward Frenchglen on Highway 205 for 23.2 miles, and turn left 6 miles to refuge headquarters.

11   Steens Mountain

Congress protected much of this 50-mile-long mountain with the 174,573-acre Steens Mountain Wilderness in 2000. Most visitors begin in Frenchglen *(see p266)* and drive the Steens Mountain Loop Road, a 65-mile gravel circuit that slices through the wilderness almost to

A primitive trail from South Steens Campground leads 6.5 miles up Big Indian Gorge and peters out in the sage.

At the East Rim Viewpoint, the tilted plateau of 9733-foot Steens Mountain ends with a 5700-foot cliff.

the mountain's summit. Because this is the highest road in Oregon, cresting at 9550 feet, snow gates close the upper part of the loop from November through June, depending on snow levels. Even when the gates are open, many visitors drive only the northern part of the loop to avoid the Rooster Comb, a very rough, steep 6-mile road section not suitable for trailers, RVs, or low-clearance vehicles.

Highlights along the Steens Mountain Loop Road, clockwise from Frenchglen, include the Page Springs Campground (open all year), the Fish Lake Campground (open June 15 to November 15, no motorboats allowed on the lake), the Jackman Park Campground (open July 1 to October 30), the Kiger Gorge Viewpoint, the East Rim Viewpoint, the trail to Wildhorse Lake *(see pp270-71)*, the Rooster Comb, and the South Steens Campground (open June 1 to October 30). Expect to see wild horses, deer, and antelope.

GETTING THERE: From Burns, drive east on Highway 78 toward Crane for 1.7 miles, turn right on paved Highway 205 for 61 miles to Frenchglen, and fork left onto the gravel Steens Mountain Loop Road.

Quaking aspen at Fish Lake.

Landmark for all of southeast Oregon, Steens Mountain looms snowy and sudden above the Alvord Desert.

HIKE 64 Wildhorse Lake

Easy (to Steens Mountain summit)
0.8 miles round trip   240 feet elevation gain
Open mid-July to late October
Use: hikers
Map: Wildhorse Lake (USGS)

Difficult (to Wildhorse Lake)
2.4 miles round trip   1100 feet elevation loss

Getting There

From Burns, drive 1.7 miles east on Highway 78 toward Crane and turn right on paved Highway 205 for 61 miles to Frenchglen. Check your gas gauge here. Just beyond the Frenchglen Hotel, fork left onto the gravel Steens Mountain Loop Road for 2.9 miles to the Page Springs Campground entrance. Keep left, past a snow gate that's closed from about mid-November until mid-June. Continue another 21.6 miles to a 4-way junction. First turn left for a 0.3-mile side trip up to the East Rim Viewpoint and a dizzying look down to the Alvord Desert. Then return to the 4-way junction and follow a "Wildhorse Lake" pointer left on a rough dirt road for 2 miles to a parking lot at road's end.

The windswept cliffs at the summit of Steens Mountain seem perched on the edge of the planet. More than a vertical mile below, the Alvord Desert shimmers

Wildhorse Lake fills a cirque carved by an ancient glacier.

faintly, a mirage in the void. At 9733 feet, this is the ninth tallest mountain in Oregon, and the easiest to climb. In fact, after strolling through an otherworldly landscape half a mile to the top, you're likely to have enough energy left over to scramble down into a hanging valley of wildflowers at Wildhorse Lake.

Two trails start from the parking lot. If you're headed for Steens Mountain's summit, simply hike up a barricaded, steep, rocky roadbed 0.4 mile to a crest. The actual summit is 100 feet to the left. To the right, you'll find a different viewpoint just beyond five small radio buildings.

If you have a little more time and

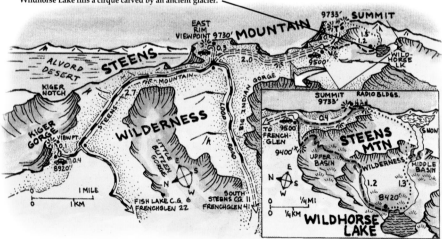

energy, however, try the other trail from the parking lot. This path heads downhill past a hiker registration box for 0.2 mile to a rimrock cliff overlooking Wildhorse Lake. Here the trail suddenly turns left, traversing down a precariously steep rocky slope. Soon the path begins following a brook through increasingly lush meadows, ablaze with pink monkeyflower, orange paintbrush, and yellow Oregon sunshine.

At the 1.2-mile mark, the narrow sandy beach of Wildhorse Lake makes a good turnaround point. If you're backpacking, camp well away from the fragile shore—and bring a cookstove, because there is no firewood of any kind.

Wildflowers line the trail down to Wildhorse Lake.

THE DESERT TRAIL

This National Recreation Trail extends from Mexico to Oregon, exploring arid mountain ranges, rimrock canyons, alkali playas, and wide-open landscapes where sagebrush rules.

Unlike the more famous Pacific Crest and Appalachian trails, however, the Desert Trail does not have a defined tread. Instead it is a general route—a corridor marked every few miles by large rock cairns. Hikers choose their own route through the sagebrush from cairn to cairn. Carrying water, maps, and survival gear is essential.

Sagebrush's pungent leaves are 3-pronged.

To date the route has been marked and mapped for 656 miles in California, 685 miles in Nevada, and about 150 miles in Oregon. Plans call for continuing the trail route through Idaho and Montana to the Canadian border.

The Oregon section traverses the Pueblo Mountains, the Alvord Desert, Steens Mountain, and the Malheur Wildlife Refuge to Highway 20 east of Burns. For maps and information, contact the Desert Trail Association at PO Box 34, Madras, OR 97741 or check *www.madras.net/dta*.

Hikers on the Desert Trail pick their own route from one rock cairn to the next. The trail corridor crosses Steens Mountain at Wildhorse Lake and extends south across the Pueblo Mountains (above) to Nevada.

WILDFLOWERS OF SOUTHEAST OREGON

When Oregon's desert blooms in May and June, seemingly barren, rocky slopes turn green with sudden growth. In July the lowlands fade again to brown, but the alpine wildflowers atop Steens and Hart Mountain are just breaking free of snowdrifts to bloom.

OREGON SUNSHINE (*Eriophyllum lanatum*). The wooly stalks of this common bloom conserve water.

BITTERROOT (*Lewisia rediviva*). Noted by Lewis and Clark, these 3-inch blooms have edible roots.

PRICKLY PEAR (*Opuntia polyacantha*). Most cacti find Oregon's desert too cold. This one's rare too.

PENSTEMON (*Penstemon sp.*). The desert varieties of this showy flower often grow two feet tall.

DEATH CAMAS (*Zigadenus sp.*). This poisonous lily can be fatal if you mistake it for edible camas.

EVENING PRIMROSE (*Oenothera tanecetifolia*) forms a golden carpet on a Hart Mountain lakeshore.

MARIPOSA LILY (*Calochortus macrocarpus*). These showy lilies vary by area. Clockwise from upper left are blooms from Steens Mountain, the Wenaha River, the Wallowa Mountains, and Hells Canyon.

12 Alvord Desert

Oregon's driest spot, this 9-mile-long alkali lakebed receives just six inches of annual precipitation. A rough dirt spur descends 0.5 mile to the alkali flat, which is open to hiking or driving except in rare winters when it fills with water.

To the north is Alvord Hot Springs. Privately owned, but generally open to

Alvord Hot Springs' bathhouse overlooks the desert.

the public for free (or a small donation), the springs fill two 8-by-8-foot concrete pools at about 102°F. Bring no glass containers and leave no litter.

GETTING THERE: From Fields, take the paved road 1.3 miles north toward Frenchglen

Below Steens Mountain lie the cracked mudflats of the Alvord Desert—often so dry you can drive across.

and keep right onto the wide gravel Fields-Follyfarm road toward Highway 78. Drive north 19.6 miles to the turnoff for the Alvord Desert on the right. Look for this unmarked side road 1.4 miles after your first view of the playa. Next, return to the main road and drive another 2.6 miles to the unmarked Alvord Hot Springs. Just beyond a cattle guard, look for a tin shed 200 yards to the right of the road.

Scalding pools and steam jets make the Mickey Hot Springs area too dangerous for children or pets.

13 Mickey Hot Springs

The moonscape at Mickey Hot Springs features boiling pools, steam jets, mud-pots, and the scalding, 30-foot-deep turquoise Morning Glory Pool. All pools are too hot for humans, with the possible exception of a single bathtub-sized basin carved by frustrated bathers.

GETTING THERE: Drive the gravel Fields-Follyfarm road north of Fields 23.5 miles (or north of Alvord Hot Springs 10.5 miles), passing the Alvord Ranch and two 90° highway curves. At a green cattle guard immediately after the road has curved sharply to the left, turn right on an unmarked gravel side road. Follow this washboard track through several zigzags. After 2.6 miles, keep left at a fork. After another 3.9 miles, park at a railed turn-around on the right.

HIKE 65   Borax Hot Springs

Easy
3 miles round trip   60 feet elevation gain
Open all year
Use: hikers
Map: Borax Lake (USGS)

At Borax Lake, a rare species of fish thrives in warm alkaline water. Steam rises from boiling turquoise pools. In the distance, the snowy crest of Steens Mountain shimmers like a mirage.

Park at a wire gate with the sign, "Danger! Hot Springs. Scalding Water.

Ground May Collapse. Control Children and Pets." In fact, dogs and any attempt at swimming are banned to protect the area's fragile ecosystem.

Hike along the road 0.9 mile to Borax Lake, passing a lower reservoir and iron vats used by Chinese laborers in the late 1800s to refine borax. From here, dozens of smaller hot springs, strung out in a line to the north, are visible as wisps of steam rising from the grass. To see them, walk back 100 feet toward the vats, turn right on a faint road, and keep straight toward

Boiling vats remain from a 19th-century borax mine.

Fields' cafe/store/gas station is famed for its milkshakes.

distant Steens Mountain. Dangerously hot at 180°F, the pools are to the right of the road, so be careful if you leave the track. After 0.5 mile a wire fence crosses the road. Turn back 200 yards later at two large, final pools.

Getting There

From Burns, drive east 1.7 miles toward Crane on Highway 78, turn right on Highway 205 for 59 miles to Frenchglen, and continue another 50 miles to the gas station in Fields. Then turn around and drive back toward Frenchglen 1.3 miles. At a junction, go straight onto a broad gravel road toward Highway 78. After 0.4 mile, turn right beside a power substation onto a dirt road that follows a large powerline. At the first fork (after 2.1 miles) veer left away from the powerline for 1.8 miles and park beside a closed wire gate.

△ Colorful algae grows in the hot springs pools.
Bathing is banned in scalding Borax Hot Springs. ▷

Three Forks

At the oasis-like confluence of three canyons, Three Forks is one of the most remote places in Oregon, wedged against the borders of Idaho and Nevada.

The Owyhee River won its name when Indians killed two Hawaiian trappers near here in 1819. "Owyhee" was a 19th-century spelling for Hawaii. A gold strike at Silver City, Idaho in the late 1860s brought miners, a wagon road, and an Army outpost to the area.

For a hike from the boat ramp, walk upstream (to the south) for 300 yards, wade an ankle-deep side fork of the river, and continue up the main river on a trail. When the path ends at a cliff after 2 miles, wade the river (knee-deep in summer). A hot springs pool is to the left along a faint road 200 yards, just above the waterfall of a side creek. Note,

Western fence lizard.

however, that the hot springs itself is on unmarked private land. Although hikers have been allowed to visit in the past, this may change.

A hot springs pool overlooks the Owyhee River. △
◁ Cliffs reflect in the river at Three Forks.

GETTING THERE: From Burns, take Highway 78 east through Crane 93 miles to Burns Junction and turn left on Highway 95 for 30.5 miles. Near milepost 36 (west of Jordan Valley 16 miles), follow a pointer for Three Forks south onto a dirt road that serves as part of the Soldier Creek Watchable Wildlife Loop.

Although the lonely dirt road to Three Forks becomes an undrivable trough of slick goo after rainstorms, this area only sees 11 inches of precipitation each year.

After 27.6 miles you'll reach a signed junction. Ignore the loop route that heads left toward Jordan Valley, and instead turn right toward Three Forks. In 2.7 miles you'll reach a corral at the edge of the Owyhee canyon rim. If you're driving a passenger car, it's best to park here and walk the final 1.4 miles. If you're driving a high-clearance vehicle, continue down what suddenly becomes a very steep, rocky track. At the bottom, fork to the right at a boater registration signboard and keep right for 300 yards to a parking area just before a boat launch site (GPS location N42°32.78' W117°10.04').

15 Leslie Gulch

Driving through this narrow canyon of colorful rock pinnacles is like touring a giant's labyrinthine rock garden. Cliffs of welded volcanic ash here have been colored orange, yellow, purple, and red by minerals. Soft spots have weathered into niches known as "honeycombs."

The best camp nearby is at Succor Creek (see p279). Slocum Campground, a gravel flat 0.2 mile up the road from Leslie Gulch's boat ramp, is a free but bleak and shadeless place to overnight.

If you have time for a hike, drive 3.6 miles up from Slocum Campground to the marked Juniper Gulch trailhead pullout on the left. This trail hops across Leslie Creek and follows a narrow

Leslie Gulch's gravel road can be closed by rainstorms.

right on a gravel road down this canyon 14.5 miles to its end at a boat ramp.

If you're driving here from Jordan Valley (140 miles southeast of Burns), take Highway 95 north for 27 miles and turn left at a sign for Succor Creek for 8.4 gravel miles. At a T-shaped junction, turn left toward Succor Creek another 1.8 miles, and then turn left on the gravel Leslie Gulch road for 14.5 miles to road's end at the reservoir boat ramp.

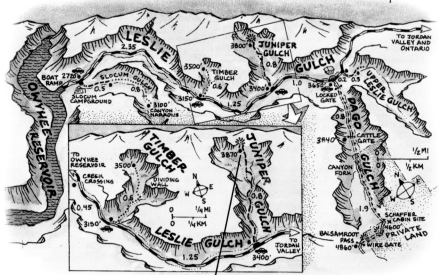

sandy wash up past overhanging cliffs. After 0.6 mile keep right at a fork. Then follow the path up a ridge to its end at an orange cliff.

GETTING THERE: From Interstate 84 at Ontario, follow signs south 14 miles to Nyssa. In Nyssa, turn right at a pointer for Adrian onto Highway 201 for 20.6 miles. Then turn right on gravel Succor Creek Road for 15 miles to Succor Creek State Recreation Area, continue 10 miles to a sign for Leslie Gulch, and turn

A trail climbs Juniper Gulch to a viewpoint amid "honeycomb" rock.

WHERE TO STAY

Campgrounds (map p261)

	Campsites	Water	Showers	Flush Toilet	Fee
3 **FISH LAKE.** At the 7400-foot level on the Steens Mountain Loop Road 18 miles east of Frenchglen, this small lake (no motorboats) has a campground among the quaking aspen. Open June 15 to November 15.	23	●			$
1 **HART MOUNTAIN HOT SPRINGS.** Camp by a desert creek amid quaking aspen and walk to a free natural hot springs (see p265). Open May through November. Drinking water is at the refuge headquarters.	14				free
5 **LAKE OWYHEE.** Motorboats tour the Owyhee River's 53-mile-long reservoir amid desert badlands from this state park, open April through October. Two teepees are also available ($29 rental includes use of canoe; reservations 800-551-6949). From Ontario, follow signs 14 miles south to Nyssa, drive Highway 201 south 8 miles to Owyhee, turn right on Owyhee Avenue 4.5 miles, and take Owyhee Lake Road 23 miles.	64	●	●	●	$$
4 **SOUTH STEENS.** This spacious camp amid sparse juniper is open June through October and has 15 horse sites. From Frenchglen, drive Highway 205 south 10 miles and turn left on Steens Mountain Loop Road 18 miles.	36	●		●	$
6 **SUCCOR CREEK.** Colorful canyon cliffs surround this primitive state park, open March to November. From Ontario, follow signs 14 miles south to Nyssa, drive Highway 201 south 20.6 miles, and turn right on gravel Succor Creek Road 15 miles.	19				free
2 **PAGE SPRINGS.** On the beautiful Donner und Blitzen River at the foot of Steens Mountain, this camp is open all year. Free in winter. From Frenchglen, take the Steens Mountain Loop Road 3 miles and fork to the right 0.6 mile.	36	●			$

Page Springs Campground. ▷

B&Bs and Quaint Hotels (map p261)

	Rooms	Private bath	Cont. breakfast	Full breakfast	Rate range
7 **OREGON TRAIL INN.** Mail-ordered from a 1900 Sears catalog, this Victorian home is a bed & breakfast inn 17 miles west of Ontario at 484 N. 10th, Vale, OR 97918. Pets OK. Info: 541-473-3030 or www.searshomebb.com.	5	1	●		$59-70
5 **HOTEL DIAMOND.** This rambling 1898 hotel and cafe is the town of Diamond, between the Malheur Refuge and Steens Mountain. Open April 1 to October 31. From Burns, drive Highway 205 south 44 miles and turn left 13 miles. Info: 541-493-1898 or www.central-oregon.com/hoteldiamond.	8	3	●		$68-90
6 **FRENCHGLEN HOTEL.** Restored by the state parks, this 1916 hotel has spartan rooms, but offers friendly, family-style meals (see p266). Open March 15 to October 31. Info: 541-493-2825 or sghotel@centurytel.net.	8				$67-70
4 **MALHEUR FIELD STATION.** Oregon's best birdwatching is at your door at this wildlife preserve (see p268). The headquarters offers 9 rental trailers and 150 dormitory beds April to mid-October. Info: 541-493-2629.	17	9			$40-60
3 **SAGE COUNTRY INN.** On a full block in downtown Burns, this 1907 Georgian-Colonial home is decorated with antiques. Now a bed & breakfast inn, it's located at 351½ W. Monroe, Burns, OR 97720. Info: 541-573-7243 or www.sagecountryinn.com.	3	●		●	$85
1 **SUMMER LAKE INN.** This inn's ten modern cabins have views across ponds to Summer Lake and the cliffs of Winter Rim. Breakfast is available Tuesday-Sunday for $8.50. Located south of Summer Lake (see p264) on Highway 31 between mileposts 80 and 81. Info: 800-261-2778 or www.summerlakeinn.com.	10	●			$105-165
2 **WILLOW SPRINGS GUEST RANCH.** This remote, 2500-acre cattle ranch 30 miles north of Lakeview has two duplex guest cabins decorated with Western art. It's open all year, but from May through October the hosts lead horse trail rides and cook dinner outside in Dutch ovens. Info: 541-947-5499 or www.willowspringsguestranch.com.	4	●		●	$115

INDEX

Page numbers in *italics* refer to maps.

◁ **Traverse Lake in the southern Wallowa Mountains.**   △ **Crater Lake's Wizard Island in winter.**

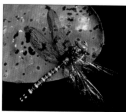

Dragonfly on pond lily.

Broken Top in winter.

Mossy spring below North Sister.

Church in Grants Pass.

Hells Canyon from a trail near Buckhorn Lookout.

Bear tracks in the snow.

Glacier Lake from Eagle Cap.

Mickey Hot Springs.

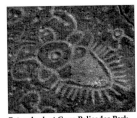
Petroglyph at Cove Palisades Park.

Old-growth forest near Mount Hood.

Broken Top from Broken Hand in April.

Sunset from the Kalmiopsis Wilderness.

Blacktail deer on oceanfront bluff.

Fog on a forest path near Eugene.

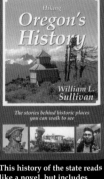